PORTRAIT OF CORNWALL

OTHER *PORTRAIT* BOOKS

Portrait of
CORNWALL

by

CLAUDE BERRY

ILLUSTRATED AND WITH MAP

LONDON
ROBERT HALE LIMITED
63 Old Brompton Road, S.W.7

PRINTED IN GREAT BRITAIN
BY EBENEZER BAYLIS AND SON, LTD.
THE TRINITY PRESS, WORCESTER, AND LONDON

CONTENTS

ILLUSTRATIONS

ACKNOWLEDGEMENTS

Illustrations numbered 1, 10, 14, 16 and 17 are reproduced from photographs by Mr. J. L. F. Rowland of Truro; 2 and 15 by Mr. Reece Winstone, A.R.P.S., of Bristol; 3, 5, 8, 9, 11, 12, 13, 18, 19, 21, 23 and 24 by Mr. George W. F. Ellis of Bodmin; 4, 6 and 7 by Mr. E. Osborne of Falmouth; 20 by Mr. George Warren of Penryn; and 22 by Mr. Griffith Sandy of Truro.

FOREWORD

THE virtue of this book is its authenticity. There are many books—
too many indeed—written by people who come down to view the
Cornish scene and write about it from the outside. This book is not
only written from inside, it springs out of the life of the Cornish
people: its quality is given by its author's sympathy with, and love for,
that life, in all its ways and hardships, the struggle with the soil or
with the sea, the farming, mining, fishing folk of Cornwall.

How could it be otherwise? Claude Berry has these folk in his
blood, especially the fishermen and mariners of Padstow from which
he comes. I envy him that Padstow background: the crowded life, so
close-knit and intimate, of that little community shut in between the
Elizabethan park of Place and the blue and sand-gold estuary of the
Camel; with its memories of John Hawkins putting into harbour and
Sir Richard Grenville, of the Spaniard who lived there and seems to
have known Christopher Marlowe, the sagacious and variegated
Prideaux in their great house up the hill. Anyhow, Claude Berry
views all Cornwall for us through the eyes of a Padstow man.

He is Cornish of the Cornish; more Cornish than "Q" even, for
on his mother's side, as his *Memories* remind us, "Q" was a Devonshire-
man. Mr. Berry is, if possible, as irretrievably Cornish as I am myself.
All his life, save for some dozen years, he has lived in Cornwall, and
pretty representatively: Padstow, Bodmin, Truro: north, middle,
west. He can speak with an authority that few can; for there are
differences, not only of dialect, between one part of the county and
another, such as only a Cornishman would know. But the dozen years
outside we may regard as not ill-spent; he served through the 1914-18
War in France; next London University, then Fleet Street. Good
judges know that he was on the way to winning a high place in his
profession when ill-health brought him home for good. We are the
gainers in the most distinguished journalist in the West Country.

Claude Berry—"C.B." as he is known with affection down this
way—has many advantages. He has eaten (cf. Chapter VI) a much
greater variety of Cornish fare than I have: I regret that I have never
eaten squab-pie. He explains to you, in the proper place, how to make
Cornish cream. But you have to have the cows and the pasture and the
tang of the sea in the milk, as well as the knack.

The exuberances of Cornish cooking are getting flattened out, along with much else. Yet it is pleasant to think that Cornish pasties and saffron cake still make their faithful appearance among our folk as far from home as Mineral Point, Wisconsin, the Upper Peninsula of Michigan, in Grass Valley, California, in Colorado—and, I dare say, in the right spots in Canada and Australia, wherever around the world Cornish people have settled. It is consoling that, however far away they may be, they still look homeward to Cornwall as "home".

Not even Mr. Berry can altogether explain—though he devotes some of his best pages to the subject—the extraordinary pull that Cornwall exerts over her children, and not only over Cornishmen either. I know a man who gave up a fine Elizabethan house in Suffolk to come and live in a derelict old Cornish house—true, it had some magnificent memories, but for the rest it was inhabited by bats and rats and owls—and a ghost. I said to him something about his paying me a visit in Oxford; he answered, quite simply, "I hope never to cross the Tamar again, so long as I live." He was quite a youngish man then, and otherwise sane enough; he had entertained a passion for that house since he was a boy.

What is it that draws us all so inexplicably? It is something more than the spirit of place, powerful as that is, of just any place. That under-current of feeling is present on every one of these pages: it is what makes the book so authentic. We who are Cornish have that feeling in crossing the Tamar into Cornwall. But what of the others? I have sometimes thought that there may be some primal impulse that carries us westwards, some primitive urge to get as far West as we can. Think of the drive that carried so many hundreds of thousands—a good sprinkling of Cornish along with them—across the plains of the Mid-West ever westward in the nineteenth century: the most significant folk-movement of modern times, the epic of the English-speaking peoples.

It is a very Cornish book, then, that "C.B." has written. What better guide could there be?—not only to the county, but what guide books so rarely give us—to its essential and inner life.

A. L. ROWSE

Trenarren House,
St. Austell.

AUTHOR'S
ACKNOWLEDGEMENTS

I AM most grateful to Dr. Rowse for his Foreword to this new Edition of my book and for his permission to quote from his great *Tudor Cornwall* and *A Cornish Childhood*. In every case, I hope, I have acknowledged in the text my indebtedness to other Cornish scholars from Richard Carew to Charles Henderson. Death came to stop the ready flow of help from the endearing Canon G. H. Doble, our greatest authority on the Celtic Saints; but his *Lives* of the saints remain, and will, I hope, one day be collected in a single volume. I am grateful to Mrs. Christopher Vivian and Mrs. J. R. Bennetts for having read and improved my typescript, and to Mr. F. L. Harris and Mr. Ashley Rowe for valuable suggestions. My debt to my wife goes far beyond the bounds of Cornish cooking. I cannot sufficiently thank my colleague on *The West Briton*, Miss Muriel Goldsworthy, for extending her comradeship into the making of this book. What I owe to my paper will be guessed from the many quotations I have made from its invaluable files since 1810.

C. B.

Truro.

I

THE SEA-GIRT LAND

CORNWALL, on a map, always reminds me of a fisherman's sea-boot, and from an aeroplane above the county the resemblance, on a clear day, would be even more marked. There, thousands of feet below, would lie this most south-westerly of the counties of England; just like a sea-boot on its side, and full of crinkles and bulges. More remarkably, though afloat on a wide and ever restless sea, it would be perfectly still. The long, inshore breakers of this sea would lend to much of the contour of the boot a fringe of pure ermine. Where the top of the boot should fit snugly round the English limb thrust Devonwards, a narrow edge of white, like the top of a fisherman's long stocking, would be trailed in gentle curves or bold half-loops by the River Tamar. Looking down from the air, you might suppose that, in one place, a few inches of the stocking had slipped below the top of the boot. This is a neck of land, about four miles wide, which lies between the shyly revealed source of the Tamar in Woolley Barrow and the wild and impressive coast of the north-eastern corner of the county. By those four miles alone Cornwall fails to qualify as an island.

It may have been of this narrow strip of littoral joining Cornwall and Devon that a London comrade of mine in our county regiment during the First Great War was thinking when, in France one day, he enunciated a profound truth. Or he may have had in mind the lovely, five hundred years old Greyston Bridge which the Tamar hurries so ungraciously by; though more likely it was Brunel's imposing structure away down at Saltash which now has for near neighbour the great road bridge completed in 1961.

"Cornwall ain't England at all, reelly," declared the Cockney, half in commiseration. "It's jest attached to England for rations and pay." I demurred no further than to suggest that he should add, in fairness, "And for duty". So there we left it. He had got the truth of the matter in him.

For I knew that he had in mind not only Cornwall's almost complete physical separateness from England. Although he did not say so, it was much more than that. Some, who have gone into the matter more comprehensively, have invested the source of this separateness with an

CORNWALL
Scale
0
5
10
15Mls
Pentire Pt
Stepper Pt
Trevose Head
St. Merryn
Padstow
St. Eval
St. Mawgan
St. Columb Major
Newquay
Cubert
St. Den
Newlyn East
Perranporth
Zelah
St. Agnes Hd
St. Agnes
St. Erme
Grampour
Portreath
Illogan
Truro
Redruth
Camborne
St. Day
Kea
Ruan Lanihorne
Treg
Roseworthy
St. Ives
Lelant
Gwennap
Stithians
Devoran
Gurnard's Hd
Zennor
Hayle
Penryn
Mylor
Morvah
St. Erth
Crowan
St. Maw
Ludgvan
Falmouth
St. Anth in-Rose
Cape Cornwall
Penzance
Marazion
Germoe
Breage
Wendron
St. Just
Sithney
Constantine
Newlyn
St. Michaels Mt.
Helston
Mawnan
Helford
Manaccan
Mousehole
Loe Pool
Sennen
St Buryan
Porthleven
GOONHILLY
St. Keverne
LAND'S END
St. Levan
Cury
DOWNS
Mullion
Coverack
Ruan Major
Ruan Minor
Cadgwith
Lizard
THE LIZARD

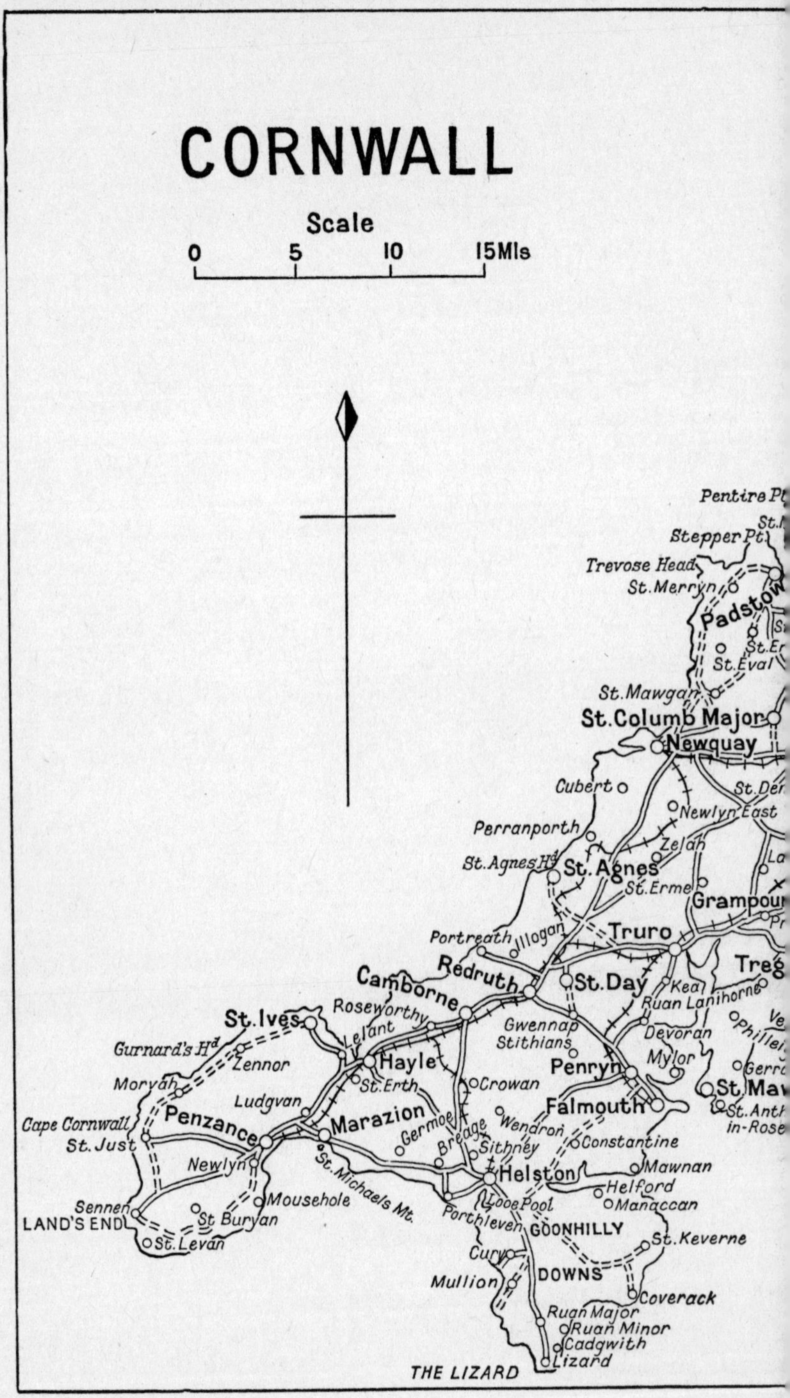

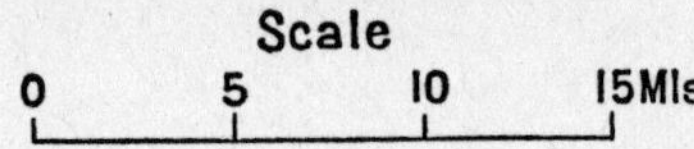

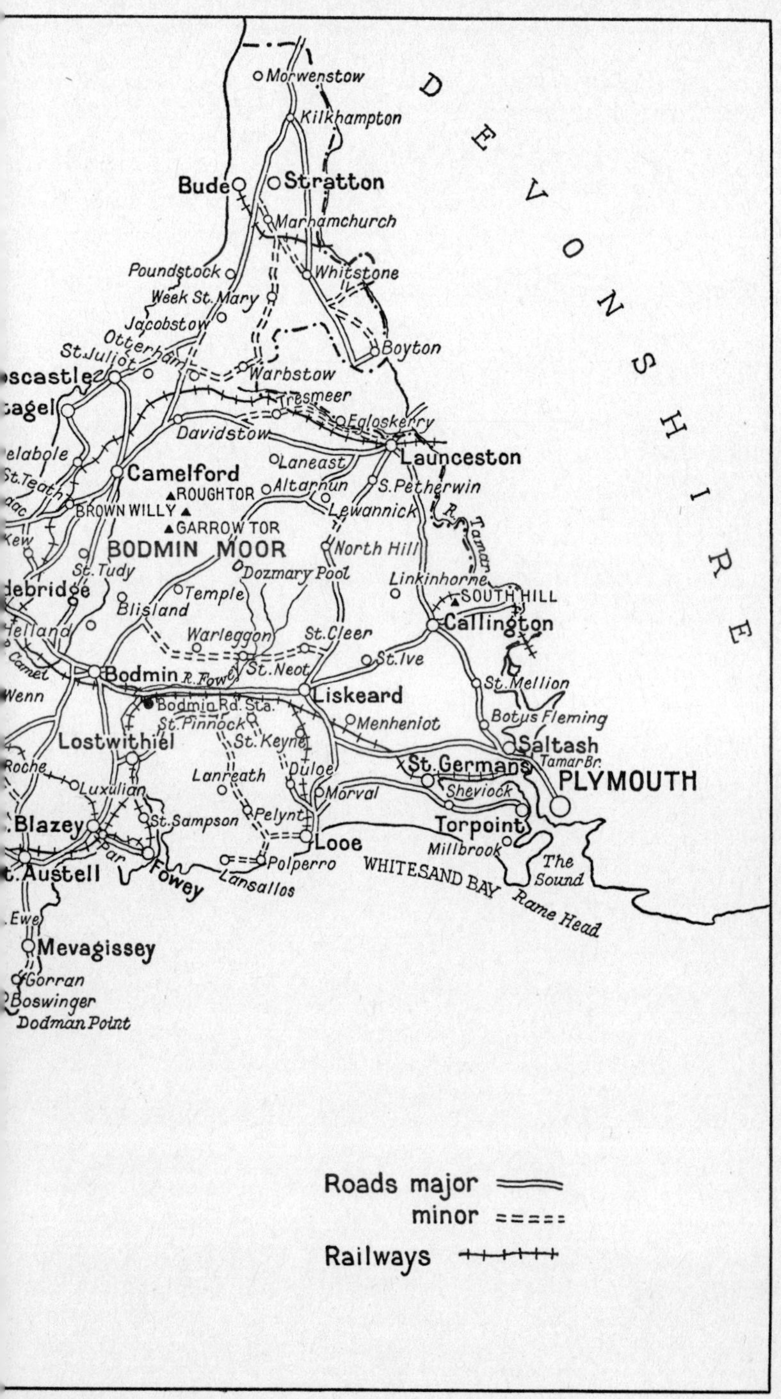

DEVONSHIRE
Morwenstow
Kilkhampton
Bude
Stratton
Marhamchurch
Poundstock
Whitstone
Week St. Mary
Jacobstow
Boyton
Otterham
St. Juliot
Warbstow
oscastle
Tresmeer
cagel
Egloskerry
Davidstow
Launceston
Laneast
elabole
St. Teath
Altarnun
S. Petherwin
Camelford
ROUGHTOR
BROWN WILLY
Lewannick
dac
GARROW TOR
R. Tamar
Kew
BODMIN MOOR
North Hill
St. Tudy
Dozmary Pool
Linkinhorne
Temple
SOUTH HILL
debridge
Blisland
Warleggon
St. Cleer
Callington
elland
St. Neot
St. Ive
Camel
Bodmin
R. Fowey
St. Mellion
Wenn
Bodmin Rd. Sta.
Liskeard
St. Finnock
Menheniot
Botus Fleming
Lostwithiel
St. Keyne
Saltash
Roche
Lanreath
Duloe
St. Germans
Tamar Br.
Luxulian
Morval
Sheviock
PLYMOUTH
Blazey
St. Sampson
Pelynt
Torpoint
Par
Looe
Millbrook
The Sound
t. Austell
Fowey
Polperro
WHITESAND BAY
Lansallos
Rame Head
Ewe
Mevagissey
Gorran
Boswinger
Dodman Point
Roads major
minor
Railways

almost mystical quality. Yet much of it can be explained, surely, by a group of quite simple, material facts mainly geographical and geological. I should err grossly by over-simplifying and suggesting that situation, or structure, or configuration, or composition, is all. But who, looking at a map of Cornwall, can miss the significance of her shape (so much like Italy's), and of the dramatic exposure of four-fifths of her outline, some two hundred miles or more of it, to the varying moods and the latent and unleashed might of the sea?

Nowhere in the eighty-mile length of Cornwall can you put between yourself and the sea more than twenty miles of land. At Truro, our cathedral town and county administrative centre, the coast is but nine miles to the north and nine to the south. Not much farther west, midway between Hayle and Marazion, across the instep of the sea-boot, the sea is only three miles away on either side. Wherever you may be in the county, you have the sense that, if the sea is not on your doorstep—as at Padstow, my native place, it sometimes, quite literally, has been on mine—it is just over the broad brow of that lonely hill, or just beyond the edge of this stretch of heath and gorse-clad moorland. In its influence, if not in physical fact, the sea is omnipresent in Cornwall.

It would be easy, and agreeable to me, to surrender my judgement—though certainly not from sentimentalism—to this potent omni-presence, even though it is here no more than the distant thunder of the ebb, and there no more than the slightly salty tang from the rollicking nor'-wester. For I come of seafaring stock. Through all my memories of childhood, youth, and young manhood ripples, or roars, or sighs the Cornish sea. Along the sternsheets and bottomboards and over the thwarts of our old ship's boat, I moved with ease and confidence long before I was man enough to stand up at the wicket. Quite early in life I had experience of the sea as an element that men fought; some of them a losing battle. One night in early spring, cowering close to my father, and clutching tightly at his coat so that I should not be swept from his side by the gale, I watched masthead lights rising and falling in the darkness near the harbour mouth. I was oppressed and scared by the tension of some terrific drama which I could only fragmentarily comprehend. That was the night when, in a vain endeavour to save the crew of a fishing-smack which was being swept to destruction, the Padstow harbour life-boat and the steam life-boat—the first of its kind to serve along the coast of Britain—were both lost.

Later on, in the fading light of a November afternoon, I saw a schooner and a French brigantine, which were running for shelter from

Bedruthan Steps, with Queen Bess Rock

the gale, swept, within half an hour of each other, to their doom. Those are but two of many harassing memories. But there are other memories, full of pleasure and colour, chiefly of the Cornish sea in June, or on "a day lent" in early October, when the light has a clarity, a purity, which is rarely equalled during most other periods of the year in the county.

It is almost impossible to over-estimate the importance of the sea in Cornwall's history and character. Thrust out into it, as she is, and surrounded by it on three sides, with the longest coastline of all the English counties. Cornwall has had her contacts chiefly by sea and not by land, and with other countries than England. Civilization reached this remote peninsula from the Mediterranean before the rest of the country felt its influence, and Cornwall was thus favoured because it had to offer, what England had not, a supply of tin. Much later (and in what marvellous ways, some of them!) came to us by sea the Celtic saints, who ensured that Christian worship should have with us a continuous history of at least fifteen hundred years.

Before exporting saints to us, Ireland in the dimmer ages sent us, mainly for transit across the county and re-export, her gold. With our other Celtic cousins, the Welsh and the Bretons, especially the latter, contacts have always been close and mutually profitable. In-evitably our long coastline has invited incursions planned with ill-intent, notably the burning and plundering raids of the Danes, of which my native place was a particular victim; and, centuries later, the landings of the Spaniards near Penzance.

Up to comparatively recent times it was by sea, and not to England, that Cornish people usually went when they left their native county. Hundreds, if not thousands, of people of the tin and copper mining districts who, during the great depression in their industry, emigrated from our little ports in the nineteenth century to Canada, or the United States, had never set foot in England; while large numbers who did cross the River Tamar went that way only to embark immediately at English ports for Australia, South Africa, or the Americas. Corn-wall's setting in the western sea and the late development of its roads were chiefly responsible for the centuries of virtual isolation from England. It has never been true that the sea-boot to which I have likened the county has encased a solidly English leg and foot. But even in ancient times county and country were linked by coastwise traffic along the south coast; after the Norman Conquest came the close link with the Throne: the creation of the Earldom, then a Dukedom, of Cornwall for the monarch's eldest son. So the contacts with England

2

"Passon" Hawker's Church, Morwenstow

and the English grew and never were they so numerous as today when, in the space of a few summer months, some three hundred thousand English people seek recreation in this bony extremity of their land.

They flock, of course, chiefly to the coast with its innumerable coves and its score or more of spacious bays which are almost equally distributed along the north and south coasts, with the incomparable Mount's Bay in between. Generally, the north coast is more bare and majestic than the south, with stretches of cliff from which in places you look down as much as five hundred feet to the Atlantic breakers pounding and smothering the tumbled masses of rock below, or swirling up gullies floored by golden sand. The south coast is softer in other ways, notably in its climate. And yet along the south there is nothing quite so soft as stretches of the north coast like the eastern arm of St. Ives Bay; Holywell Bay, between Fistral and Perranporth; and again at Constantine Bay and Harlyn. These are the districts of the sand-dunes or, as we call them, towans.

Thousands of tons of sand have been swept in by north-westerly gales over the rocks and the surrounding fields of these districts—at Perranporth "marring the land adjoinant", wrote Richard Carew in his delectable *Survey of Cornwall* (1602), "so as the distress of this deluge drove the inhabitants to remove their Church". They have, in fact, had to do this twice, and a tablet in the present parish church of Perranzabuloe (Perran-in-the-Sand), which is about two miles inland, records that the first stone was laid in 1804, after two former churches "had been successively overwhelmed with the sand of the desert in which they were imprudently built". I like that "imprudently"—a rebuke of the Age of Reason for the jolly old sixth-century St. Piran, patron saint of Cornish miners, for having built his oratory where he did; and for his thirteenth-century successors who erected their church as far away from "the desert" as their rights in land would allow.

Because of blown sand along the eastern shore of the Camel Estuary, opposite Padstow, my maternal grandfather and grandmother, I have been told, had to enter the chapel-of-ease of St. Enodoc, for their marriage, through the roof. But there is, I think, about this a touch of pardonable romancing. Almost buried in the sand for years, the little fifteenth-century church was indeed entered at times through the roof for services, but my grandparents were probably the first couple to be married there after the sand had been virtually cleared and the dismantled church restored to use. St. Enodoc is now a little tamarisk-fringed island of sanctity in a sea of secularism-at-ease: for within a stone's throw of its tiny, two-stage tower and octagonal broach spire, flutter the red flags on three or four greens of a most interesting and exhilarating golf course.

Throughout my boyhood everybody at home spoke about St. Enodoc Church, significantly enough, as "Sinking Neddy", a phrase which had obviously been handed down through generations. Here, as in other districts which were overwhelmed with sand, *arundo arenia*, sand rush, or marram grass, or, as we call it, "spires", has long since stilled this golden sea, and there its great and little waves are today as though suddenly frozen by some miraculous gesture.

The Cornish coves and creeks were linked in the past—and still are occasionally in fiction—with smuggling. While only a few of the more romantic visitors cherish the notion that "goods" or "moonshine" are nowadays run into the coves, it is perfectly true that in the eighteenth and early nineteenth centuries, smuggling was a flourishing industry in Cornwall, enabling the thriftless to settle debts or pay for goods in fistfuls of uncounted guineas; and Mevagissey specialized in building fast-sailing vessels for the trade. It was a flash, sometimes a lurid flash, of Cornish opportunism, one factor in which was our long and close association with the Bretons, because of our family origins. In the course of the centuries down to the nineteenth, Cornish fishermen had also been at various times pirates, privateers, and (I use this word with reservations) wreckers. But all these skilful, daring, and sometimes bloody enterprises occupied, in the long history of the Cornish coves and Cornish fishing, only the briefest space.

Besides the bays and the coves, there are four or five indentations in the Cornish coast that look almost as if the fishes had intended to nibble a way right across the sea-boot; but had given up after a very promising start. On the north coast there is only one: the long, winding estuary of the Camel (Cornish *cam*, crooked; *heyle*, estuary), the only river worth mentioning that does not flow south to the sea. Carew, away south-eastwards at Antony, in the serenity of his study or among his placid fishponds, looked with evident disfavour to the bleak and treeless north coast. Of the Camel Estuary he was acidly parenthetical. "A town and haven of suitable quality," he commented, "for both (though bad) are the best that the North Cornish coast possesseth." This was truth, but truth laced with vinegar.

Padstow, the town in question, was probably in those Elizabethan times a boisterous, rough-and-tumble little port, with its own shipyards and ropewalks, and it would have had little to commend it to a cultured and fastidious, though charmingly inquisitive squire. Carew, moreover, knew its worst blemish. Here was a harbour spacious enough for a great fleet to ride at anchor in it; and it was so choked with sand that entrance was difficult and perilous and, as Sir Martin Frobisher found in 1577, "riding there, a very dangerous Road", was a worse evil than putting to sea again. In the three hundred years since Carew's time countless billions of shells, ground to tiny particles and whirled in by the Atlantic seas, have obstructed trade here almost as effectively as skyscrapers of tariff barriers.

You might cite Padstow as an example or a victim of geographical determinism. But we Cornish look at realities rather more obliquely. We have, in fact, invented a fable of a mermaid, who was mortally stricken by the longbow of a greedy and obtuse Padstow man. Whereupon she cursed the harbour and foretold its doom from sand which, even as she spoke, began to drift inexorably in from sea.

Of Carew's curt appraisal of the North Cornwall coast as a whole even its most devoted native can hardly complain. It has a reputation as sinister and melancholy as its great sweeps of majestic cliffs and its succession of noble headlands are awe-inspiring. How does the old rhyme go?

> From Padstow Point to Lundy Light
> Is a sailor's grave by day or night.

Even in this twentieth century when the life-boats of the Royal National Life-boat Institution are so carefully designed and constructed, and when mechanical propulsion has been so much developed, five of these boats on rescue missions have come to grief along this coast of ill-fame. Between 1800 and 1826 on the forty-mile stretch between Perranporth and Bude, and principally in the vicinity of Padstow Harbour, a hundred vessels were wrecked and stranded. These were mainly brigs and schooners, two of them belonging to the Royal Navy. From Cape Cornwall, near Land's End, to Trevose Head, just west of Padstow, another stretch of coast of about forty miles, there were lost, between 1823 and 1846, one hundred and thirty-one vessels and a dozen fishing-boats. Some two hundred seamen and fishermen were drowned.

Single storms accounted for a surprising number of victims. Thus, on an October day in 1823 a gale finished fourteen vessels and twelve fishing-boats. One February night in 1840 nine vessels were lost; and seven were destroyed by a storm two years later. The trouble was that nowhere along the whole north coast was there a harbour in which, particularly after high water, vessels caught by gales on a lee shore could find safety if they ran for it.

By contrast, the two most important south coast estuaries offer excellent harbourage, neither having a sandbar flung like a boom across its entrance, and both affording shelter and good anchorage at any state of tide. Falmouth Harbour is easily the best in Cornwall and is among the finest landlocked harbours in the world. "Falmouth braggeth", Carew observed, alluding to the harbour and not the town, which did not then exist, "Falmouth braggeth that a hundred sail may anchor within his circuit, and no one of these see the others' top." Nowadays Falmouth does not brag; she is much too civilized and busy and prosperously mellow, grouped there in her terraces round the great bay; though with the harbour as one, and Gyllyngvase Beach as another, she has a pair of healthy lungs that should provide a braggart with a remarkably loud voice. Arwenack Manor House is much more than an architectural treasure. It is the very heart of Falmouth. For it was the Killigrews of Arwenack who gave her life and fostered her through infancy and youth.

Until that far-seeing monarch, Henry VIII, built castles at St. Mawes and Pendennis, on either side of the harbour, it was dangerous to develop a port there, for it would have lain open to predatory raids from sea by pirates and other enemies of the king and his merchant subjects. So Penryn, a mile or two up the river, and more particularly Truro, several miles still farther away from open sea, were thriving ports and market towns long before Falmouth was thought of. The shrewd, pushing, and piratical Killigrews drew the proper conclusions from the provision of the defensive castles at St. Mawes and Pendennis, and went ahead developing Falmouth from a tiny fishing village. Naturally, both Truro and Penryn, not to say Helston, did all they could to strangle or cripple the upstart down where the confluent Fal and Truro rivers, from their many-fingered creeks, opened out to the sea. But nothing could stop Falmouth, with its superb situation and nearly ten square miles of sheltered water, from outstripping all other Cornish ports. So Falmouth Harbour has long been Cornwall's Golden Gate to the wider world; though not much that passes through it is Cornish.

Falmouth never fails to enchant me. But its climate is too mild for me. This comes of being native of the exhilarating north coast, and others born there may wonder, as I do, how the Killigrews, in the soft air of Falmouth, could ever have been sufficiently stimulated to scheme and to push so dubiously and dourly in founding and fostering the town. They may wonder, too, how residents since have had the energy to go on developing the place, instead of yawning, "Tomorrow", and giving themselves up again to the languors and loveliness of the gardens and to the enchantments of the bay.

Does that sound far-fetched? Well, consider that my native north coast stands so exposed to the rigours of the Atlantic that we cannot grow there even the most ordinary trees except in a few sheltered plantations; while in and around Falmouth rare and exotic plants and shrubs flourish opulently out-of-doors. Even before the Second Great War, when the importation of bananas was suspended for a few years, Falmouth had been cultivating her own. Some were fattening in the park during the war, when small boys, unable perhaps to recognize a fruit they had so seldom seen, set about the tree and damaged it beyond recovery. As I looked across the county then from my bleak and exposed north coast, the thought flitted through my mind that, in such a deplorable end to a daring experiment, Mother Cornwall might have been warning this "nestle-bird" of her sadly shrunken brood of boroughs not to pursue too far the devious and absorbing passage to exoticism.

Neither by glance nor gesture has Mother Cornwall ever had to give such a warning to Fowey, though she may have had anxious moments during that rollicking period when the Gallants of Fowey, in the days of the Third Edward, refused to strike their colours on demand as they sailed past Rye and Winchelsea. Instead, they routed the ships sent out to punish them by these two arrogant places, and thereafter flaunted with their own the arms not only of Rye and Winchelsea but of all the Cinque Ports. Again in the Fourth Edward's time Mother Cornwall may have drawn a deep breath of suspense. Although Louis XI and Edward had come to a truce, these full-blooded Gallants fell upon the French. What could an English king do with such men? Told by a Royal messenger (whom they relieved of one ear) that the French were no longer the enemies of England, and that they must act accordingly, the Gallants sent back word that the French were still the enemies of Fowey—and went on acting upon this long-cherished conviction. For they had old scores to pay off.

Royal displeasure vented itself in an order for the confiscation of all Fowey's ships and naval stores and for their transfer, together with the great chain which Edward III had provided for the harbour, to Dartmouth. This put an end to Fowey's account as a respectable auxiliary naval base, but there remained her commerce by sea, which went back to the days when Fowey stood on the trade route from the Continent to Ireland and the West of Britain. For generations now Fowey has been the chief port from which china clay (kaolin), produced in the nearby St. Austell district, is sent to all parts of the world. Like Falmouth's therefore, though on a much more modest scale, Fowey's shipping is cosmopolitan.

Both ports are favourite haunts of yachtsmen, for South Cornwall waters are ideal for the absorbing recreation. It was from Falmouth that Robert Peverell Hichens, a local solicitor and a keen and accomplished yachtsman, went off to serve in the Royal Navy during the Second Great War and, by his leadership and daring, won for himself the unofficial rank of "Nelson of the Navy's little ships". Fowey produced no comparable figure; but her fishermen, seamen, and yachtsmen gave once more to their country's service that expert knowledge of, and long familiarity with, the ways of ships and the sea, which is really national capital distributed among Cornwall's coves and harbours—and almost forgotten in peacetime.

While my response to Falmouth's superb setting and politely masked prosperity is a passive yielding to something subtly distinctive in the Cornish scene, I run and leap towards Fowey, so boyish and ebullient still is my affection for her. It is not, of course, that Fowey lacks distinctiveness, or that her appeal is to the crude and callow of mind and heart. In the end, I suppose, it all comes back to that sense of "belonging", which we Cornish find it so difficult to put into words without blurring its significance and making ourselves look like vague and sentimental fools. From my experience of it, the rhythm of Fowey's life is essentially Cornish. In her streets and along her waterside I can hear the steady, comforting beat of Cornwall's heart.

When I cross in the ferry, scramble to the top on Polruan side of the harbour, and sit looking across at Fowey, strung out and yet snug and compact along the western slope, I feel how exactly right and almost inevitable it was that to two or three generations of English-speaking peoples this place should have become the microcosm of Cornwall. And I ask myself whether "Q" (Sir Arthur Quiller-Couch) could have achieved just that result with Falmouth, if his study windows had opened out upon the bay there instead of looking across Fowey Harbour to this precipitous Polruan.

The answer, I think, is that he could not. For one thing the real pattern of Cornish life is always best revealed in the small community. Our Celtic forbears were widely scattered over the face of Cornwall in tiny groups. Even villages came late in our history; and towns, in a sense, were foisted upon us by influential people who had to get a lot of "foreigners" from beyond Tamarside to live in them and show us how useful, from their key positions, they could be to the surrounding countryside. Even now our towns are mostly no more than fair-sized villages. Fowey is one of these; Falmouth is much more. Moreover, Fowey's harbour, which is markedly the smaller, is linked with an industry that is particularly Cornish; her life as a port throbs very much in time with the pulse of the china clay trade. In other words, she is manifestly and essentially a Cornish port. Falmouth also is Cornish, and notably so in her front street; but she is pre-eminently an English possession, and has been prized as such since the days of the Packets and since she began, as Conrad once put it with unusual candour, to thrive on the casualties of the sea.

Both Falmouth and Fowey, like St. Ives and Penzance and other places all round the coast from Bude to Looe, have a non-Cornish element in their populations: valetudinarians, retired people, and so on. Falmouth has also a large number of "strangers" among her working people, and altogether her non-Cornish residents must form an appreciable proportion of the whole—the figure may be as high as fifty-fifty. The pattern of Cornish life at Falmouth, then, tends to wear thin, and another is becoming insistently interwoven with it. It is because Fowey is still richly, though unobtrusively Cornish, that I get there a sense of "belonging", of being at home, which Falmouth, for all its prestige and enchantments, never engenders.

In these two ports, together with Par and a few smaller ones, the south coast of Cornwall affords safety and facilities for shipping which the north coast, in the absence of a harbour of refuge, has never been able to offer. Yet in the course of the centuries storm and fog have strewn some of these south coast coves and bays with the wreckage of hundreds of proud ocean-going ships and sleek and modest little coasters. All in all, it is likely that the Manacles, those treacherous rocks not far off the shore about ten miles north-east of The Lizard, have claimed more victims than any other single spot along the south coast. People in this part of Cornwall, on winter nights when the gale roars across the peninsula, still talk about three disasters of the Manacles in which altogether five hundred men, women and children were drowned.

On a January morning in 1809, during the Peninsular War, a brig of eighteen guns, and a transport homeward bound from Portugal, were lost here within a couple of hours of each other. In the transport were three officers, seventy-five other ranks, and thirty-six horses of the Seventh Dragoons. Two hundred lives were lost from the two ships. Six brave fishermen from Porthoustock put out in their small boat to render what assistance they could. Another victim of the

Manacles was an emigrant ship bound for Quebec, with many children among her passengers. Four short of two hundred lives were lost in this disaster, which was the more unaccountable and distressing for having taken place in the bright moonlight of a May night. And thirdly, there was a seven-thousand-ton, brand new steamship that struck the outer rocks, where a hundred of her passengers and crew perished. I should say that while the bolder and wilder north coast of Cornwall has sealed the doom of the greater number of vessels and fishing-boats, the south coast has levied the heavier toll of human lives, because it has been here that the bigger ships have come to grief.

One portion of the Cornish coast which is neither north nor south is the long sweep between The Lizard and Land's End. This is the sole and heel of the sea-boot, with Mount's Bay as the initial curve of the arch of the foot. For some people this stretch of thirty miles, with its hinterland, is all they know of Cornwall, and all, they think, they need to know. I do not agree; but I commend their choice. For here you get the beetling and jagged severity of the north, in stretches of cliff from Lamorna to Pordenack Head, and from Kynance to Gunwalloe; and, by contrast, the Mount's Bay shores, with "few harsh and untamed features" and having as background thousands of acres of Cornwall's most richly productive land.

Penzance, mild and equable child of the prosperity flowering from this garden of West Cornwall and from her favoured place in the bay, is the key also to the West Penwith peninsula. This is mostly a great mass of granite moorland and hill and is almost oppressively rich in remains of ancient Cornwall. Standing sentinel a little to the east is St. Michael's Mount, by description "too often profaned for me to profane it". Canon Taylor's almost colourless evaluation of it as "the greatest natural curiosity and the most commanding object in the county" must serve: or better still, perhaps, Spenser's

> St. Michael's Mount, who does not know?
> That wards the Western Coast.

To the south and east again is The Lizard district which, because of its metamorphic and intensely sheared sedimentary and igneous rocks is, to the geologist, among the most difficult and fascinating complexes in the whole country. To the layman it is "a wonder and a wild surmise", for here, as nowhere else in England, there is—besides the abundant Cornish heath of Goonhilly, *erica vagans*—a mass of serpentine, that beautiful, veined, and variegated rock in soft greens, and browns, and reds; speckled so much like the skin of the serpent, that it was thought to warrant the linking by name of reptile and rock. The full beauty of the serpentine is dramatically, even melodramatically, displayed, in all its variety of colour and form, at Kynance Cove, which, in consequence, is often considered the chief glory of all this area. As miniature lighthouses, and in many other shapes, serpentine finds its way to all parts of the country; for upon the rock has been based a small but locally important industry since its pioneers were given encouragement a century ago by the Prince Consort.

This sweep of the coast between The Lizard and Land's End— between the heel and toe of the boot—and particularly the eastern portion of it, has a record of destructiveness to shipping as grim as any in the county. In one period of three years, three hundred lives are known to have been lost in shipwrecks in the Porthleven district alone, the ships and cargoes involved having a value of some £300,000. Both the Penzance and The Lizard life-boats have been capsized in the westerly and south-westerly gales that have swept across the bay. One of the heroes of the disaster to the Penzance life-boat was a horseman who, in the vain hope of rescuing at least one of the men struggling in the seas, gallantly swam his animal out through the surf.

As The Lizard is the most southerly point in the kingdom, so Land's End is the most westerly. It is curious into what ecstacies some people can still work themselves—freely discarding litter in the process—over the second of these two, simple geographical facts. The modern pilgrimage to the "first and last" bit of cliff in England seems to me, in any profound satisfaction that it affords, altogether inferior to the ancient pilgrimage to St. Michael's Mount—even if you leave out of account the generating and sustaining piety which was involved in this. For the "guarded mount" is an exquisite poem in Cornish granite; Land's End, itself and not the district, is unremarkable prose. The neighbouring Pordenack Head and, even more, Tol-pedn-Penwith (the holed headland of Penwith), not much farther away, make the Land's End for me anti-climactic. And you get much the same effect if you bear down upon Land's End from the north. The jagged pre- cipices of Botallack Headland, of granite, like the rest of the district, fill me with much more awe than when I stand on the "first and last" promontory in England. For down among the crags of Botallack is one of the most spectacular, and for that reason perhaps the most pathetic now, of Cornwall's innumerable "knackt bals".

How can I translate out of the Cornish this phrase which has for us such haunting melancholy? "Disused mines", "abandoned mines", "finished mines"—each is a good literal translation, and each seems to kill outright all the poignant significance of the phrase; almost in the same way as would a sentence of doom pronounced by a judge with a bad lisp or in a falsetto voice. Down there is the gaunt ruin of Botallack, whose deepest workings ran far out and far under the sea, so that the miners could hear above their heads at times the rocks and pebbles being driven ashore by the ground sea. Botallack's tin, copper, and arsenic, in a period of sixty years, fetched well over a million sterling. Still along the coast, and a mile or two to the north-west, is Levant Mine, not so spectacularly sited, but with workings which used to run for more than a mile under sea-bottom. Levant was a money-getter, too; in ninety years her tin and copper—our mines are always feminine —were sold for two million pounds. During forty years her growth called for £400 from the mining people concerned in her welfare, and in that period she brought them the handsome profit of £200,000.

I hope I have not given the impression that Land's End itself stirs in me no emotion. (It assuredly does on the rare occasions when I am there in high summer—rage and disgust are the emotions evoked by that fair-ground spectacle, inevitable, it may be, but none the less repulsive). When there in other seasons of the year, I remember what an ordeal to the small craft of the old days was implicit in what we in Cornwall call "goin' roun' land". I remember too our special figurative use of the phrase. When anybody is desperately ill in my part of Cornwall we say dismally, "I'm 'fraid he's goin' roun' land." This is as near to admitting as words can that scarcely any hope is left. It was, I believe, the hazardous business of getting vessels round Land's End and safely into the English Channel, or into the Bristol Channel funnelling from the Atlantic, that gave us our saying. It means that the chances of recovery of the person ill are as slender as were the chances of small ships rounding Land's End safely in foul weather.

Dread of that venture was most marked in prehistoric times, when two tracks were made across the county so that it might be avoided. One was from St. Ives Bay to St. Michael's Mount, the other from the neighbourhood of the Padstow Estuary to Fowey. Both these "roads", it is true, passed through ancient tin-streaming districts and were therefore useful for the conveyance of tin ore to the coast for export. But I agree with Dr. Hencken who, in his *Archaeology of Cornwall and Scilly*, gives as first among reasons for these two tracks the profound dislike, if not the abiding fear, of the old mariners of rounding such a promontory as Land's End. Thus, the traffic from Ireland and West Britain to the Continent would be by sea to Padstow and St.

Ives, overland to the two southern ports, and thence by sea, probably, to the Continental depot isles off the Breton coast.

There is a theory that the genesis of the two roads lay, not in the dangers of rounding Land's End, but in the piracy which may have been practised off that peninsula, perhaps by tough fishermen of Sennen, who would wax fat on the interception of Irish gold or Continental goods. This may be so; but it does not accord with the account given by the oft-quoted Diodorus the Sicilian of "the inhabitants of that part of Britain which is called Bolerion" (Land's End), who, he says, "are very fond of strangers, and, from their intercourse with foreign merchants, are civilized in their manner of life". In and for those far-off days this was a considerable tin producing area, and what with this activity and with fishing, I should say the Land's End people had little impulsion to bother themselves with piracy which, if it was profitable, was also fraught with many and great dangers.

There has since been a fair amount of piracy off the Cornish coast, but a nimbus that has hung more heavily and more continuously over the heads of the sea-board people, and some of those inland, is that which gathered round their evil reputation as wreckers. One could find plenty of evidence that for centuries the Cornish regarded what was thrown ashore from wrecks—cargoes and portions of the doomed ships—as "God's grace", of which they were to avail themselves as freely as possible.

Charles Henderson, whose early death was an irreparable loss to Cornish scholarship, pointed out in one of his *Essays in Cornish History*, that in regarding wrecks along their coasts as blessings to be enjoyed the Cornish were not in the least a peculiar people; this was the natural attitude of former coast-dwellers all over the world. Right of wreck along the Cornish coast seems originally to have been vested in the Crown; but it gradually passed to the sea-board lords of manors, one of whom even claimed all wreck from Mount's Bay right round Land's End to the Gwithian sands—the richest prize in this kind along all the Cornish coast. Naturally, the lords' agents tried to allow as little wreck as possible to fall into the hands of the poor and eager coast-dwellers, often reinforced as they were by great crowds of miners who streamed to the coast when news reached them of ships a mile or two away being in imminent peril.

These impoverished wreckers, I daresay, were a lawless, grabbing lot, and got away with as much loot as their strength and ingenuity could ensure. They may even have been so callous as not to concern themselves much, if at all, with the human wreckage tossed in by the waves. For this, at any rate, they would hardly have been censured (whether they were held in anger or contempt, or not) by their superiors, who themselves could not exercise right of wreck if from a ship in distress any creature, human or animal, got ashore alive. In the olden times, there was this legal incentive to callousness which may have been too much for the servants of the lords of manors as well as for frail mortals so very poor as undoubtedly were the generality of the Cornish.

As to coast-dwellers having been unregenerate in this respect down to comparatively modern times, what seemed like acres of reports of Cornwall Assizes have yielded me in support of this assertion not a grain of evidence. Nor is there anywhere, I feel sure, a scrap of documentary evidence that would have been missed by Mr. Henderson's expert hands and eyes, to bear out the viler suggestion that Cornish coast-dwellers lured vessels to their doom in order to plunder them. This is the very stuff of the sensational novel, and I believe it to be little or nothing more.

Dark stories may since have been inspired by the eighteenth-century phrase "wreckmen" which originated in Cornwall and which seems to have given to the parish of Breage a most unenviable notoriety. But a passage in *The Gentleman's Magazine* (February, 1796) is, I think, conclusive proof that "wreckmen" were concerned with life-saving and not plunder. In this case, a transport with hundreds of Dragoons on board foundered in a storm near Porthleven. Joining themselves by a rope, nine Breagemen, called "wreckmen", attempted to reach the ship before she went down, "When a sudden gust and a dreadful sea coming over them, their rope broke and they were never seen more."

If in the distant past sailors have found the Cornish coast singularly destructive and some of the coast-dwellers inhospitable, their successors have been greatly blessed by the establishment of an altogether more merciful and magnificent tradition. The Cornish record of tenacity and gallantry in life-saving, and of succour and sustenance to sailors in distress has been outshone during the past hundred years nowhere in these islands. It is to a Cornishman, moreover, that the seafaring community owes the invention of the rocket-firing apparatus for life-saving, which, between 1870 and 1920, was the means of saving some ten thousand lives.

Henry Trengrouse, who had a cabinet-making and upholstery business at Helston, made great sacrifices in order to perfect this invention, and to persuade the authorities to adopt it. When he was thirty-five he witnessed on Loe Bar, near his native town, the wreck of H.M.

frigate *Anson*, with the loss of a hundred lives, including that of the commander. Trengrouse was horrified by this wastage of human life under his very eyes, and for long he was haunted by that terrible scene in which he and so many others had been harrowed and impotent onlookers.

From that stormy day in 1807 he was dominated by plans for the rescue of sailors who should be in peril near the shore. To his experiments and his invention, which was to mitigate if it could not avert such disasters, he devoted his little fortune of £3,500, and sacrificed time, comfort, and even health, with a singleness of purpose that was almost sublime.

By the time of his death in 1854 he had received £50 from the Government as compensation for 20 sets of his apparatus which it had ordered; the large silver medal of the Royal Society of Arts, with an award of thirty guineas; and an autographed letter and diamond ring from the Emperor Alexander I of Russia. What probably gave Trengrouse most satisfaction was that he was widely known as "The Sailor's Friend", a designation given to him during the sittings of an Admiralty Commission. Since boyhood I have often seen the perfected life-line performing its work along the Cornish coast, and never without a stir of pride because it was a Cornishman who invented it, and who gave the best of forty-seven years of his life in order that crews of vessels stranded where the use of boats was impracticable, might, in what we now know as the breeches-buoy, be brought safely to shore.

Few English people, and for that matter not many Cornish, know anything of Trengrouse. Better known everywhere is our tradition of rescue-work by life-boat; though even this has received little notice compared with that given, by those who like curdling the blood, to the Cornish tradition of wrecking. Since the first decade of the nineteenth century nothing has been more revealing than the life-boat service of the character of the Cornish coast and of the humble people whose homes are there. They have not been more gallant, more skilful, or more steadfast in rescue-work than the coast-dwellers of other counties along the British coast, but they have an impressive record of life-saving, and have not lacked heroes of the first quality.

Of phantom terrors, apparitions, and omens, of which the Cornish coast has been stated to be prolific, I, who was born and bred there, have had no experience, nor have I even heard them mentioned there. If the coast has the power to stir, sometimes incongruously, memories of "old, unhappy, far-off things", that is no more than you would expect of a coast with such a record of storm and destruction. Let me give only one example from many in my own experience. The rocks and sands of Gwithian, with Godrevy Island and its stone-circled lighthouse just off-shore, are among my favourite haunts. Often to me they are as much pure joy on a summer day as they are to any stranger: but sometimes the radiance will fade from the sunshine, and the blue sea change to grey and become whipped to fury by a seventy-mile-an-hour gale. St. Ives, across the bay, becomes hidden behind a curtain of haze. Above the Knill Monument and massive Trencrom a winter sunset flares, and all the land below is a silhouette softened by blurring spray.

That was how I saw it one January afternoon in 1939, following the night when seven of the eight men in the crew of St. Ives life-boat lost their lives on service in the bay. As I stood by the boat, her bows holed, both sides stove in, and tossed by the breakers on to a great platform of rock, I looked towards St. Ives and knew from old experience, what a town of sorrow was there obscured by the spray. Gwithian Sands, Godrevy Island, and St. Ives have from that day meant much more to me than ever before, and now even their names evoke one more memory of how, along this wild, majestic north coast of Cornwall, "the Lord hath his way in the whirlwind and the storm".

II

UP-ALONG AND DOWN-ALONG

IN THAT little classic of the Westcountry, *Footprints In Far Cornwall*, Robert Stephen Hawker, Vicar from 1834 to 1873 of the bleak and wave-beaten parish of Morwenstow, in the north-east corner of Cornwall, relates of the widow Joan Treworgey, hostess of the Ship Inn at Boscastle, that she was born two doors away from the inn, "and except that she travelled up the hill to Forrabury Church to be married there, it appeared that a diameter of five yards would define the total circumference of her wandering life". No doubt Hawker was consciously writing for a circle of mainly non-Cornish readers, to whom he was by that time famous as the poet of *Cornish Ballads* and more particularly the "Song of the Western Men". (This song, by the way, has been heard in many parts of the country since Hawker's day, chiefly by Rugby spectators on grounds to which Cornish supporters have travelled in the hope of seeing their county XV one stage nearer the final of the English Counties Championship.)

Had Hawker been writing for Cornish people only, he might easily have used, instead of "she travelled up the hill", our much more familiar "she went up-along". One of the first significant things to be noticed about the Cornish is our frequent use of "up-along" and "down-along". It is a key to our way of life. In this, as in other ways, our speech bewrayeth us: physical life in Cornwall is principally and often strenuously undulating. As a prim and precise pedagogue of early Victorian times put it: "The inland aspect of the country is that of a continued succession of hill and valley." It was this that made for, among other things, the relative fixity of the Cornish before the advent of the motor omnibus, for if you went with a party in horse-drawn brakes on an outing that involved travelling twenty miles, it was almost certain that the menfolk and perhaps the nimbler women would have to walk at least seven miles to ease the strain on the horses going uphill.

Of the sixteen Cornish hills which are over a thousand feet high, my oldest friends are the two highest, Brown Willy (1,375) and Rough Tor, pronounced Rowtor (1,312). It was chiefly to see them that I climbed quite often to the Three Turnings above our school at Padstow.

The once-buried St. Enodoc Church

I had got it firmly into my head that these were our only Cornish mountains, and this seemed to lend distinction to my part of North Cornwall, even though they were some fourteen miles away towards the Devon border. Nevertheless, I had an uneasy feeling that they were only "courtesy mountains". Impressive as they sometimes looked away there above the dunes and St. Minver Highlands, they did not dominate the landscape quite as I felt mountains should. From their broad bases they appeared to rise far too slowly and comfortably, and I guessed (quite rightly) that no dangers assailed anybody who climbed them. I never once saw snow even on their summits, but this is not remarkable considering how rarely snow falls anywhere in Cornwall.

Whenever I have wandered over the moors fairly near Brown Willy and Rough Tor, I have wondered why so few visitors to Cornwall are attracted to these parts. They are easily reached from Camelford, through Tregoodwell. The air here is as exhilarating as along our Atlantic seaboard, and from these hills on a fine day there is a wonderfully comprehensive view of our Cornish land. On the most easterly of Rough Tor's jagged peaks, moreover, remains evidence of our long tradition of Christian worship: the foundations of the ancient chapel of St. Michael the Archangel, Cornwall's patron saint. In much more recent times, on the slopes of Rough Tor Cornish teetotallers used to gather in thousands annually to celebrate their apparently most cherished virtue.

Nobody told me when I was at school that these two were the highest of a ridge of granite hills which runs brokenly, and losing height all the time, down to the Land's End. In a school which was steadfastly built of the surface granite that we call moorstone, faced by quarried granite, and roofed with blue-grey slate, and in a town where granite, abundant in the streets, appeared also in the bollards all round the quayside, nobody connected these things for my edification with our proximity to granite on the Bodmin Moor and to slate which had been quarried at Delabole for some 400 years. Young as I was, I should have been interested, I think, if one of my teachers had told me to picture Cornwall as a sea of clay-slate—which is roughly true— with five "islands" of granite rising above that sea and together making up quite a large portion of the county.

Ages ago rocks, chiefly granite, that were very hot and possibly molten, were erupted through Cornwall's clay-slate, which itself then underwent various changes. The eruptions were on the Bodmin Moor in the north-east of the county, the moorlands north of St. Austell

3

Falmouth Harbour

in the centre, and a roughly circular area, with a diameter of about ten miles, to the south of Camborne-Redruth in the west, where also there is the Tregonning Hill district (very small), not far from St. Michael's Mount, and finally the whole of the Land's End peninsula, which is the only part of Cornwall where our granite confronts the sea.

A teacher with a warm touch of imagination—dangerous but divine gift—might also to advantage have given us at school a picture of Cornwall, after those powerful punches from fists of granite, as a creature with its back broken, and badly, in three places. From this I should have understood later on, that the familiar sub-division of the county into East, Mid, and West Cornwall—areas with their differences in dialect and with their own historic centres of mining administration—was not another example of human weakness for method and convenience, like the old three-decker sermons on Sundays; but was based upon something as solid and enduring as Cornish granite.

The great upheaval of igneous rocks ages ago has had an enormous effect upon Cornish history and character. One result was that the county has a greater variety of minerals than anywhere else in the kingdom. Tin and copper are the most widely known, but Cornwall has also lead, antimony, iron, and zinc; silver, cobalt, and manganese; bismuth, wolfram, and arsenic. Uranium also; and gold in small quantities in tin streaming works and river beds. If you know where the granite islands are, you may be confident of finding the mineral areas nearby. The railway line from Liskeard to Penzance runs almost in the middle of the mineralized zone. It is difficult to realize it, though: and the stranger to Cornwall need not reproach himself with deficient observation if he notices no outward and visible sign of the zone until he is within a score of miles of the end of the journey. Unlike him, I have come to look out for the engine-house and stack or two, sil-houetted against the sky for a few seconds, mute and melancholy witnesses of the great days of Cornish mining, when the roar of the stamping machinery was heard in the land, and when, deep "below grass" and sometimes in a temperature of 112 degrees, the next-to-naked miners toiled and sweated themselves into a consumption that made theirs the shortest working lives in industry.

All that activity and nearly every vestige of it have gone and the railway line, as it curves above and below the middle of the mineralized zone some five or six miles broad, passes through or skirts some of the most beautifully wooded and fertile countryside in Cornwall. Before the zone is reached from Plymouth, there come the estuaries and creeks of our Tamar and Lynher, which have flowed down from the bare northern upland between banks that grow ever more leafy and fruitful as they approach the south. Then, west of Liskeard, comes the gracious Glynn Valley; and thereafter for a cherished mile or two, through a green shade pierced here and there by shafts of sunlight, the Fowey river, an angler's paradise, dimples, dances and glides, almost alongside the rails until it reaches Lostwithiel and broadens out in its lovely southward valley to Fowey and the sea. Beyond Lostwithiel, the uninitiated traveller may be bewildered by the scene north of St. Austell, where the tall clay-waste tips stand like a vast encampment of Cornish giants, but soon he is passing through good farming country again, with woodland and copse, and from the carriage window at Truro he gets a fleeting glimpse of the Truro river going down to meet the Fal through perhaps the most enchanting of South Cornwall's deep and bosky river valleys.

It is a few miles farther westwards that the traveller, even though singularly unobservant, cannot fail to notice signs of the mineralized zone, in spite of the painfully achieved success of hundreds of small-holders who have reclaimed in "penny packets" much of the country-side which was laid waste by mining. Beyond Redruth and along the foot of the massive granite Carn Brea, with its castle and obelisk and its rock-strewn slope, there is a graveyard of mining enterprise, with scores of smokeless stacks and roofless engine-houses as headstones which, for us, need no inscription. Cornishmen remember, as they pass, that among the "knackt bals" here is the Great Dolcoath, deepest and richest of their mines, where the men worked half-a-mile below day-light, and where they brought to surface in two hundred years tin and copper ore which was sold for over six million pounds, with a hand-some addition for arsenic, silver, and cobalt. Grim and perplexing this mile or so may be to the impressionable traveller, who will the more delight in the remainder of the journey to Penzance which is set in green and pleasant places, including "The Golden Mile", probably the richest market-gardening area in the whole country.

What is it about this rail journey through the southern half of Cornwall—or the excursion by road, from which the railway line does not wander far—that makes it so perennially fascinating to one born and bred, as I was, along the Atlantic seaboard? For one thing, it is the trees. On the windswept uplands which run out to make our northern cliffs "as high as the Great Pyramid", we are for the most part destitute of trees. Save in a sheltered valley or two, or around a semi-exposed farmhouse where they lean away from the wind so that from a distance they look like a hand stretched over the buildings in blessing, trees from Land's End to Morwenstow are rare; though not, indeed, nearly so rare as our "national" bird, the glossy, jet-black Cornish Chough, that handsome member of the crow family, with his red legs, and long, sharp, red bill.

Because the watershed of the county has a southern drainage, only our own River Camel has managed to get diverted in a quadrant to a northern estuary, after having flowed for much of its course southwards. Unlike the Tamar, Looe, Fowey, Fal, and Helford rivers of the south with valleys beautifully wooded, the Camel within five or six miles of the sea can find scarcely a tree to mirror; though higher up, in the sheltered Allen Valley, there are trees to delight the eye and spirit. So there are, but a mile or two from the sea, at Mawgan-in-Pydar, that exquisite village deep in the Vale of Lanherne. By and large, though, we of the north coast must go over the upland of clay-slate and beyond the granite islands to the gently sloping southern portion of the county, and especially the river valleys, for long walks or idle dreamings among trees.

Parts of Cornwall were better wooded in the time of our Celtic ancestors, notably districts between St. Austell and Camborne, and chiefly along the southern edge of the mineralized zone, where woodlands were cut down for fuel and their sites dug up for tin and copper. Some of this woodland has been restored; but much has not and our descendants are not likely to see again a large area of the county in its pristine state of grace, with oak and ash, willow and hazel, birch and alder, elm, and sycamore and beech.

The mineral zone, while it is only about one-fifth of the area of the county, holds about one-third of our population. This is as you would expect. Where the minerals have been exploited near the granite islands, there the people have collected and multiplied. True, there was a large-scale exodus to mining camps overseas when the great era of our own mining prosperity closed during the late seventies of last century; but even so, Camborne-Redruth is still, with nearly forty thousand people, the largest urban district in the South-West of England. This town was once—and, beating feebly, still is—the heart of our mining world. Its present considerable engineering works have on g supplied deep mines the world over, as did its former fuse-making factory. From the Camborne School of Mines, young mining engineers have gone for over eighty years, with the assurance of welcome, to wherever the search for minerals has made "a hole in the ground".

By the time Cornish mining had fallen upon bad days, St. Austell had become the centre of a greatly extending china clay industry based upon the weathered granite of the "island" north of it, and the town has since greatly grown and prospered. From the Middle Ages Truro, a busy market town and port, with a fortified castle overlooking the river where it curves above the old Forest of St. Clement, did re-markably well out of mining in the neighbourhood. Westward again, Penzance has enjoyed prosperity derived from several sources, among them the mines operating round our remotest granite islands. East of St. Austell are the two ancient boroughs of Lostwithiel and Liskeard, neither a big centre of population even on our reckoning (there being some 350,000 of us all told in Cornwall), but towns which have had good days in close association with mining. They have retained some of their old prestige, though now as market and tourist centres only.

It is to the north of the mineral zone that you must look for our ancient capital, which is Launceston (pronounced Lanson), and for its successor in 1838, Bodmin. On one of the four principal roads into Cornwall from Devon, Launceston is our only hill-top town, and is a mere mile or two on the Cornish side of the border. Although it was the capital of our Duchy for about five hundred years, Launceston used to seem to me to be, in spirit as in location, remote and aloof from the Cornish scene. But in this I was wrong. It has now one of the strongest and most enthusiastic Old Cornwall Societies in the county, and the 1947 Gorsedd of the Cornish Bards, held near the town, was a gratifying success.

Seven hundred years after they had been subjugated by the English, the Cornish Celts were still smarting from their defeat: and the English, particularly in the early days of their extended supremacy, must have thought us very bad losers. Since bad losers require watching, where a better watch-tower than the castle at Launceston? The English, in fact, left us pretty much to ourselves and our humiliation, until they realized that there were valuable things in the Cornish earth, that the Cornish themselves were not without good qualities, and that it was not sensible to leave excursions to the county only to pilgrims to St. Piran's Oratory and St. Michael's Mount, who were prepared to endure hardship as a spiritual exercise. Even so, the English did not venture far into Cornwall until it had provided itself with a system of roads that was tolerable by their standard (or the Roman). Thus, from the inauguration of Assizes in the thirteenth century until the beginning of the eighteenth century (and then only as a consequence of much agitation), the King's Judges came no farther west than Launceston.

In 1715 a petition from the county was sent to the House of Commons, humbly praying "your Honours that leave may be given to bring in a Bill that the Assizes and Generall Gaol Delivery for the County of Cornwall may be kept and held atte leaste once in every year atte the Town of Bodmin, within the said County". This last phrase may have been no more than technical and customary; but it may well have been, besides, a polite reminder to the Commons of the remoteness of Launceston from the more thickly populated parts of Cornwall, and of the hardship of bringing witnesses, jurors, and others almost to the Devon border. "To the great joy of the whole county"—an indubitable snub for Launceston here—the Commons decided that thereafter the Summer Assizes should be held at Bodmin.

Followed quickly another petition, this time to the Bishop of Winchester and the Justices concerned, "that they immediately issue warrants, or take some effectual care that the roads and wayes from Launceston to Bodmyn be levelled, and the trees and hedges cut fit for travelling with coaches, etc". In July, 1716, Bodmin Corporation paid John Alford ten shillings for "rideing to Polson Bridge (across the Tamar) against the Judges to shew the way". At heavy expense the Corporation of Bodmin had had the ancient refectory of the Convent of Grey Friars adapted as an Assize Hall, and this served until 1838, by which time another prolonged and powerful agitation in the county had resulted in the choice of Bodmin as the sole Assize town.

Judges and counsel, I do not doubt, heard of the change with distaste and even dismay, for crossing the Bodmin Moor is one thing in summer and quite another in winter. In spite of the money and labour spent upon the new road across the moor—it was along the older one, by way of Camelford, that their predecessors had driven—it was a wild, rumbling, jolting, and even dangerous coach journey of some twenty miles which the judges and lawyers had now to make, with a blanket of mist liable to descend at any moment upon the desolate scene.

Gilpin, the eighteenth-century author of *Forest Scenery*, must have been at least as anxious to ascertain what Cornish woodlands were like as the early nineteenth-century judges were to regulate Cornish conduct, but even Gilpin was appalled by the Bodmin Moor and, instead of pushing boldly westwards from Launceston in pursuit of his researches, he seems to have hurried south to Liskeard and out of the county as fast as horses could take him. Some people have supposed that it was the deep dislike judges and counsel had of crossing the moor, that led one or another of them to originate the saying, long resented by our county town, "Out of the world and into Bodmin"; but I think the saying has older roots, and was a reminder of the days when Bodmin lay well off the main road through the county.

There, then, in Bodmin and Launceston, are our present and our ancient capitals, at either end of a great granite moor, inside of whose circular periphery of tiny villages is a big tract of wild and fascinating country, with an average of one person or so to the square mile. Obviously, neither Launceston nor Bodmin is the ideal county town. The one is almost out of Cornwall; the other is far from central, and is not even on the main railway line. Moreover, the bulk of our population is in the area from St. Austell westwards, and for its convenience Truro is the town best suited by far to be our capital. It is, in fact, from Truro that the county is largely administered. For more than seventy years, too, Truro has had towering up from its St. Mary's Street the Cathedral Church of our restored diocese.

Despite the loss of the Assizes, Launceston has remained a unique outpost of the Cornish land and, much as in Norden's time, is "a pretie towne, neatly kepte, and well governed by a Mayor and his brethren, that upon festivalls goe in their scarlet Roabes". Bodmin, in acquiring both the Assizes, added to its ancient prestige as the ecclesiastical centre of Cornwall, and increased its few memorable buildings by two in granite in the simple style which so well suits our county.

What I like most about Bodmin is its magnificent parish church, the largest in Cornwall; its high and windy Beacon, from which you can see so much of North and Mid Cornwall; its Mount Folly Square, so well described in the autobiographical opening of "Q's" charming romance, *The Ship of Stars*; and a headstone or two in slate in its churchyard, with seraphs and cherubs picked out with an inspired nail by that wayward Cornish genius from Altarnun, Nevill Northey Burnard.

What I like most about Launceston is its altitude, its crisp air, its castle ruins, its medieval south gate, and, of course, its Church of St. Mary Magdalene, with an exterior of granite so elaborately carved as, by contrast, to make the average Cornish parish church look bleak. The explanation is simple and touching. St. Mary Magdalene was the gift four hundred years ago of Sir Henry Trecarrel, who had been suddenly bereft of both son and wife. No other tears that I know of have left such lovely traces through the centuries upon our Cornish granite—a stone which the Norman craftsmen, in the great age of church-building in Cornwall, found so unresponsive to their tools that they rejected it for stone easier to work, even though some of it—you find it mostly in the Falmouth district—had to be brought all the way from Caen.

North of the mineral zone there is only one more borough; and but three other towns still classified in 1962 as urban districts. The borough is St. Ives, down near the instep of the sea-boot. Just as at Padstow we talk of Up-town and Down-town, so they do at St. Ives of Up-along and Down-along, and know almost to an inch where the one begins and the other ends. Fishing made St. Ives's Down-along, and with the decline of the fishing its functional basis—and old Cornish fishing-places are perfect examples of functional architecture—has gone.

Its continued existence is due not so much to artificiality as to art, or should one say to artists? Pictures have succeeded pilchards in giving vitality and activity to what might otherwise have become museum pieces, or worse. I hope that art will be more constant than the pilchard —that small and scaly, but tasty and nutritious fish, which used to come in its millions to St. Ives, whence it was dispatched to the country districts and to distant Italy. It is absent now when "the corn is in the shock", its favourite season for calling in the old days, and when the artists are nowadays holding their exhibitions in or near its old lodgings. It would be comforting to think that St. Ives, in spite of the decay of fishing and its ever increasing popularity as a holiday resort, had not much changed for generations, but I still cherish a lively hope that something of the old St. Ives will be there for years to come, to match an old memory and reward an old loyalty.

Now, we must go a score of miles along the coast to Newquay, pausing a moment on the eastern arm of St. Ives Bay to commiserate with Hayle, which gets its name from the Cornish word *heyle*, estuary. Nearly thirty years ago Hayle was humiliated by the loss of its urban status, and was merged for administrative purposes in the big rural district of West Penwith. For a century at least Hayle was the chief industrial handmaiden of Cornish mining, and its name was familiar to and respected by engineering men all over the country. The town also provided port facilities for the mines. The names of Copperhouse and Foundry might well have sufficed, I think, to spare this people with a notable tradition in engineering and shipping the ordeal of having to develop a "rural bias" and to "babble of green fields". For years the Home Rule question burned at Hayle as brightly and steadily as did once its foundry fires. As a Cornishman I often warmed my hands at the flame; but I confess that I liked to turn away from the fire before long, to wander over the extensive towans which front the broad and blue Atlantic.

For Newquay I have had much affection since boyhood, when we used to drive there on summer mornings so early that the gipsies on St. Columb Downs were barely astir, and in St. Columb Major, with its fine old church, only a few townsmen were about to wave a sleepy acknowledgement of our greetings as our horses clattered through that narrow front street. Between hedges where the dew lingered we drove through St. Columb Minor into Newquay, and I cannot help thinking how much more pleasant was the drive than now. Newquay, at that time, was no longer, as it was just before my father's boyhood, the grey fishing village of eight hundred souls. Already the huer's house on the Headland had become a survival, and I was never to see the huer at his station, watching for signs of pilchard "schools" in the bay, and never to hear his strong baritone voice shouting "Heva, heva!" through his speaking-trumpet, the moment he saw the significant, reddish-brown troubling of the waters.

The sound that I was always to associate with Newquay—with Bodmin it has been "the bugles speaking comfort"—was the tinkling of little bells on sleek and spirited ponies which used to trot along with "jingles", carrying perhaps three passengers and the driver. The jingles, alas, have gone; but still the huer's house is there, a dazzle of whitewash in the sunshine, with the blue bay as background. Above the worn flight of steps is the huer's platform, in the shelter of a stuggy tower, which goes well with the castellated curve of the little building's thick, stone walls, and the diamond-shaped peepholes towards the sea. If the town's buildings were twice as interesting as they are—and that would be no difficult objective—this would remain for me still the most attractive of all.

As a holiday resort Newquay was years ago warmly commended by a President of the Royal College of Physicians; and more than one over-strained statesman has revived, if he has not been rejuvenated, in this Atlantic air. But a finer testimony still to its pleasure-giving as well as its health-restoring qualities, is the fact that in this former fishing village of eight hundred people you will find in summer thousands of visitors from all parts of Britain. They leave this rugged court of the "Queen of North Cornwall" with a new light in their eyes, and usually with a resolve to return at the first opportunity. That is to their own and, of course, to Newquay's benefit. So it does not much matter, that one Cornishman who has loved her since all his world was young, laments that the town has so little of the character of that incomparable coast.

The next dozen miles also tempt me to dawdle, for who, with an eye for grandeur, can hurry past Bedruthan Steps or over the cliffs of Porthcothan? But there is a spur to hurry me, for the next town of our three is Padstow. In boyhood I used to hear my progressive elders and betters bewailing that Newquay was extending east, west, and south, while Padstow was shamefully static. That indignation I used to share; not very intelligently, but with a strong conviction that somebody was "letting the old place down". It did not then occur to me that developing Newquay was, by comparison with developing Padstow, not much more than child's play. For one thing, Newquay fronts the open sea (alas, that any of that superb position should have been squandered), while Padstow is tucked away in a valley a mile or so from the broad harbour mouth. Padstow has lacked both the natural environment and the social conditions which alone could have given rivalry with Newquay muscle and sinew. With its growing attraction to holiday-makers from all parts of the country because of its character and charm, the old part of the town still retains the stamp of its former response to the simple standards set for the small builder by traditional Cornish architecture. There are growing flaws and blemishes, I know; but the town is yet, in its own unpretentious way, pleasing, as befits a place which, thirteen centuries ago, was the settlement of the most important of the Celtic saints.

Strong as the temptation is, I shall not linger now along the quayside which cradled me, or in the narrow streets and courts which were the playground of my childhood. Instead, on the way to Bude, we must pause at Wadebridge, about eight miles from Padstow, to admire the late fifteenth-century bridge over the Camel, which here flows down to the sea through seventeen pointed arches. Like Hayle, though in a much more modest way, Wadebridge has also been a foundry town; but equally it is a market centre, and babbling of green fields is here an old and easy accomplishment. Another market town on the road north-east to Bude through the lovely Allen Valley is Camelford, a good centre from which to explore the Cornish hills and moors, and also from which to make sudden sallies to the coast. For three centuries Camelford was a borough returning two Members to Parliament, and its town hall, over the market house, was the gift of a former Duke of Bedford. Camelford House, solid and grey among the trees by the river, belonged to a member of the illustrious Pitt family.

On the coast not far away, Tintagel, with its ruined castle, tends more zealously than Camelford the garden of legend, in which bloom bright and fair the flowers of chivalry, rooted from the days of King Arthur and his knights of the Round Table. Better to my liking is Boscastle, which is almost a rock garden above the little harbour with its oblique entrance between two massive promontories, one looking as though it were hiding behind the other for protection from the fury of the sea.

A little way from Boscastle is the Church of St. Juliot, the restoration of which the youthful Thomas Hardy supervised, and whence he took his bride, the Rector's sister-in-law, honeymooning through other romantic haunts of the Cornish land. In the church are memorials both to Hardy and his first wife. Much as I like *A Pair of Blue Eyes*, I always fail to include it when I am asked for a list of novels with settings in Cornwall. At first I used to attribute this to forgetfulness; but it is the forgetfulness induced by an old conclusion. This was that, good as it is, and illuminating about the early Hardy, *A Pair of Blue Eyes* does not help at all to interpret the Cornish and Cornish life to a stranger. Cornwall is no part of Wessex.

If it were not essential for my present purpose to push on to Bude, I should go no farther towards it, I think, than to Crackington Haven, which was once to have been given a Royal name and transformed into a harbour of refuge, and which provides such a dramatic revelation when, having come down that lovely combe, so deep and quiet, you find the beach flanked on your right by a cliff stupendous even by the standard of this coast of grandeur. I like to go back along the combe and up to the old church of St. Gennys, peerless in situation, and with a lovingly tended churchyard from which the coastal panorama north-wards is unforgettable.

It is odd to recall, as one stands in the wind and the sun looking up towards "Passon" Hawker's cliffs at Morwenstow and beyond to Hartland, that schism once tore this parish in twain. One of the eigh-teenth-century rectors ranged himself with John Wesley, and the anger and scorn of his brethren in that part of the diocese found vent in the memorable phrase of one of them, who wrote in 1745 of the convert's "circumforaneous vociferations".

But this has nothing to do with Bude, you say; and you are quite right. The truth is that Bude stirs in me scarcely a flicker of enthusiasm, it is a seaside town so modern and undistinguished. Even its castle is modern, though it is rightly cherished as the former house of Sir Goldsworthy Gurney, a Cornish genius in the field of invention whose Bude Light markedly improved the assistance given to mariners by lighthouses all round the British coast. It has a fine stretch of sands and a spacious bathing pool, and there can be scarcely an English pastime for which it does not provide, so no wonder it is popular with our cousins beyond the Tamar. It has a canal, too; the only one in Cornwall. Seven years and about £130,000 were spent on its construction, its chief purpose being to facilitate, in the days before railways and motor lorries, the carriage inland of sand from the beaches. Bude sand, like that from Harlyn and other bays along the north coast, has a high percentage of carbonate of lime, and consequently it has been a potent fertilizer of the good wheatlands of the neighbourhood. Along the canal bank they used to house the Royal Bude Life-boat, the only one that was ever given to a port, I believe, by an English monarch.

King William IV paid Wade, the famous Sunderland shipbuilder, a hundred guineas to make the craft, which had, however, an undistinguished career. In 1844, "manned by those sailors of the port who are likely to be employed in her in the event of a wreck occurring", the boat put out into the bay for practice. Very soon a heavy sea broke the steersman's oar and four others on the larboard side of the boat, which was brought broadside on, became utterly unmanageable, and was soon capsized. Fortunately, it was possible to rescue the trapped crew, for the boat was quickly swept in close to shore; but I feel sure that for weeks afterwards in the Bude district tongues were wagging vigorously.

For there had been a long and heated controversy about this Royal life-boat, and it had been freely alleged that in her house along the canal, she had suffered as much neglect as had the training of her crew. How true this, was, I do not know; but Bude life-boat work at this time certainly seems to have been handicapped because the place had only a handful or so of skilled seamen, who were often away in coasting vessels on their lawful occasion when storms were beating on their native coast and the assistance of the life-boat was being sought. Some years after the capsizing of the *King William IV*, Parson Hawker of Morwenstow fell foul of the Bude life-boatmen. His solicitude for those in peril on the sea was one of the noblest traits of a richly complex character. When a number of lives were lost from the big ship *Bencoolen*, bound from Liverpool to Bombay with machinery for the cotton mills, Hawker raged in a letter about the "dastards of Bude", who would not launch their life-boat to go to the rescue. But I fear that Hawker's anxiety about seamen in distress, and his notorious detestation of Bude Dissenters, between them clouded his sea sense and warped his judgement. For this was one of the occasions when Bude could muster only two skilled seamen for service in the life-boat. Even had a full complement been available, however, I doubt whether they could have got the boat out through the breakers before it was too late to save the crew of the *Bencoolen*, who have been sleeping these many years in Bude Churchyard.

So much, then, for Bude. Except in summer, the aggregate population of all these towns of the north cannot much exceed thirty thousand, which is less than that of Camborne-Redruth alone. Nor would more than a few thousand heads be added if I included as towns north of the mineral zone St. Columb, almost a hill-top town and the last real stronghold of our ancient Cornish game of hurling; Perranporth, where deep combes open out to a long stretch of sand which is a playground for thousands of English people in summer; or St. Agnes, straggling about the lower slopes of its Beacon and "stippy-stapping" down to "Quay", a game and friendly little place which has survived the cessation of both its mining and its shipping. It is clear now, I hope, why we in the north are urban *in petto*, and that what small concentrations of population we have depend upon agriculture, the holiday traffic, or remnants of a former appreciable coastal trade and fishing industry.

Between the sea and the granite islands, both north and south of the mineral zone, there is good farming country; though near the granite, the soil is thin and acid. In the north, Padstow corn, partly because of easy access to sand, is proverbially the best in the county; and from the deep clay just behind Bude, along the banks of the Camel, in the area from Lanteglos to just south of Newquay, and again south of Hayle, a normal season will produce good crops. The enchanting valleys running inland from the south coast are full of alluvial deposits from the hills, and are very rich and fruitful. The Tamar Valley, in particular, is famous for early flowers and fruit, especially strawberries. From the River Fal to the River Fowey the country for generations has been known as "the granary of Cornwall", and eastward again, between the Fowey and the Tamar, the clay-slate produces first-class wheat and barley right down to the edge of the cliffs.

A rich tract not many miles south-east of the Mount's Bay parishes, with their specialized and early crops of flowers and vegetables, is the district around Helston, which is its market and was, until late in 1962, its railway centre. Most strangers know Helston as "the quaint old Cornish town" where people dance through the streets and in and out of the houses on May the Eighth every year—not even a World War could stop them—to a tune made widely familiar by the late Peter

Dawson. Helston people do not spend the other 364 days of the year rehearsing the ancient dance. Their town is, in fact, a busy enough little place, though with a population not much larger—excluding the Royal Naval Air Station at Culdrose—than it was in the Middle Ages, when Helston was a leading town of the West. Among the oldest of our twelve surviving boroughs, it became in the reign of Edward I one of four coinage towns in Cornwall.

This does not mean that it has ever had the right to issue its own coins. What happened was that, four times in the year, tons of tin ore were brought here from the mines in the neighbourhood. In the coinagehall, a corner (French, *coin*) of each block of tin was cut off for testing by officers of the Duke of Cornwall. If the quality of the ore was up to standard, the Duchy arms were stamped on the tin, and the tinner was taxed at the rate of four shillings for every hundredweight stamped. Helston's Coinagehall Street, like that at Penzance, is a reminder of those days, when the heir to the throne, as Duke of Cornwall, derived a tidy revenue from this source.

I am quite ready to join in the praise of Helston as an attractive, well-planned town, but not to agree that the planning of other old Cornish towns shows notable blemishes or defects. Truro, for example, another of the few Cornish towns with broad front streets, the sides of which are being continuously cleansed with running water, is quite well planned, and the pity is that the deep bowl in which the city is set has been allowed to overflow in two thin streams of dwellings at opposite sides of the bowl. A pity, too, that in one quarter the city should have departed from the Cornish traditional roofing of native slate; though I must say that the Hendra Estate does not look so pink and "foreign" as does the northern fringe of Falmouth which, even from as far away as Carn Marth on a clear day, reminds one of a rash sunbather who has exposed too long a portion of her back to the ardent rays. Why will not those responsible for building in Cornwall bear always in mind that ours is essentially a county of soft greys and greens and browns? Right up to the First World War this was accepted as a canon as naturally as was simplicity, though not monotony, of design. Between the two wars standards crashed about us, and, scattered over the face of Cornwall, we have several crude and silly legacies of the resulting chaos.

I must not leave Helston without remarking that, for a Cornish town, it has a unique situation, in being near a lake—and that the largest in the West of England. (Falmouth's pool, which used to mirror the graceful Killigrew swans, is hardly a lake.) In the valley running down to the sea from Helston, Loe Pool is said to induce in Canadians a deep homesickness; not least, I suppose, because of the lovely woods of Penrose and the presence near Loe Bar of the wild service-tree, with foliage resembling the maple. With one or two smaller streams, the exuberant and troublesome Cober river is responsible for Loe Pool, which is about two miles long and two or three hundred yards wide. The water ought to flow sweetly down the valley and out to sea, but the waves have thrown a bar of sand and shingle across the far end.

In the old days, when the streams were swollen and the waters of the lake unregulated, the valley towards Helston used to flood, and the town mills were put out of action. Whereupon the Mayor would hurry away to Penrose to present a leather purse containing a few pence to the lord of the manor, from whom he would receive permission to have Loe Bar cut so that the water could rush out to sea. Before the mines in the district were closed, the streams were ochreous, and it is said that the people of the Scilly Isles, some forty miles away, knew when the Loe Bar was cut, because the sea round their islands was dis-coloured by the outrush from the lake. A more interesting illustration of the force and direction of currents in the sea used to be provided when the lake water was clear. The fact that the bar was broken was then known in the Scilly Isles by two tides, and trout borne along in this current of fresh water were caught by the islanders.

In a whispered aside I add, for those who are interested, that there are also trout, and eels, in our only other lake, Dozmary Pool; but you must not expect a Cornishman to talk of fish in reference to this almost circular sheet of water, a mile or so in circumference, and nearly nine hundred feet above sea-level, in the lonely Bodmin Moor. For this lake, though but rarely visited, is almost as sacred to us as is the Ganges to the Hindus. Here, was it not? the sore-tried Sir Bedivere, hearing

> the ripple washing on the reeds,
> And the wild water lapping on the crag,

at length summoned resolution to obey his dying King, and to fling the great sword Excalibur out into the lake; and here rose an arm,

> Clad in white samite, mystic, wonderful,
> And caught him by the hilt, and brandished him
> Three times, and drew him under in the mere.

If you go to Dozmary Pool as the light is fading, you will not, I think, be in much doubt (unless you are a scholar of the Arthurian legend) that it was here, in the folds of the desolate moorland of East Cornwall, with Brown Gelly hill brooding massively beyond the pool, and unbroken silence all about you, that the wheeling sword "made lightnings in the splendour of the moon" the night they bore the great king away for ever from the Cornish land. Here, too, between the lights, may sometimes be discerned the giant form of our legendary giant Tregeagle, doomed for his sins to stoop over these lifeless waters (the Dead Sea of Cornwall, somebody called Dozmary of old) and to empty the lake with a limpet shell the base of which has been cleanly holed.

I am thoroughly Cornish in that, while I realize how impoverished we should be were we suddenly to forget our legends and to shed our superstitions, I claim the right at times to exercise in relation to them a gentle scepticism, in which is no element of hostility and certainly none of ridicule. Legends and superstitions, thus regarded, are better fare than catchwords. Not for nothing have we Cornish lived for ages close to the granite, from which we may somehow have derived the hard, grey core of commonsense that is one of our characteristics— though just as the granite by its fiery intrusion added new and rich complexities to the country, so in our character there is a variety which strangers find interesting and sometimes a little bewildering.

Not far from my Truro home, along a lane flanked by tall foxgloves, clumps of rose campion, and the bright yellow cat's ear, a gateway leads into a field the hedge of which is here neatly rounded off with small slabs of granite. The granite post upon which the wooden gate is hung is some two feet thick and four feet out of the ground. The slabs on one side of the gateway are granite wholly exposed, so that, in the afternoon sunshine, its bare surface glints pin-points of white fire. That, it seems to me, is the Cornish character at its core, and it finds expression when somebody is trying to persuade a Cornishman away from the course which commonsense and duty commend to him, in the rebuke, "And I doan't want none of yer ole nonsense."

On the other side of the gateway the granite slabs are visible only on close inspection, being overlaid with ivy, tufts of delicate grasses, honeysuckle, and dog roses, while about the base are scattered greater celandines. The whole is crowned with the yellow fire of furze. This granite is fulfilling its function as steadfastly as are the stark stones opposite; but here it has taken on new colour, and warmth, and life. That is how I like to think of the Cornish character at its fulness and best; the granite quality of commonsense softened and animated by,

Fowey

and in constant touch with, other qualities less stark and forbidding. There is then something receptive about it, as the flowers in the gateway are receptive of sunshine, rain and dew, and of the fertilizing touch of the bee.

We Cornish as a people have a full measure of this receptivity, and not least to the legends and superstitions which come to us from the twilight of our past. "Old nonsense", the sceptic in us may provoke us to exclaim about them, though often with only feigned disparagement; and I myself wonder whether any of them are markedly more "old nonsense" than some of the things which have been said about our county by people who have come far to see us, and to put us in the way of understanding ourselves. There is, for example, that widely known description of Cornwall as the "English Riviera". In spite of the tropical and semi-tropical shrubs and plants which flourish along the south of Cornwall, no Cornishman would have dreamed of making this Riviera claim for his county, and I am always curious as to its origin. Oddly enough, I find that Sir Arthur Quiller-Couch, over sixty years ago was anticipating, though unwittingly, the coining of the phrase, and, as was his way, dealing faithfully with such counterfeiting. This is what he told the ship's crew and passengers of the *Cornish Magazine* one day from the bridge of that gallant but short-lived craft of which he was master:

> "We have on our side unique and magnificent natural scenery, and a pleasant and extraordinarily temperate climate. The Riviera has exquisite scenery, but somehow its scenery lacks the depth, the 'values' of ours. It wears at the best a painted appearance, and the difference between the Mediterranean and the Atlantic is just the difference between flat cider and champagne. It has more sunshine, far more sunshine, than we enjoy . . . but the alternations of heat and cold are swift and treacherous."

Yet it was, I suspect, upon this supposed similarity of climate that Cornwall was first proclaimed another Riviera. No doubt this has had the effect of swelling the crowds of holidaymakers and the thinner streams of invalids and retired people who come to the far south-west; but none of these can possibly find here either the peculiar virtues or vices of the climate along the shores of the Mediterranean. Our winters are usually milder than they are anywhere else in the kingdom, and our summers are cooler. The late Mr. Tregoning Hooper, when he was superintendent of the Falmouth Observatory, once declared that "the general conditions in Cornwall for man, beast, or crops, are such

4

The Lizard

as few countries are favoured with, and make our county a veritable Elysium, compared with less fortunate parts of the British Isles".

Mr. Tregoning Hooper went on to explain that in Elysium "people lived a life of perfect happiness: there was no snow, no frost, nor storm, no rain, but the cool west wind breathed there for ever". Well, for about four days in the seven the wind in Cornwall is probably westerly. Snow we seldom see, and frost not much, though a farmer friend tells me that if we have any in March we have a similar recurrence in May, when it is really damaging. The average number of fine days in the year has been estimated by one geographer of Cornwall as 114; of rainy days, 164; cloudy and changeable days, 87; but I think some twenty or thirty of the days described as rainy might well be added to those which are called cloudy and changeable. Our normal rainfall is over forty inches, and is heaviest on the granite uplands. We need plenty of rain because of our porous soil and our hilly country sloping south to the sea. One of our old sayings, indeed, lays down that "Cornwall can do with a shower every day—and two on Sundays!"

Our south coast is much milder than the north, which does not, I confess, induce in me favourable comparisons with Elysium when I am struggling to move forward along the familiar cliffs with a showery north-westerly gale blowing in my face. If from Truro, which is about midway between north and south, I go to my native coast for an afternoon in summer, I return braced as by a potent tonic. If I go south to Falmouth I come back dazed as by some sweet soporific. Lovely the bay is there, and full of strange delights are those rich, sub-tropical gardens which the Foxes have fostered; but nothing here, or anywhere along the south—not even the Helford Estuary, or Gillian Creek, or unforgettable Manaccan—can shake my constancy to the rugged cliffs and the comparative bleakness of my own Atlantic coast.

You will have noticed that when the slightest pretext for so doing presents itself, it is always there that I turn. It would be strange if it were otherwise, for my family have been coast-dwellers in North Cornwall—and in one small portion of it—at least since Tudor days. Yet I am, I hope, as responsive as any other Cornishman to the call of the hills, moors, and valleys. Certainly I am convinced that a good half of the beauty and fascination of Cornwall is withheld from those who race in their cars along our two or three main highways, turn north or south to the sea, and there remain until it is time to hurry back again over the Tamar bridges.

How much more of the character of Cornwall, in its variety, is revealed, for example, by an hour or two spent on the Carn Marth, the granite hill which slopes westward to Redruth as the more rugged and romantic Carn Brea slopes eastward towards the town. On the summit of Carn Marth the pellucid waters of the pool mirror the blue sky and the abrupt, cleanly-hewn cliffs of the quarry. At moments they mirror also swallows which you may later see resting on the wires of the electric grid, ranged like notes in music.

From the western edge of the Carn's summit you look down upon Camborne-Redruth, where there are no airs and graces about the solid buildings of local stone, but where the grimness of smokeless stack and silent engine-house has been comfortingly offset with trees and shrubs. Towards the North Cliffs, only a mile or two away, the town is flanked by the woods of Tehidy, where lived that Lord De Dunstanville, of the Basset family, in whose memory—and particularly his interest in the miners—was raised the obelisk on Carn Brea. Southwards from that carn, which has yielded so many relics of ancient Cornwall, the broad shoulders of Carn Menellis baulk the eye of any glimpse of the Meneage or The Lizard districts, in the same way as the nearer portions of the Land's End peninsula are hidden from view by Trencrom and its huddle of boulders—remaining perhaps from those used by the giant of the hill in his game of "bob-button" with the giant of St. Michael's Mount. So the eye moves quickly down the slope of Trencrom to rest gratefully upon the grey roofs of St. Ives and the shining waters of the bay.

One afternoon in 1940 I chose a perch on the eastern edge of Carn Marth. Bombs had been scattered about in the night, and a possible danger lay then in a dawn landing by the Germans somewhere along those miles of coast in the south, and a determined swarming across the narrow peninsula. The very insecurity made dearer the panorama of rolling countryside and sea, from St. Ives to Trevose Head, and from Falmouth Harbour to St. Austell Bay. Far away to the north-east were Brown Willy and Rough Tor, giant sentinels of the Bodmin Moor; in mid-distance the glistening china clay waste encampment above St. Austell; and stretching for miles from the foot of the carn were the thick, Cornish hedges, separating hundreds of tiny fields which looked like gaily-coloured, dark-bordered handkerchiefs spread out, country fashion, to dry in the sun.

Between the foot of the hill and the sombre pines round Baldhu Church was the once immensely rich mining country of United Downs, with its tall chimneys and Doric engine-houses, surrounded by a wine-dark sea of heath, in which bobbed here and there yellow lightships of gorse and broom. Where a narrow road skirted the downs of the south, the eye lingered compassionately upon a solitary tree, bent (as we say) almost two-double by the wind. Low, grey farm-houses in their scores were scattered about the land from St. Agnes Beacon in the north, through the broad parish of Kenwyn whose eastern bounds slope into Truro City, and so to the woods of Kea and Killiow and the silver reaches of the Truro river. Above the waste and the arsenic ovens of the old mine of Poldice ("The men of Poldice are as quiet as mice"), rose the burrows of Creegbrawse, a mine more ancient even than her pallid sister in the lowlands—for among the company of tin traders who came to Creegbrawse from the Eastern Mediterranean was there not the lean and grave Apostle Paul?

Nearer the foot of the carn drowsed the village of St. Day—which one of my friends once called "the town that died"—dreaming, perhaps, of the prosperous days when its then empty streets were thronged with miners and their families, or of an earlier age when pilgrims rested here and were refreshed in spirit at this famous shrine of the Holy Trinity before they braved again the rough track that had led up and down from distant Rough Tor and would drop to the sea at last in the shadow of St. Michael's Mount. A little west of St. Day, and indistinguishable to a stranger's eye, was the neat, grassy amphi-theatre of Gwennap Pit, of all his preaching-places in Cornwall the one that John Wesley loved best. Here, when he was past his eightieth year, and was making the last of his many visits to the pit, he preached to a congregation which, on his own estimate, exceeded thirty thou-sand. About this figure I have often had doubts; but against them I set the possibility that the pit, most carefully tended, has since been much constricted, and recall the well-known entry in the *Journal:* "I think this my *ne plus ultra*. I shall scarce see a larger congregation till we meet in the air."

From Gwennap Pit I looked across to the woods of Scorrier House, once celebrated for its collection of Cornish mineral specimens, and to the oaks of Wheal Unity, from the edge of which Killifreth Mine points a long finger to the sky; then, far over the countryside, towards Holywell and Newquay Bay, and so to Bedruthan Steps and Trevose Lighthouse, a faint gleam above the sands of Constantine Bay. Beyond is my home country, and I fall to thinking of old delights: the Marble Cliffs and Gunver Head, with low-flying oyster catchers far below, and restless herring gulls and noisy jackdaws above and around the mighty Cat's Back; glimpses of the shining heads and shoulders of seals among the rocks; the old cliff wall towards Butter Hole, with its cool green cushions and nodding heads of sea-pinks (our cliff-daisies), and its clumps of pale sea-campion, which we call grannies' nightcaps; blue water cupped between the sturdy shoulders of Tregudda Gorge, or the cream and pale green slopes of the Constantine sandhills; lively sandpipers on the firm, wet shore at St. Minver; the flash of lovely blue and red as a kingfisher passes the little boat I am rowing up the creek between Saltwater Mill and Little Petherick; tense seconds as a buzzard is poised for the kill above the bottoms at Creddis and Sunny Corner, and blessed relaxation as he sails northwards and is lost to view beyond Dinas Hill.

Strangely enough, my thoughts in the end on that far-off afternoon on Carn Marth, came back, as they so often did in the anxious days that followed, to the steep hill I used to climb to school, and to the little group of Tudor cottages, where wrinkled and kindly old women would be sitting knitting and gossiping in the sunshine as I hurried from afternoon school to the quayside, the centre of my universe. There was peace for you, there security; for these cottages had survived the wars and changes of nearly four centuries, and would surely be there when the dear, familiar sounds of life were no longer dulled by the mighty clash of arms. But one night in that year of 1940 this heart of peace and security was broken; for two bombs fell on School Board Hill, and Tudor Close was a heap of rubble.

III

BACK-ALONG

Up-along and Down-along are Cornish words that reveal, in a flash, the kind of physical setting into which we were born, and in which we live, move, and have our being. They are essentially words of movement and direction, a kind of repetitive commentary upon our comings and goings.

"Coming up-along, are 'ee?" asks a West Cornwall man of his friend at the foot of the hilly street.

"I zeen 'un goin' down-along jes' now," a Mid Cornwall woman informs her neighbour.

Another of our key-words, "Back-along", is not nearly as constantly used as the other two. We sometimes use back-along to denote direction and movement.

"Darn 'ee, I've a-comed all this yere way an' fergot me ole purse, and now I've a-got to go back-along fer to fetch 'un," exclaims a Mid Cornwall woman, in vexation, on her way to shop or to pay her rent. But this is the occasional and short term use of the word. As I, and most other Cornish people, know it better, back-along is used in relation to time rather than to distance or direction and most commonly in relation to our Cornish past. I sometimes think we Cornish are all born with our heads looking back over our shoulders into the mists and the mysteries, the splendour and the poverty, of our past. We are haunted by it. It pursues us, generation after generation, as caressingly and unrelentingly as the little waves of a flowing tide pursue the feet of children during their reluctant retreat to the warm sand that stretches above high water mark.

There is, it seems, no high water mark above which we can stand secure and remote from our past. It is an unseen tide that floods the Cornish land from Harlyn Bay, with its Iron Age cemetery and Early Bronze gold crescents, to Dozmary Pool, on the circumference of the little circle of Bronze Age villages that once braved the bleakness of the Bodmin Moor; from Tregiffian Vean, near the Land's End, with its stone burial chamber of four thousand years ago, to the great sixth-century fort of Castle Dore, high above Fowey, and its associations with the immortal romance of Tristan and Iseult; from the base of St.

Michael's Mount, only a few miles from the Celtic village of Chysauster, to the stone circles of Stannon and Fernacre, in the morning shadow of Rough Tor.

Only the learned among us fully appreciate the significance of these and a hundred other relics of the far past, some of which were still being discovered to the astonished gaze of men of the British Army when they were making roads for the passage of tanks and guns to the landing craft used in the invasion of Normandy during the Second World War. Several hoards of Roman coins have been found in Cornwall; but only this one, near Feock in 1944, ever gave itself up to the soldiery.

Few of us in Cornwall are versed in the archaeology and the history of the county, but most of us, if only in a vague, inarticulate way, are more conscious of our inescapable entanglement with the past than are the people of probably any other county in England.

It is this "tie-up" with our past, of which visible and tangible fragments remain under the Cornish skies after four thousand years, which gives, perhaps, to some English people when they are among us, the sense of being in a land that is haunted, a land in and over which broods an ages-old mystery. In his *Twenty Years at St. Hilary*, the late Fr. Bernard Walke told how, on the way over to his parish one day from Sennen with Walter de la Mare, the latter confided that "he thought Cornwall was a haunted land, and he would never venture to stay there again".

Everybody who knows de la Mare's poetry and prose must realize how acutely perceptive, how delicately attuned, he was, and I am not surprised that he found this haunted quality of Cornwall so overpowering as not to wish to repeat his experience. For one thing, he had been staying in a district, West Penwith, or the Land's End peninsula, which has more prehistoric stone burial chambers, stone circles, longstones, and fortified castles, than any other area of its size in the country. It is, moreover, a granite peninsula, and except for its southern valleys, is mainly wild and lonely moorland and hill. The fisherman after trout there in a little moorland stream becomes oppressed with the burden of the past, of which even the water seems to murmur. And northwards, beyond moorland and hill, where, in fantastic shapes, the past has been petrified, the Atlantic beats against granite cliffs which were withstanding just such onslaughts long before the first adventurous seamen from the Mediterranean reached this south-west extremity of Britain—after what prodigies of skill and endurance!

How does our past differ from that of the people of any other county in England? Notably, of course, in that radically we are not English people at all; though even in our place-names we tend to become more English towards Tamarside and "glorious Devon". Our remotest ancestors were the British people who came here from the Mediterranean shores. The county is strewn with their survivals in stone, principally their chambered tombs, of which Lanyon Quoit, in the parish of Madron, near Penzance, is a good example. These tombs, which look like enormous tables, or rude altars, puzzle as well as impress me, because the transport and erection of such gigantic slabs of stone must have been a problem even for a small army of men three or four thousand years ago. Then there are the tombs of the less notable of the old Britons, the great mounds, or barrows, of which Carn, in the parish of Veryan, south-east of Truro, is the most extensive; though the one that attracts me most is that on Denzil Downs, near St. Columb.

Most of the stone circles the old Britons also left to us are in the Land's End peninsula or the Bodmin Moor. The Nine Maidens at Boscawen-Un are the best known in the one area, where there are seven; and the Hurlers, not far from Liskeard, in the other area, which has ten. Some learned people who are not Cornish have professed to be shocked and pained by our having given to stone circles the names Nine Maidens and Merry Maidens, and have frowned darkly upon our cherished legend that the latter group are naughty Cornish maids who dared to dance on a Sunday, and that two pipers were also turned to stone for their share in the revels. Behold, say these critics, the blighting effect of John Wesley and the Sabbatarians upon the descendants of this ancient people whose graves, or meeting-places, perhaps, are marked by the stone circles. The fiction seems innocent enough to me. Anyhow, the Nine Maidens, the Merry Maidens—are not the names charming?

Besides chambered tombs and stone circles we have other remains of the old British people: weapons, tools, ornaments, and incinerary urns, many of which may be seen in the Museum of the Royal Institution of Cornwall at Truro. After the early Britons came the Celts. They remained almost undisturbed in this far corner of the land until the heathen English, who overwhelmed the Celtic occupants of other parts of the country, had been Christianized. Before this, of course, the Romans had conquered all the kingdom, except Cornwall and the North of Scotland. The great Roman roads and towns ended in the West at Exeter, but the Romans did penetrate into Cornwall and, in a small way, built a road or two here. Four of their milestones have been found, two in the north-east corner and two in the south-west. It was in our tin and antimony that the Romans were really interested, and they probably sent a few of their officials down here to facilitate production and conveyance to the coast for shipment.

That they did this in my part of Cornwall was proved by the discovery of a large, wedge-shaped ingot of tin at Carnanton, St. Mawgan-in-Pydar. Stamped on the ingot was the Roman helmeted-head and small buckler, and the inscription marked it the property of "our Lords the Emperors". The hoards of Roman coins discovered in Cornwall—one tin jug containing as many as 2,500—were mainly near the south coast ports and the tin-streaming districts of the rest of the county. In 1931, when a farmer was ploughing at Magor, not far from Camborne, he came upon a piece of Roman tessellated pavement. It is possible, however, that the villa, the floor of which was subsequently opened up to the light of day, was built by a Celt, who had learned to admire the Romans and had imitated their way of life.

Although the Romans did not greatly concern themselves with Cornwall, and did not interfere much with the production of tin and the manner of life of the natives, they left us with something much more precious than their coins and milestones and a camp or two. They left what had become under Constantine their official religion, Christianity, which was to survive here when it was swept away elsewhere by the English hordes who overran the country, except Wales and Cornwall. It was not until four hundred years after the arrival of the English that they finally vanquished the Celtic-Cornish, and it is with a portion of this period of resistance in the south-west that the name of King Arthur has been linked in legend and song. A friend of mine has said, quite rightly, I think, that if there had been no King Arthur, it would have been necessary for the Cornish to invent one. There has probably been much invention in the things we have heard and read about this glorious Celtic champion of the West, and particularly his associations with Cornwall. The celebrated King Arthur's Castle at Tintagel was built centuries after Arthur lived and fought the English, and its site was formerly that of a Celtic monastery. I do not suggest that this matters much, in the balance with the mighty Arthurian legend, which figured so largely in medieval romance and flowered so beautifully again in the work of later poets. That there was a King Arthur is in little doubt; that he was specially linked with Cornwall by birth and residence no historian will affirm. What cannot be gainsaid is that his memory was cherished here for centuries after the English had finally subjugated this western land.

In the twelfth century some of the Cornish were still clinging to the belief that he who had championed Celtic freedom so magnificently was alive and would come again to save them. Canons of Laon were in Cornwall early in the century, receiving gifts for their cathedral, and having with them sacred relics which had already effected at Exeter seventeen miraculous cures, They came to Bodmin, with its large monastery, then the chief town in Cornwall, and there a blind girl had her sight restored and a deaf mute had regained his hearing, while a man with a withered hand awaited in the church the miracle that should make him whole. Unfortunately for him, he began to quarrel with the Archdeacon of Laon's servant, who had scoffed at the Cornish-man's assertion that King Arthur still lived. At once there was an uproar among the Cornish, "and so many people with arms rushed into the church that, if Algar the Clerk, had not prevented it, there would have been bloodshed in the end". Needless to add, the poor man with the withered hand, "who had made the tumult on behalf of Arthur, did not receive his cure". Sad; but I feel certain he was Cornish enough to go home with the conviction that he had done the right thing.

The Cornish, it is evident, were still looking to Arthur to restore their old integrity and to avenge the humiliation they had nursed (as the Cornish do) since their final defeat by the English. That had been the end of nearly a thousand years during which they had been virtually left to themselves. For generations after the defeat they must have gone on talking wistfully, and more and more ignorantly perhaps, of "the good old days"; but, little by little, they got used to the new order, and by the end of seven centuries they had become so reconciled to their lot that "they had much conformed themselves to the use of the English tongue". Even so, let an English stranger in their midst "inquire the way or any such matter", and he was met more often than not with the firm but polite, *Meea navidna cowzasawzneck*, which is Cornish for "I can speak no English"—non-co-operation, not as the policy of a people, but as the predilection of the individual.

The contemporary English stranger will meet with no such em-barrassment. Indeed, a minor terror of my life is that one day an interested stranger from the other side of the Tamar will ask me to speak to him in Cornish, so that he may know what the language is like. He will have to be satisfied with my assurance, on the word of the best authorities, that Cornish is a most pleasant-sounding language, Cymric and not Gaelic, and without the guttural quality of some other Celtic variants. It was "stored with sufficient plenty to express the conceits of a good wit, both in prose or rhyme"; and I wish that more of whatever literature we had, had been preserved so that we might savour the good wit. You would hardly expect to find much of this in the mystery plays which have survived; though some of these are marked by a real Cornish independence of treatment, and all enriched by those local touches which, even now, wherever they may be found, delight the Cornish heart.

I tried once to read aloud the Apostles' Creed as our forefathers used to say it in their long, low, simple churches. Had it been in Latin I could have said it with much more ease and confidence; and yet somehow, inept as I was and almost shyly diffident, I found a queer sort of familiarity as I went on, and during the long pauses there seemed to be in my ears the faint echoes of faraway Cornish voices, for this one solemn occasion in unison. They loved the service of their Catholic Church, which was benevolent and wise enough to allow them to use their own language, instead of Latin, for the Lord's Prayer, the Apostles' Creed, and the Ten Commandments. It was perfectly natural, therefore, that Cornish opposition to the first English Book of Common Prayer should have been passionate; and in 1549 this feeling flamed into armed rebellion. "We will not receive the new Service," the Cornish had protested, "because it is like a Christmas game, but we will have our own Service . . . as it was before." ("As it do belong to be," say their successors), "And we, the Cornyshe men," they repeated, even more emphatically, "*whereof certain of us understand no English*, utterly refuse this new Service."

In the end they had to accept; though not before much blood had been spilt, and not before the long, dark shadow of the gallows had fallen upon the Cornish land as never in the centuries since. Liturgical change came, and many another disruption of the old way of life, social, economic, as well as religious; but so acquiescent had the Cornish become in Elizabeth's time that Scawen, a not disinterested observer, I take it, records their *desire* "that the Common Liturgy should be in the English tongue, to which they were then for novelty's sake affected, not out of true judgement desired it". As long afterwards as 1640, however, the Vicar of Feock had to administer the Sacrament in Cornish, because his older parishioners had no English with which to follow the service in the little church by the riverside, one of the few dedicated to a woman saint, and one which suffered grievously at the heavy hands of the Victorian restorers.

The language lingered on in the west of the county until the middle of the eighteenth century, though by its beginning almost every Cornishman could speak English, and the number who were bilingual was probably small. A century ago, I find, the Rev. Robert Williams, of Oswestry, who was compiling a Cornish dictionary, was greatly dismayed and discouraged because he could not ensure for his work even two hundred and fifty subscribers, the minimum he required in order to publish. He "was much surprised that the Cornish gentry took so little interest in the language of their forefathers", and he uttered a warning that his "would probably be the last attempt that was ever made to collect what remains of the ancient Cornish". It was twenty years before the reverend gentleman issued his *Lexicon Cornu-Brittanicum;* and if he still supposed that this would be the last work dealing with our ancient language, he was wrong.

After an interval of another twenty years came Jago's Dictionary, and early in the present century, Henry Jenner, whom many of us remember as the perfect patriarchal Grand Bard of the Cornish Gorsedd, published his scholarly *Handbook of the Cornish Language.* In the late 1920s, during the high summer of the Old Cornwall revival, two other Cornish scholars, A. S. D. Smith and R. Morton Nance, the latter Jenner's successor as Grand Bard, compiled an English-Cornish Dictionary. Mr. Morton Nance also produced in 1938 a Cornish-English Dictionary. Both have been published by the Federation of Old Cornwall Societies.

To all intents and purposes, however, the Cornish language is dead. Only its ghost, like other ghosts from the Cornish past, troubles us a little, even while we may feign indifference. If we had been bequeathed a body of Cornish literature of real importance, it might be well worth while for many of us to master the language; but in the absence of such a bequest, what real inducement is there to any, except a handful of enthusiastic Cornish scholars, to undertake a serious study of our language? To me, at any rate, it seems a work of cultural supererogation; though I hope there will always be a few people eager and happy to undertake it. The practical value of a knowledge of the language is, of course, in getting at the meaning of our place-names and surnames. In much of his work, from which, alas, he was so prematurely snatched and laid to rest in the Protestant Cemetery in Rome, Charles Henderson put his Cornish to excellent use.

More than once I have half-resolved to learn Cornish, so as to meet place-names with true native politeness and understanding, and then I have blenched at the prospect of having to give so much time to the business, when there were so many other things, which I considered more important and urgent, clamouring and jostling for my moments of leisure. In consequence, I am meagrely equipped for getting at the meaning of our place-names unless I am near my books. It is easy enough to remember, of course, that

> By Tre, Ros, Car, Lan, Pol, and Pen,
> You well may know all Cornishmen.

But even if you know that *tre* means a homestead, *ros* a heath, *car* or *caer* a camp, *lan* a monastery, *pol* a pool, and *pen* a headland, the other parts of the names to which they are prefixed may convey nothing unless you have at least a smattering of Cornish.

My own name is gloriously Saxon; and it does not, I hope, vex the spirit of that alien ancestor who brought it into the family (from Celtic Wales, too!) if he should know that it will die with me. In the family, however, will go on the names of Tremaine (*tre* homestead, *maen* stone, the homestead by the stone) and Helbren (*heyle* estuary, *bron* hill, the hill on the estuary, where is situated the home of my maternal grandfather's family above the dunes at St. Minver). It is entertaining and enlightening to have some Cornish; but it is easy enough, thanks to the scholars I have named, to find what you want in a dictionary or a handbook.

Back-along, then, we Cornish had a language of our own, which has gone out of common use only in the past four hundred years. Back-along, too, we had our own Celtic form of Christianity; and one of the little Cornish places of prayer of some fifteen hundred years ago may still be seen among the dunes between Perranporth and Holywell. Bishop Benson once said that there was no older sanctuary in the land, except, perhaps, St. Martin's at Canterbury; "but if St. Augustine had come here in Cornwall, he would not have had to have made his way among crowds of heathen people who wondered what he was come for; for here in Cornwall he would have found people to meet him with the full knowledge of the Gospel, worshipping here day after day, as well as from Sunday to Sunday, in this little church".

The Perran Oratory was buried in the sand for three centuries or more and was revealed when the sands shifted in 1800. St. Piran I have already described as a jolly old Celt, on the authority of Dr. Max Muller, who expressed the opinion that the saint was "not always steady on his legs"—in other words, was addicted to too much mead and metheglin. There may be some truth in this, for we still describe a man who has been drinking to excess as being "as drunk as a Perraner".

We may charitably suppose that it was St. Piran's voyage from Ireland to Cornwall which left his "land legs" thereafter unsteady; though I like to think, as Cornish miners of old doubtless did of their patron saint, that for all his holiness and his legendary wisdom as geologist and instructor in the smelting of tin, Piran was as jovial a missionary as you could have found in a day's march through Celtic Cornwall.

St. Piran was one of a hundred or more Celtic saints who gave their names to Cornish churches, villages, and parishes. They were the fount and origin of the saying, "There are more saints in Cornwall than in heaven". In the fifth century many of these holy men came here as missionaries from Ireland and Wales, concerned for the spiritual welfare of their Celtic cousins in Cornwall. Christianity had, indeed, survived here from Roman times; but there were probably many pagans, who provided the missions with an element of peril. The saints came in diverse ways. St. Piran, whose legendary first disciples were a boar, a fox, a badger, a wolf, and a doe, made the voyage on a millstone. This was doubtless his altar stone, like the one upon which one story says that St. Petroc reached Padstow Harbour. St. Kea chose a stone trough as his vessel. Upon pagan sites which they found here, these missionaries seem to have set up their hermitages, some of which were later developed into big Celtic monasteries.

So far as modern scholarship can throw light upon that dark period of history, the Celtic saints who came to Cornwall have had their biographies written by the late Canon Gilbert H. Doble, upon whom the University of Oxford conferred her Doctorate of Divinity for his work. Most of us, Cornish people and strangers alike, are content with the more picturesque legends, such as that of St. Keverne speeding with great slabs of moorstone his departing guest, St. Just, who had made off with a goodly chalice prized by his host. St. Just figures in another "battle of stones", this time with his near neighbour, St. Sennen. Each, in a rage, flung at the other a big granite boulder, the two missiles being miraculously guided so that neither saint was injured.

There are several legends of St. Neot, the exquisite dwarf some fifteen inches high, whose favourite devotion was to stand in water reaching to his neck, while he recited the Book of Psalms. Once while he was thus engaged, a beautiful doe, hotly pursued by hounds, fell down before him and mutely pleaded for his protection. One glance from the saintly eyes was sufficient to halt the hounds and to send them slinking back into the woods; and the huntsman who followed, ready to loose an arrow at the doe's racing heart, threw away his quiver and humbly handed to the saint his hunting horn, to be hung as a memorial in the church. The legends of the saint are recorded in rich colour in the windows of St. Neot Church—windows which have come down to us, as so few others have, from the fifteenth century. They are famed throughout the country and among the glories of Cornwall.

The Celtic saints, of whom a few were women, were so numerous that it is no wonder the names of many of them are quite unknown to English people. They were wise as well as holy, these saints who came so precariously to the wild Cornish coast from over the sea. They did not ask of their pagan cousins here that they should abandon their old meeting-places or avoid such old haunts as the streams and wells. Instead, they accepted the framework of life as they found it, and concentrated upon changing the quality of the life. Their own hermitages and altars were set up on pagan sites. The stream and the well, hitherto sacred as the haunts of fairy and piskey, became consecrated to Christian purpose. In this sense, there was no complete break with the past, which is the hardest demand conceivable to make upon a Celt. Instead, there was a gradual process of transition during which the marvellous powers of stream and well became transferred to the saints who "sanctified the water to the mystical washing away of sin", and who had built their little chapels nearby. Thus the wells became holy wells, often receiving the names of the saints who came to be associated with them.

There are about a hundred of these holy wells in Cornwall, nearly half of them with buildings over them. They are scattered all over the county from Morwenstow to Land's End; and at one at least, the Well of St. Euny, Canon Doble used to conduct a service every year. Several of the well-chapels are architecturally interesting, with local stone in much of the work; and they are often picturesquely situated, in some lovely valley with their own leafy groves, or among the sand dunes between the shoulders of which you get a glimpse of the sea. A few holy wells have been restored and are being preserved by local societies of the Old Cornwall Federation and other lovers of Cornwall. St. Mawes Holy Well had long been bricked up in a wall and buried under a garden before it was reconditioned and re-consecrated in 1938.

The water of the wells had special virtues, but not all of these have been remembered. Nobody at Padstow, for example, can now say what miraculous properties pertained to the water of Lady (or Lanad) Well, or of Fentonleno, both with the trees of Prideaux Place as background; or St. George's Well, in the cove near the Old Battery; or St. John's Well, at Hawker's Cove. Best known of Cornish holy wells, because of Southey's verses, is that of St. Keyne, one of the twenty-six children of St. Brechan, and one of fifteen of these who became saints. The legend is that the man or wife

> First of the sacred stream to drink,
> Thereby the mastery gains.

This would account for the brisk sale of water from the well at two shillings a bottle, when two dozen bottles were once sent by an enterprising Rector of St. Keyne to a bazaar at Mount Edgcumbe—the one Cornish mansion many years later, in the Second World War, to have been destroyed by German bombs.

It was—and may still be—customary at several of the wells to drop pins, usually bent, into the water, and to wish as the pin dropped; or else to watch where the bubbles rose to the surface, denoting either good or ill. Fame came to some of the wells because of the cures their waters wrought in a variety of afflictions from sore eyes to whooping-cough. Jenner suggested a rationalistic explanation of the good done by water to sore eyes "in days when personal cleanliness was a very bad second to godliness". If you want to know how absent friends are faring, you go to St. Gulval's Well, near Penzance, and make the proper invocation to the bubbling waters. As an insurance policy against hanging for your infant son or daughter you should have the baptism with water from Ludgvan Well, also near Penzance, or Venton-Uny, Redruth. Some of the wells were resorted to as cures for all the ailments flesh is heir to. Dipping had to be done on special days—May was a most propitious month—and the proper ritual observed; for example, after dipping you walked backwards three times round the well. Then you were cured—or you were not.

From "away back-along" we have left to us, besides the holy wells, about fifty of which are called after Celtic saints, many inscribed stones, and more than three hundred of an original total of five hundred stone crosses. In the moorland not far from Land's End is the *Men Scryfa* (inscribed stone), which commemorates "Rialobranus, son of Cunovalus", who died there fourteen hundred years ago. Near the railway viaduct at Hayle is another such stone, the inscription on which never fails to set me wondering as to what manner of woman was this Cunaide who "lies here in the grave" and of whom all we know is her lovely name and that "she lived thirty-three years".

Of our Cornish crosses, the stump of what was possibly the finest of them all is just inside the south gate of Padstow Churchyard. To me

Land's End
Cornish Hills: Rough Tor, Garrow Tor, and
Brown Willy

as a boy it was an attraction more potent even than the apple trees tempting me to scale the high wall just outside the gate, and more terrifying than the possibility of being caught red-handed by the owner of the orchard. For they used to tell us that if we sat on the great slab of granite on which the shaft of the cross is based, we should hear faintly the roarings of the Devil, who was incarcerated beneath.

This, probably the original churchyard cross, was found buried in 1869. Near the south porch of the church is the head of a "four holed" cross, also found buried in the churchyard. This one and the smaller cross in the gardens of Prideaux Place, are, according to Henderson, "the oldest ecclesiastical memorials in the parish, the sole survivors of Celtic or Saxon Petroc-stow". The largest cross in Cornwall, the one in Mylor Churchyard, near Falmouth, is ten feet out of the ground and about seven feet under it. In Pentewan stone, instead of the customary granite, the cross at Lanherne, Mawgan-in-Pydar, is a beautiful specimen; though it was probably no more richly decorated than originally was the broken and weathered cross of St. Neot. There is a legend of this diminutive saint that he used to stand upon the base of the churchyard cross, and throw the key of the church door into the lock, which it then turned unaided. Churchyards are not the only settings of these crosses; you may find them along moorland tracks, by church paths, and, I fear, without their heads in the middle of fields and used by cattle as rubbing posts.

In the Morrab Gardens at Penzance there is a cross which is much admired. It was formerly in the main street, and on market days pigs were tied to it until a buyer came along to claim them. The crosess, like so many other memorials of back-along, are most thickly distributed in that part of the county. If you come upon "crowse" or "grouse" in a place-name, you may find a Cornish cross nearby. For example, Crowz-an-Wrah, near St. Buryan, and Crowza Down, near St. Keverne, are names both derived, as Henderson once pointed out, from the Cornish *Crowz-an-Wragh*, "the Witch's Cross".

It is a pity that Cornwall, unlike Ireland and Brittany, no longer possesses any of the holy handbells which, with their staffs, the Celtic saints were seldom without. Nothing seems to have been heard of Cornwall's bells—except two which found their way to Brittany— since the end of the thirteenth century, when an inventory of church treasures mentioned "the little copper bell" of St. Piran and the "little bell of St. Symphorian". Deaf pilgrims who go to Stival, near Pontivy, in Brittany, still doubtless have jangled above their heads, to cure them of their infirmity, the little copper bell of St. Meriadec,

5

Dozmary Pool
Whit Monday service in Gwennap Pit

who was the founder of Camborne Church and the saint of its holy well. And in St. Pol-de-Leon Cathedral there is a little bell which belonged to King Mark of Cornwall. While he was over here St. Pol admired this bell, which the king declined to part with. Immediately the saint got back to Brittany, behold, there was the bell, brought to him in the mouth of a fish. I cannot help thinking that only a saint could get away with that one!

Of the bells in Cornish towers some fifty are said to be of the period before the Reformation. In the little detached tower which stands on the edge of the cliffs at Gunwalloe, not far from The Lizard, are still the "iij Bellys", recorded by the Commissioners of 1551, with their ancient symbols and their Latin jingles, thus translated by Henderson:

> With my living voice,
> I ward off what annoys
>
> Let the bells of (St.) John
> For ever ring on.
>
> All people cheer,
> When me they hear.

Landewednack, not far away, has a like trio; and a little eastwards at St. Anthony-in-Meneage, one of the Medieval bells, recast not many years ago, with two others recast in the seventeenth century, keeps company with younger bells in calling good people to the little church by the waterside built to the glory of the saint by the owner of a ship overtaken by a storm in the Channel. Praying for succour to St. Anthony, he promised the church as a gift if his petition was granted; and the saint saw to it that the vessel survived wind and sea and came safely to berth in Gillan Harbour.

The period of the Civil War and of the Puritans was a bad one for Cornish church bells, as the Reformation had been for Cornish crosses. Thus, of Mevagissey the Rural Dean in 1665 had to report "the tower to be dilapidated and the bells imbezzled and sold to one Laurence Grouden of St. Austell in the time of the late rebellious wars". Later, though the times were happier, some of our old bells received rough treatment on occasions of great rejoicing. In one parish all the bells, which were in decayed cages, are said to have been cracked by the sledge hammer used by the blacksmith and his friends during the celebration of weddings. A fair amount of money was spent on the bells and on the ringers, especially in the seventeenth and eighteenth centuries, and since then ringing has still been a favourite accomplishment in Cornwall.

For the origins of our Cathedral Church at Truro you do not have to go "away back-along", because it was as recently as 1880 that its foundations were laid, and seven years later that the choir, with other portions of the building by then completed, was consecrated. Twelve years afterwards were laid the foundations of the western towers and of the nave which was finished a few days before the central tower, and dedicated with great pomp in 1903. By then the western towers had reached the level of the nave roof, and they were completed in 1910. The cathedral, except that a choir screen is lacking, is now as J. L. Pearson, the architect, designed it. A noble and beautiful example of modern ecclesiastical architecture, in the Early English style, it is a fine memorial not only to Pearson but also to the devotion and self-sacrifice of the people of a county relatively so poor as Cornwall.

Although I have called it modern, the Cathedral is not entirely so; for most cunningly incorporated into it is the south aisle of the sixteenth-century parish church of St. Mary, the exterior of which shows what decorative effects may, with the right tools and skill, be obtained from Cornish granite. Its site might have been some lofty spot where the beauty of the building could have been shared by dwellers in the countryside over a wide area. Some, I believe, would have had it thus elevated and set apart from the everyday life of a city which has grown in and about a deep hollow. Instead, the great nave and the lovely towers rise from street level where the hollow is deepest, and they are mirrored in the little Allen river which almost laps the east end as it flows between shops and houses and under bridges towards the busy quayside. Of no Continental minster or cathedral can it be said that it is closer to the heart of a town or city; and I am thankful that this should be so, as also that Cornish stone—granite, china clay stone, Polyphant, and serpentine—has been so largely used in the building. The roof of the spire of the clock tower is of Cornish copper, which has weathered to a brilliant green.

Truro Cathedral is dear to us in Cornwall as the symbol of the restoration of our ancient bishopric, after it had been united first with Crediton in 1027, and then with Exeter in 1046. During the intervening eight hundred years—and mainly between the end of the Middle Ages and the uprooting whirlwind of the Reformation—our parish churches had been built, and rebuilt, for Cornwall, though somewhat late in the day, shared in the fifteenth-century outpouring of wealth upon church building, despite her slender resources. Except for the little Celtic oratory at Perran, and one still buried in the sands at Gwithian, we have no pre-Norman churches, though there is masonry in a few churches, and there are fonts in many more, from a period earlier than Norman. This, however, was our great age of church building, and R. F. Wheatly, our authority on the architecture of parish churches, has traced Norman work in about one hundred and forty-four of the total of two hundred and twenty. Our best example of the Norman Church, which, as a rule, was cruciform, with nave and chancel of the same width, and small north and south transepts, is the one at Tintagel (ancient Bossiney). The tower is now at the western end, but for two centuries it was probably central—and a failure. The walls of the Norman churches were about three feet thick, and they were not of granite because the Norman craftsman would have nothing to do with this common stone, which was too hard for his axe and pick. Instead, he used other local stone, or else had stone brought from Devonshire and even from as far away as Caen in Normandy. Not until the fifteenth century did granite come into its own, in the course of the widespread and drastic additions and restorations; and the outside walls of St. Mary Magdalene at Launceston and of St. Mary's, Truro, and the tower of Probus, loftiest and probably finest in Cornwall, show how triumphantly the stone will bear its enrichments through the centuries.

The typical Cornish church is long and low, with grey native slate roofs running side by side, and there is a tall, simple, and rugged western tower. This was not built to take a spire, and we have only about half-a-dozen spires in the county. The one that I always look for, as I pass in the train, is that of Lostwithiel Church, which, with three other churches, has clerestory windows, found nowhere else in Cornwall. St. Austell, like Probus, is a notable exception to the customary simple towers, which, "down west"—that is to say, in the Penwith area, where there are often no buttresses—are of big granite squares, with offsets marking the three stages.

Originally, and indeed right down to Victorian times, the Cornish church roof was barrel- or waggon-shaped, slightly pointed, and deeply carved. The screen, of course, was one of the artistic glories of the church; and frescoes such as may still be seen at Breage, near Helston, and at Poughill, behind Bude Bay, where they have been lovingly restored, adorned the plaster of the inside walls of the church. What the rood was like may still be appreciated by a visit to Crantock Church, near Newquay, but our forebears would miss the backing of board, with its painting of the Doom, and the beautiful colours and gilding of the whole. The church seats, of oak, were more than three inches thick, and the square ends of the benches were carved by men who, if for the most part they lacked subtlety, were full of variety and vividness in their execution. It would have been beyond their powers of comprehension that not a little of their work, centuries later, should have been carelessly, if not contemptuously, consigned to secular uses most prosaic and even indecorous.

Of the interior adornments of the fifteenth-century churches not all are gone, but in no county did churches suffer more grievously from the Reformation, the Puritans, and the Victorian restorers. For all that, there remains much of interest in some of our old churches. To many of us Cornish they are among the most cherished bequests to us from back-along—as well they may be: scores upon scores of them, some braving all winds and weather in the bleak uplands or above the rugged cliffs, others deep in the valleys with their trees and streams, have given their names to "Church-towns" (villages, sometimes mere hamlets), as well as to parishes, from Hawker's Morwenstow, in the far north-east, to Sennen, the most westerly, and Landewednack, the most southerly, in England.

Raised primarily to the glory of God, as all our towers were, a few of them have, by intention, served also the needs of ships and fishing-boats off our wave-beaten shores. St. Eval, on the high ground behind the northern cliffs, between Padstow and Newquay, was the gift of the merchants of Bristol, anxious for the safety of vessels using the Channel. During the Second World War St. Eval's tower served as a mark also for aircraft, chiefly of Coastal Command, using the aerodrome in which the church and vicarage were enisled.

The close relation between piety and practical service has been more marked in Cornwall in the provision of bridges, some score of which—two or three partly or largely rebuilt—have come down to us from the fourteenth and fifteenth centuries. Here, as elsewhere throughout Christendom, in the late Middle Ages, the Church granted Indulgences in return for offerings from the faithful for the construction or maintenance of bridges. The one that I know best, Wadebridge, had been finished "with xvij fair and greate uniforme arches of stone" some eighty years before Leland first saw it in 1538. Then, as in Carew's day, it was "the longest, strongest, and fairest that the Shire can muster", and it is so still.

Until the Reformation there was a chapel at either end of the bridge. (Near one end now there is a railway signal box, near the other a public convenience.) A passage of Leland reminds us that the building was at times a source of deep anxiety to Lovebone, the vicar, who, "movid with pitie, began the bridge". Somebody told Leland that "the foundation of certein of the arches was first sette on so quick sandy ground that Lovebone almost despaired to performe the bridge ontyl such time as he layed pakkes of wolle for fundation". The bridge was widened in 1800, and modern traffic has again made this necessary in 1962.

Fifty-three years after the first widening, the old bridge at Looe, at the seaward end of that lovely valley where you may often see the brilliant blue and orange flash of the kingfisher, was pulled down altogether—almost exactly four hundred years after the first Mass was said in its chapel, which was the only one in Cornwall erected in the middle of a bridge. As most of our rivers are east of the ancient track from Padstow to Fowey, so are nearly all our bridges. Delightful are many of the little ones, like Panter's Bridge, made of rubble and with parapet copings of granite, which carried the old road from Bodmin to Liskeard, north of the modern main road andthe main railway line. Where two rivers which time has robbedof their proper names join and flow south to the Fowey, Panter's Bridge, "riding gaily over its rock-strewn torrent", as Mr. Henderson has described it, "makes as pretty a picture as can be found". A little farther west, on the outskirts of Lanhydrock, the well-wooded estate of the Robartes family, the Fowey is spanned by Respryn Bridge, no two of whose five arches are of the same size or date. The bridge carried an old road from Bodmin to Looe, and its tactical importance was proved during the Civil War, when the Earl of Essex too lightly protected it, and King Charles was able from nearby Boconnoc to gain contact with Sir Richard Grenville at Bodmin, while Royalist troops could take Lanhydrock, and so tightened the stranglehold on the army of Essex at Lostwithiel that his infantry had to surrender, though he and his cavalry were able to cut their way out.

Lostwithiel's was then, as now, the pride of the bridges over the Fowey. It is probably the best known in the county, and has happily been preserved in recent years by the diversion to a modern structure of traffic with which it could not satisfactorily cope. Of the six old bridges across the Tamar, the motorist entering Cornwall is right in regarding Greyston, both in setting and structure, as among the most nearly perfect he has seeen in the whole West Country. Over two hundred feet long, with five semicircular arches, Greyston is not so old as Polston, a few miles north of it, and the first bridge that Cornwall had, or shared with Devon. Over it, on an August day in

1354, the first Duke of Cornwall, the famous Black Prince, rode into his Duchy on the way to Restormel Castle, the remains of which you may see from the train a mile or two east of Lostwithiel. "In the time when the Earls and Dukes of Cornwall did make their abodes at Restormel Castle, the town was famous and glorious," declared Norden, who was particularly interested when he visited Restormel in "the reliques of a ruined oven of four yardes and two feet diameter", which led him to comment wistfully, "In those days they builded for use, and not as men now doe their great and glorious houses for ostentation, great halls and little meate, large chimnies and little smoke".

When the Duke of Cornwall arrived at Restormel, there came with him a Cornishman carrying the customary grey riding cloak which awaited His Royal Highness when he crossed to the Cornish side of Polston Bridge. The cloak, in the Black Prince's time, used to cost 3s. 4d., and it was service for the tenure of the Cabilla Manor on the Bodmin Moor. It was in completion of the service that it was carried by a Cornishman during the stay of the Duke, who, however, had to foot the bill for this. The old custom was revived when King George V, then Prince of Wales and Duke of Cornwall, came down to see the Royal Cornwall Agricultural Association's annual show, which is the crown of Cornwall's farming year; and again when King George VI, but lately ascended to the Throne, returned to the Duchy which His Majesty and the brother whom he had succeeded had both known well since boyhood.

Closely linked as Cornwall had been with the Throne since the days of the Black Prince, and fervently as it had adhered to the "old religion" before it came at length to embrace the "new", there could have been little doubt as to the reaction of the deeply Cornish part of the county when Charles I and his Parliament decided to fight their quarrel out. Parliament found most of its support in East Cornwall which, for one thing, had been the home of Sir John Eliot, whose zealous leadership of the Commons had landed him in the Tower, where he died far from the wood, rock, and water, which made Port Eliot, near St. German's, such a pleasant country seat.

Most of the "big people" in the county, however, flocked to the King's standard, and, in the following years, sacrificed proudly and heavily in the Royal cause. When "the Cornyshe men", a century before, had come into collision with Edward VI and his advisers about the New Prayer Book, they had drawn up, in favour of the retention of the old service, a petition which, in parts, was minatory in tone. But they had professed their loyalty to the Throne, and there is little doubt that this profession was perfectly genuine and widely felt. The Prayer Book Rebellion cost the Cornish dearly, but not so dearly as their loyalty to Charles I. He has left on record what he thought of his Cornish subjects' devotion to his cause. In several of our churches you may see the boards on which are painted the letter he addressed "To ye inhabitants of ye county of Cornwall" from Sudeley Castle in 1643. He commanded copies of this "to be printed and published, and one of them read in every church and chapel therein, and to be kept for ever as a record". The letter is a glowing tribute to "ye extraordinary merits of our county of Cornwall, of their zeal for our Crown, and for ye defence of our person", as well as to their "great and eminent courage".

In the year that followed the issue of this message, Charles himself came down here, and won notable successes; but by then some of the Cornish were growing war-weary, and the calls of the harvest fields were awakening a response which the camp could not. Although Basset, at St. Michael's Mount, and the seventy-year-old Arundel, at Pendennis Castle, Falmouth, showed of what fibre as well as of what fire the Cornish were made, winter was soon to come to the King's cause in Cornwall, where its spring had been so bright and confident, and its summer so radiant. Cornwall came to the end of the struggle an impoverished county, and very grievous among its losses in life was that, on Landsdown Hill, of Sir Bevil Grenville, grandson of the great Sir Richard of the *Revenge*, who had gone forth from Stowe with such ardour and with the aureole of the perfect knight; and, at Chagford, of the gentle and lovable Sidney Godolphin, in days of peace "of so nice and tender a composition that a little rain or wind would disorder him and divert him from any short journey he had most willingly proposed to himself", but who, when war broke out, "put himself into the first troops which were raised in the West for the King, and bore the uneasiness and fatigue of winter marches with an exemplary courage and alacrity; until by a too brave pursuit of the enemy, in an obscure village in Devonshire, he was shot with a musket".

The Puritan period that followed the warring must have torn the hearts of the faithful, so rudely and brazenly did it strike at the treasures of our little churches. But that was not peculiar to Cornwall. Indeed, although in many ways most markedly her own right down to modern times, Cornwall's story had begun, from the Reformation onwards, to take on the rhythm and to acquiesce in the theme of the story of England. Cornish seamen and soldiers, humble and great, played their part in the Elizabethan life-and-death struggle with Spain, and again when "Boney" was a name with which Cornish mothers scared their children into docility. (They never attempted this, I think, with the name of Hitler!) In the two World Wars of our own times, Cornish men and women stood shoulder to shoulder with their "cousins of England" against all the threats and tempests of those cataclysmic days. In the projects and endurances of peace, no less than in the stresses of war, this slender extremity of our country is one with England.

But we are still, in the little, richly significant things of life, a land unto ourselves—so much so, indeed, that in spirit if not in the precise phraseology, we find ourselves at moments in complete accord with that lay preacher whose home was one of the tiniest of the Scilly Isles, and who, in the little chapel there, on one occasion, asked the blessing of God upon "this, our own dear country, and the adjacent Isles of Great Britain".

IV

HOME-ALONG

ON AN August morning that began another in the long succession of perversely brilliant days during the fateful summer of 1940, readers of *The West Briton* newspaper found on its leader page a letter of uncommon interest. Itself a sign of the times, the letter vied for their attention with other signs; among them, the destruction of a Cornish bungalow by a German bomb, which had killed its elderly occupant, and the decision of Falmouth Town Council that the port's prized relics of the Napoleonic Wars, including the guns of the *Bellerophon* and the anchor of the *St. Vincent*, should be sent for manufacture into armaments to be used in the defence of Britain against the triumphant and menacing enemy massed on the other side of the English Channel.

This was the letter:—

TO MY DEAR CORNISH PEOPLE

I have today sent the lovely diamond tiara, which the Cornish miners gave me in Johannesburg, to the British Red Cross. It will be sold to help the maimed and wounded of those who are so bravely defending us in this awful war; and I am sure that everyone of you will approve of my action.

I shed tears when I parted with it, as it brought back memories of the happy days I spent in South Africa, and my dear late husband, who made a speech at the presentation, and we all sang, "And Shall Trelawny Die?", and how good my dear Cousin Jackies were to me —which I shall never forget.

In affection,

FANNY MOODY MANNERS

This letter moved me, as it must have moved many another of Dame Fanny Moody's "dear Cornish people". In a sense markedly different from that intended by Dr. Johnson when he coined the phrase to describe Pembroke College in his undergraduate days. Cornwall is "a nest of singing birds". But only Fanny Moody, one of thirteen children of a Redruth photographer, ever left the nest to

74

become a favourite English *prima donna*. She was "the Cornish Nightingale"—the only one, for we are like the Welsh in having no real nightingales to enchant us, though nearly three hundred species of birds have been noted in Cornwall. In the eighteen-nineties Dame Fanny had brought the tiara back from South Africa: the fifteen bezants of the Cornish arms, and our motto, "One and All", in diamonds. It was a gift from her fellow Cornish on the Rand, who had crowded the Theatre Royal in Jo'burg to hear her in *Philemon and Baucis*, *Faust*, and *Maritana*. Then there had been a Cornish concert which, to that exiled community, must have brought heaven for an evening.

One can but guess which song of Dame Fanny's most deeply affected the miners. Knowing my Cornishman, I think it was "Home, sweet Home", which she sang for them from her hotel balcony under the stars and the velvet sky. Some of those who packed every corner of the Square that night may have sent soaring then the bright balloons of *spes phthisica*, which, alas, so soon are grounded. To treacherous hope was added, while Fanny Moody sang, a rare nostalgic ecstasy. Thoroughly Cornish in their ardent response to music and in their passionate attachments and loyalties, how un-Cornish for the moment they were, those stricken and sanguine ones, in daring to match the African stars with the borrowed glint in their eyes of Cornish sunshine from far-off tomorrows.

Some did, indeed, come home again; but plants which, young, had flourished even in poor and "hungry" Cornish soil, soon failed when replanted in it years later, their roots then bright and rotted with gold-dust. But that night in Jo'burg, bondmen of phthisis and free alike, as they went to bed with the strains of "the Nightingale" in their ears, were men who already trod the front streets and highlanes of the heart, on the worn way home-along.

A magic word is "home-along"; and yet, as with others of its kind, we set it on occasions menial tasks, though magnitude goes with the magic when, for example, the word is used by long absent Cornish folk talking about their "own dear country".

Home-along, then, is a word big enough to contain Cornwall; though it implies that the very heart of the county is that town or village from which, in the hope of bettering himself, the exile had torn himself up by roots already deep in Cornish earth. "An' how's things down home-along?" he asks eagerly of another "Cousin Jack", newly-arrived from a part of the county many miles from his own. Thriftily he stores up every scrap of the proffered Cornish news. To produce its full effect, however, the word must be in the mouths of exiles from the same district, and narrowed down so as to encompass, very often, a community no bigger than those of our scattered Celtic forefathers in the long centuries before men moved with ease or security over the land. Home-along, then, is a word so intimate and all-sufficient that one does not even need to use a place-name.

Home-along to me means Padstow, a name which is neither charming nor haunting, as are so many Cornish place-names. How shall a man not stir the memory at times for such names as Penelewey and Polperro, Burncoose and Belovely, Creegbroas and Carleen, Chyoone and Goonbell, Treravel and Godrevy; Lansallos, Marazion, and Merther Euny; Zelah and Zennor, and Wheal Rose? Prosaic and John Blunt-ish beside these is Padstow; which we call Padsta. It is as though, in anger or disgust, a name for the place had been spat out; and this is all the more lamentable because the district speaks in another language, in names like Trenairn and Trenyo; Trethillick, Trecerus, and Tregirls; Cateclewse, Lanadwell, and Lelissick; and in the English Rainy Field and Music Water, Sweety Meadow and Pleasant Streams.

The word "Padstow", is a corruption. The ancient name of the place was *Petroc-stow* (Petroc's church), and an older name still was *Lanwethinoc* (the monastery of Wethinoc), but the oldest was probably *Lodenek*, the fortified inlet—a name remembered down to Leland's time (1535). In the Middle Ages the town was called *Aldestow* (the old church). I wish that this name, or Petrockstow, or Lodenek, had survived until today.

An odd Cornishman I should be if I did not think my native town the most interesting in the county To declare it so is another matter; but, even if I did, not many of my three hundred thousand fellow Cornish would be moved to shake the fist in wrath against me. True, a St. Merryn man or two might rise to demand angrily, "Who is this Padstow Town Crow who caws so foolishly and boastfully on his tree-top?" For these St. Merryn Bulldogs since the olden times have not loved us in their hearts, and used for ever to be growling and barking at us before strangers; save in the Feast Week of their saint, when even a Padstow Town Crow might peck in their churchtown, and their parish; and, no matter how dismal his croak, or shabby his plumage, might feel that he was "fine and welcome" there.

In my experience the rivalry or antipathy between Padstow and St. Merryn has never been more than skin-deep; and I have felt that, on both sides, we were less than half-heartedly seeking to maintain an old tradition, in the worth of which neither of us believed. All the asperities which once marked our relations are now as smooth as the slate headstones in our churchyards. And that is true, or on the way to being true, of all parts of Cornwall where formerly there was a real, and a seemingly irrational, animosity between near neighbours. Thus, you would never get a good word for Redruth from a Camborne man; and a Redruth man, asked once if he were going the mile or two to Camborne for the funeral of a widely esteemed personage, replied, in a voice which cut like a whipsaw, "I don't *never* go to Camborne."

This antagonism between the two mining towns was probably deeper than any other in Cornwall, but antagonism existed also between Lostwithiel and Fowey, Falmouth and Penryn, Bodmin and Wadebridge, Perranporth and St. Agnes, Feock and Devoran, and scores of other places, some of them hamlets within a single parish. Nowadays, only occasionally does one detect a glow among those embers. The fires burned so fiercely in other days, however, that a stranger might well have wondered why, of all mottoes, the County of Cornwall should have chosen for itself, "One and All". And still the wonder must have grown as the stranger noted, besides our community rivalries and antipathies, the innate and intense individualism of the Cornish people. If an uncharitable stranger, he probably set us and our motto down as inept hoodwinkers—or worse.

There is this to be said. For all their rivalries and their individualism, the Cornish are as closely bound and as happy a family as any collection of three hundred and fifty thousand people in the world. And there is this to be added: a motto, surely, is less a family or a community label than an aspiration. Our Cornish motto—as to the origin of which one guess seems to me as good as another—may well have emanated from the more perceptive among our forefathers who were troubled by our antipathies and our clamant individualism, characteristics rooted in our geography and our economy. They probably regarded "One and All" for motto not so much the epitome of achievement as an alarm against our most insidious enemies, sounded by three short blasts of the trumpet.

Thirty years' experience of life in England, including London, and in other parts of Cornwall, mostly Truro and Bodmin, has strengthened an early conviction that it was good for me to have been born and bred at Padstow. Nowhere else have I felt myself and those around me to be so pre-eminently members of a community which was simply the family writ large. There are obvious reasons for this; first among them, that nowhere else have I lived in a community at once so small and compact, and so far removed from the main stream of life. Bodmin has at least twice the population of Padstow, and it has pushed far southwards and westwards of its large parish church and the remains of its priory. Moreover, it is the county town; and one suspects that Bodmin people are not so much living, purely and simply, as living up to the standard which they consider proper to a capital.

Truro may not now be the "prettie compacted town" that Norden found it in the sixteenth century, but it remains true that "there is not a towne in the west part of the shire"—nor, I add, in the east, either—"more commendable for neatness of buildings". I doubt whether, nowadays, Norden would also consider Truro "discommendable for the pride of the people". Indeed, I sometimes think Truro people are not as proud as they might be of a city which affords to the seeing eye so many delights, both great and small. In a town of this size, with its admixture of people, situation, and importance in the ecclesiastical, administrative, and commercial life of Cornwall, the quality of life cannot much resemble that of Padstow, a town of about one-sixth the size and population, closely grouped above a tidal basin a mile or so from the Atlantic coast, and, until the opening of this century, having practically all its communications by sea.

What *is* the special quality of life at Padstow? In the phrase of Cornish tradition, it is our Good Fellowship. Carew, half-amused and half-disparaging, noted in 1602 that, in imitation of the ancients and of the Italians of his own day, who "graced their Cities with several titles, some of the idle disposed Cornish men nicke their towns with by-words, as, The Good Fellowship of Padstow, Pride of Truro, Gallants of Fowey, etc". A century and a half later, when Thomas Kitchin published in London his map of Cornwall, he caused to be written opposite the name of Padstow, "By its situation at the Mouth of the River Camel in the Bristol Channel, lies very convenient for Commerce with Ireland. The Inhabitants of this Town, for the Love of Mirth and Good Cheer, give rise to the proverbial phrase of the Good Fellowship of Padstow."

Something was added by Brice when, nine years later at Exeter, he published his *Grand Gazetteer*. "There's extant," he wrote, "a Phrase, the *Good Fellowship of Padstow*, which is, with Probability, said to have arose from the social Mirth and good Cheer of the Inhabitants; and yet (as the like in numerous other places) I have heard Padstow Folk themselves complain their Town is the most ill-natured, roiling (i.e. railing and reviling) Place in England; not that it is so, indeed, but as Individuals may have suffered by the Obloquy, etc., of other Individuals: too many malevolent, back-biting, Busie-bodies existing mostwheres." If there are any Padstow people today who complain in the same way as did their prototypes of two hundred years ago. I commend to them the worldly-wise Brice. For myself, I speak of that I do know: three and a half centuries after Carew's time I have had much cause to cherish the Good Fellowship of Padstow.

Does it seem, from Kitchin's description, that there has been a Bacchanalian abandon—a wild, thriftless, happy-go-lucky quality—in the good fellowship? I do not think Kitchin intended to convey such an impression; though once in the year, without fail, in war as in peace, Padstow gives itself up to what strangers must regard as grotesque revelry. On May Days in the nineteenth century there were, besides the Shipwrights' Arms just behind the quayside, at least seven other inns at which the males of the seventeen hundred townsfolk could slake their thirst during and after the strenuous Hobby Horse celebrations: one inn to every fifty houses, which is certainly fair provision for man's "Love of Mirth and Good Cheer". But men who could afford to pay only five pounds a year or less in rent—and eight out of every ten dwellings in the town were then let on those terms—cannot have had much money for good ale and wine.

There was drinking, of course, hard drinking at times; and from it arose the sole record I possess of the use of the stocks outside the parish church. A contemporary of my grandmother once related that in the early eighteen-forties she saw three men, who had come to church tipsy and had fallen asleep during the service, waking to find that the constables had placed them in the stocks—those hallowed instruments of summary justice which are now in the south porch.

Of real crime our little town, despite an unsavoury reputation in the Middle Ages, has been blessedly free. The one exception of any consequence was the robbing of the mail by James Elliot, aged thirty-five, whose case is interesting because it put an end to a superstition tenaciously held at Padstow. It was believed there that nobody who had been baptized in the font of St. Petroc's Church would ever go to the gallows. (I think it may be plain to readers in a few moments how this superstition originated.) Elliot, who had been baptized in the font, was found guilty of robbery on the highway and condemned to death. Both to him and to the other Padstow people who had expected the magic of the font to ensure another verdict, this was a heavy blow; but they persisted in believing that a miracle would yet prevent the execution. On an April day in 1787, however, Elliot was hanged, and thereafter the font superstition quickly died, too.

A superstition connected with the "death rope" used at executions in Bodmin Gaol lingered in the county much longer. I have a record of a Cornishman in hospital in 1845 found to be wearing a cord round his neck with a little chintz bag attached. In the bag was a scrap of the hangman's rope. The man explained to the doctor that he had buried another piece, and he believed that as this rotted an ulcer in his back would heal.

At Bodmin Gaol, closed these sixty years, was hanged in 1813 a St. Merryn girl, aged twenty, for having set fire to a mow of wheat "over to Trevisca". This was the period of corn scarcity, so acute in Cornwall the previous year that there had been serious disturbances by the miners. The girl's offence, therefore, was no light one. But I have grave doubts as to her sanity, and these doubts appear to have been shared by many at the time. Even the constable who arrested the girl, and who had known her for seven or eight years, "would not venture to swear whether she was deranged or not". But in the gaol-yard at Bodmin, "with calm serenity and surprising fortitude" and "in a manner that astonished and affected the spectators to an extraordinary degree", the girl was hanged.

Poor, crazy, vindictive Elizabeth, who had sworn so forthily that her former master should not eat wheaten bread from his own fields while she, a parish pauper, had to eat of a barley loaf. Had she lived five hundred years earlier she might well, it seems to me, have escaped even going to gaol. While the wheat mow glared and crackled, and the rats scurried out of the glow into the ragged shadows, she could have fled through the darkness the few miles to Padstow. There, on the land, or in any of the houses, immediately round the parish church, she could have found refuge from constables, and even from King's Justice and Sheriffs. For she would have been within the "Liberty of St. Petroc".

In the Middle Ages it was not uncommon for felons to make for the nearest of consecrated buildings, all of them sancturaries which the constables and tithing-men dared not enter to make an arrest. But hunger and thirst in time would often drive out the evil-doers into the arms of the law, and later, by Coroner's order, they would be sent out of the country. By its remarkable spaciousness and facilities for supporting life, the Liberty of St. Petroc offered a rare chance for felons to escape punishment and to settle with others of their kind within a privileged sanctuary. It is odd to think now of the immediate vicinity of our church of St. Petroc as "a nest of evil doers". Yet, in the Middle Ages it was so described, and in Edward the First's time felons dwelling there "ravaged the surrounding country-side, and then took refuge in the sanctuary where they lived". The Assize Rolls in

The Fowey River near Bodmin Road

which Charles Henderson found this recorded also revealed that between 1277 and 1283 twenty-one felons fled there for safety.

That the Liberty of St. Petroc should have provided immunity so acceptable to wrongdoers right down to the Reformation is proof of the importance of this Celtic saint and of the powerful position his followers had established since the sixth century. When Petroc's remains were carried off to Brittany in the twelfth century, the relic-stealer described him as "the chief of the saints of Cornwall". Canon Doble went further, and called him "the apostle of the whole of Dumonia"—that is, of Devon and Cornwall. He was, moreover, a power in the lands of Wales and Brittany. As the centre of his activity for more than thirty years, Padstow became the most important place in the Celtic Church life of Cornwall. William of Malmesbury even calls it "the seat of the Cornish bishopric"; but this is an English conception of how the Celtic Church was organized. One must picture Padstow, rather, as a busy little seaport whose life was dominated by its monastery—save for St. Germans, the chief in Cornwall.

Between A.D. 500 and 800 the Padstow monks acquired dominion of a large tract along the coast from Portreath to Tintagel, and inland to just the other side of Bodmin. Of this, Padstow was the centre, and there cannot have been a place in the county during that period more full of life and interest. So it might have remained but for the tardy resolve of the English to subjugate the Cornish, and, following our defeat by King Egbert, his determination to put an end to the Celtic Church. All the northern portion of the big estates of the monastery of St. Petroc, except Padstow and its immediate neighbourhood, he assigned to the Saxon Bishop of Sherborne, in Dorset, as one of three missionary centres in Cornwall. At Padstow, therefore, the monks were insulated from most of their possessions, and possibly it was this that led them to move their shrine and monastery to Bodmin. Or they may have gone in more urgent and distressing circumstances, for in A.D. 981 Padstow was ravaged by the Danes. Whichever the reason, move they did, and Bodmin grew into the religious capital of Cornwall and so remained until the Middle Ages ended.

As St. Petroc was the most important, so he was the most interesting of the Celtic saints, and many were the stories our Cornish forbears told about him of a winter evening or on a day when gale or flood kept them from their fishing and tilling. The saint came to Padstow from Wales; not on his altar-stone and alone, but in a ship with a band of some sixty disciples. Although he knew nothing of navigation, he boarded and took charge of the frail vessel with more confidence than

6

Huer's Hut, Newquay

an experienced sailor. Down Channel she came, against a head wind, "borne along by the fear of God with great rapidity". Thus she reached Padstow Haven, and in the north-eastern shore of the estuary, at Trebetherick, where centuries later barges were loading lead ore from the mine at Pentire Glaze, Petroc and his company stepped ashore.

It must have been July or early August, for it was harvest time, and the reapers were tired and thirsty. Because of this, when the holy man spoke courteously to them, they answered gruffly and even rudely. They had the true Cornish curiosity about strangers, however, and soon they were asking Petroc—perhaps to call attention to their thirst, perhaps to make fun of him—if he would not "cause a fountain of fresh water to spring out of the rock that was there". With a prayer on his lips, the holy man struck the rock with his staff, and "immediately a fountain of the purest water sprang up before their eyes, and from it has never since ceased to flow a most salubrious stream".

Deeply impressed as the Celtic inhabitants must have been by this miracle, they would have marvelled even more had they accompanied Petroc when, following their directions, he crossed the estuary to find Samson at Lelissick or Hawker's Cove. "So greatly did this holy soul desire to converse with a holy man", that he prayed Samson might be found in his accustomed place. The effect of the prayer on Samson was immediate and benumbing. As usual, he was busy about the land, when suddenly his limbs became stiff as stone, and "in vain did he attempt to put his hands to his instrument with which he was turning over the soil". Nor was he released from this stone-like rigidity until Petroc had come to him and they had exchanged the kiss of peace.

Another holy man dwelt along this shore of the estuary, and Petroc's next call was upon Bishop Wethinoc, who received the visitor and his company with great courtesy and hospitality. So favourably impressed was Petroc, that next morning he proposed to Wethinoc that they should share his cell. This, however, the Bishop offered wholly to the newcomer who, he was confident, had been sent there by God in fulfilment of an ancient prophecy current in the neighbourhood. Having obtained a promise that his dwelling-place should bear his name, Wethinoc left for another field of service. Thereafter for thirty years Petroc, with his disciples, lived in *Lanwethinoc*, leading a life so innocent "that he did to none what he would not should be done to himself, and so afflicted his body with vigils and endurance of cold that, to repress the unlawful motions of concupiscence, he often plunged himself into the middle of a torrent, and stood there naked from cockcrow till dawn; although, indeed, he practised such great frugality as was sufficient of itself to conquer the longings of the flesh".

In quick succession, at the end of the thirty years, came two pilgrimages to Rome. The second was extended to the Holy Sepulchre at Jerusalem, whence Petroc turned his steps to the East and reached the farthest bounds of India, where he suffered much hardship from robbers, rivers, and the body's fatigue. When he came back to Western Britain, miracle after miracle marked his saintly days; as when a jar of water having been by accident overset, Petroc, making the sign of the Cross, picked it up and offered to his brethren a vessel now full of nectar; or when a woman, who had years before swallowed water in which was a small serpent, and who had found no relief from her consequent ill-health, being brought to Petroc, was given a mixture of water and earth, "and immediately she had swallowed it she vomited a serpent three feet long, but dead; and the same hour she recovered her health and gave thanks to God".

So the years passed, punctuated piously and freely with fast and vigil, until one day the great Abbot climbed, more wearily than before, the familiar track from *Nanceventon* (Little Petherick) on the way back to the monastery at Padstow. And there, at Treravel, on the uplands where, in June as this was, comes the benison of cool air flowing from the western sea, Death lay in ambush for the saint. Tenderly they carried him, full of days, home-along to Padstow. After all these centuries one still can feel the mingled sorrow and pride of that silent company as, coming to where the Three Turnings are now, they saw spread below them, shimmering in the sun, the waters of that fair haven. Perhaps they could even see on the farther shore the glittering stream which, those many years before, had sprung from a rock at the touch of Petroc's staff.

Neither staff nor bell of his has been preserved at Padstow, or any other place; but the ivory reliquary in which were his bones, and which Canon Doble rates as one of the most valuable monuments of antiquity in the kingdom, was hidden until the eighteenth century in a room over the porch of Bodmin Parish Church. It has since remained at Bodmin. Again I lament the passing of a little copper bell, so charmingly symbolic of the Age of the Celtic saints, and this one so venerated that, long after Petroc's death, it was reverently borne up the valley to Liskeard, so that a godly woman there might, in its presence, free her slaves. With my note of lamentation, then, goes one of rejoicing that this little bell, which so often sounded the call to prayer and praise down home-along where I was born, should have symbolized the cause of Freedom in that early morning of our day.

Of the stories passed on from generation to generation at Padstow far into the Middle Ages, first place must have been given to legends of the saint who was so great and good that the casket containing his remains had been "honourably gilded with silver and gold" by one English king, and by another provided with a "valuable silk pall, cunningly embroidered". St. Petroc's monastery had gone, but still above the harbour was his church, and on higher ground the monks of Bodmin had their grange, or farm. The Augustinian Canons of Bodmin had become lords temporal as well as spiritual of Padstow, and for long every dwelling and holding in the place was theirs. The broad fingers of their demesne lands stretched out to Lelissick, almost opposite the little bay where Petroc first landed, and to Stepper Point, where the waters of the ever more exiguous Narrows are merged in the restless Atlantic. Over these lands for centuries the Priors of Bodmin must have had great days with hawk and hound.

Thus lorded and protected, Padstow, the only port along that wild coast, grew in importance. It sent two ships to take part in the Siege of Calais. It developed its prehistoric trade with Brittany and Ireland, a feature being the joint-stock voyages for fish. The merchants banded themselves together in their Guild—of St. Petroc, probably, as at Bodmin—and theirs was the fifteenth-century house which, though now without its chapel, is still on the North Quay. In modern times it has been given the name of Abbey House, and there is a story of an underground passage to Prideaux Place, with the spicy suggestion that when the monks of Bodmin had their barton there, Abbey House held nuns whom they clandestinely cherished. This is nonsense. Any North Quay romance of those far-off days was of quite another kind of commerce.

Through the Middle Ages and down to the Reformation Padstow had, besides its parish church, at least thirteen chapels and several holy wells. One of these, at St. Cadoc, was reputed to have valuable curative properties in cases of worms. (A pity that the St. Erth woman did not take her child there in 1812, instead of dosing it with a "decoction of the poisonous herb called bearsfoot"—green hellebore—which killed the three-year-old within an hour. St. Cadoc water would at least have been innocuous.)

Of the Padstow chapels most of the names have lingered on in field and farm. At the end of "the pleasant Field of St. Saviour", topping the sheer cliff above Chapel Bar, is now our Chapel Stile, over the thick slate stepping-stones of which generations have passed on their way to St. George's Well, where the water gushed up, they say, from a rock against which the saint's horse had struck his hoof. There, at Stile, used to stand the Chapel of St. Saviour, its south windows facing St. Issey's cliffs and its north the Doom Bar and the open sea.

Of the chapel's history little is known, but a grim scene typical of the violence of the period was described by the Rev. George Closse in his *The Parricide Papist* (1606). Inigo Ieanes, of Padstow, having been persuaded by Will Mansel to join the Church of Rome, and having been censured by his father, James Ieanes, for so doing, killed his father with a club. Then, rushing to St. Saviour's Chapel, Inigo ripped out his bowels with a knife. Before he died he confessed his crime to "Sheriff Nicholas Prideaux, Master Arundel of Trerise, Master Mitchell and Master Cosworth, Justices of the Peace".

On winter nights, most probably, a light shone from the chapel for the comfort and guidance of fishermen and sailors. In the 1820s, when Stockdale was there, the east wall was still standing. It had gone before my father's time. Now, a few yards from the site is a tall Cornish cross in granite. It is a memorial to the men of Padstow who died in the two World Wars, many of them "men who were boys when I was a boy", and one most dear to me. My home town is gracious of heart, for the cross is also a mark of gratitude—are there many such in the land?— to those of us who came back from those great adventures.

Polruan, across the water from Fowey, also had a Chapel of St. Saviour affording for sailors a mark by day and a light by night. To this chapel one August afternoon in 1488, Sir Richard Edgcumbe made a pilgrimage immediately after landing at Fowey on his return from Ireland where, as Henry VII's Ambassador, he had accomplished a remarkably difficult mission. In the same year another Cornishman was sent as Ambassador on a special mission to Spain and Portugal. Again, owing partly to qualities which Queen Elizabeth was later to value in her Cornish gentry, the mission was a success.

On the homeward voyage Sir Richard Nanfan had much difficulty in doubling Cape Cornwall, and his ship was in trouble in the Bristol Channel, owing to the stiff, offshore wind. So instead of going on to Bristol, Sir Richard and his company landed early one morning at Padstow. Did they make a pilgrimage to St. Saviour's before taking the road to Launceston, on the way to Windsor, where a much pleased king awaited them? There must have been many a pilgrimage to that little chapel which stood broadside to northerly gales racing over

Newland Island and the Doom Bar; and it may be, that here, as at Mevagissey, there was every year a procession of the blessing of the waters and prayers for increase of their harvest.

With the Reformation and, in 1539, the dissolution of the monastery at Bodmin, the religious and social fabric created through a thousand years at Padstow was rudely torn. The place had been nursed and nurtured first by the Celtic, then the Catholic Church; and although through the centuries a certain amount of freedom of property and person had been granted to people of the port by Canons of Bodmin, the latter's dominating position in the life of Padstow had been barely impaired when the blow fell. With the extrusion of the monks there should have passed to Henry VIII a tidy sum from the Padstow estate. Instead, the King found himself the better off by miserably slender rents. Few passages in Dr. Rowse's *Tudor Cornwall* are more fascinating to me than those in which, with such delicious mastery of the detail, he describes how the Treasury was dished. Briefly, this was the way of it.

Thomas Mundy, last of the Bodmin Priors, seeing that dissolution was imminent, and being, as Dr. Rowse has remarked, "not unlike the Wise Steward of the Gospels", made dispositions whereby his own future might be less insecure and uncomfortable, and a few persons near and dear to him provided with fairly substantial buffers against the shocks of time and change. His election as Prior of Bodmin Mundy had owed in no small degree to Nicholas Prideaux, steward of the former Prior, Thomas Vyvyan, a great figure in the Church life of his times in Cornwall. To Prideaux, now his own steward, Mundy began to pass along plums which he carefully extracted before the crust of the pie, thus gently lifted, should be broken. For a small sum went to Prideaux the great tithes of Padstow, which, extended lengthily the year before the priory was dissolved, constituted a present of several hundred pounds. Then, marriages between members of the Prideaux and the Mundy families were arranged and "solidly founded upon the acres and in the tithes of the priory".

To William Prideaux, Nicholas's nephew, and Joan Mundy, the Prior's niece, was granted on their marriage "the manor of Padstow with all its appurtenances and rights, including wreck of the sea and Gulland Rock and Garth Wood, and the advowson for ninety years, at the low rent of £10 7s. 8d.". The tithe from fish, in which there was a substantial export trade, Nicholas Prideaux had already acquired. In 1545, acting with a rich speculator in monastic lands, he bought outright the fee simple of Padstow and made it Prideaux property.

"In the next generation," says Dr. Rowse, "they built their Elizabethan house upon the hill looking down over the little town and across the lovely expanse of water of that harbour. They have been there ever since."

Prideaux Place (Cornish *plas*, a palace) has not greatly changed since it was completed at the end of the sixteenth century upon the site of the tithe-barn of the Bodmin monks. The little town, long since screened from view from the mullioned windows of the house by the arc of trees which skirts the deer park, has grown, and changed in other ways, since the twenty-two acres of Place grounds were first laid out. Yet, for all the endeavours of successive generations of its sons to keep in step in what is called the march of progress, Padstow has remained rooted in the past. Even now there is something medieval about its maze of narrow streets, courts, and passages. "Under a sort of cliff" not far from the quayside, the old mill was still at work a century ago, its wheel turned, as it had been since the Middle Ages, by the water of a leat running through the town. The harbour has become more choked with sand, however, since Master Laurence Merther knew it, who was vicar of Padstow in the early fifteenth century, and of whom there is a three-quarter-length figure on a brass in the parish church.

Changed, too, since Frobisher sailed in 1577 at the onset of the autumn gales during his return from the search for the North-West Passage to China. "The weather being foul," wrote Best, his lieutenant, "we coveted harbourage, because our steerage was broken, and so came to anchor in Padstow Road, in Cornwall. But riding there, a very dangerous Road, we were advised by the country to put to sea again, and of the two evils we choose the less, for there was nothing but present peril where we rode."

A dozen years before, Sir John Hawkins, in his *Jesus of Lubeck*, of seven hundred tons, had been more fortunate. On his voyage from the West Indies he, too, had been mauled by the autumn gales and had run for Padstow Harbour, sailing up towards the town as the good people were home-going one Sunday morning from church. Sir John found the temporary refuge he was seeking, and found, too, one may be sure, a great welcome from sailors and shipwrights, fisher boys and 'prentices, who knew him not only as an intrepid seaman but also as a judge of ships without peer in the West.

Some twenty years after Frobisher's brief and anchor-straining visit to the harbour mouth, Padstow people had seen the first small contingents of their fellow Cornishmen leaving for service in Ireland, for twenty years a principal battlefield in the struggle against Spain. Cornish levies and horses were shipped from Padstow, to which in 1601 fast-running posts were established from Plymouth, and where a ship was always in readiness to take parcels and packet, and sometimes letters from the Lord Admiral of the Fleet, to the force in Ireland. Talk in the inns of Padstow must have been a fair index of what was thought in the country about the disastrous, long-drawn-out campaign, from which Cornish soldiers were coming back maimed, and from which the headstrong and handsome Essex was to return to make the supreme blunder that led to his execution.

After more than three centuries, Dr. Rowse has caught for us the voice of a Cornish captain, home from abroad and holding forth to his friends in a Padstow tavern upon the tragedy of Essex, in whose conspiracy against the ageing Queen had been joined Sir Ferdinando Gorges, captain and commander of the fort at Plymouth. On Ralegh's persuasion Gorges had turned Queen's evidence, and so had escaped the fate of his illustrious patron and friend. And there in the inn at Padstow was a Cornish captain, swearing of this treachery, that "if Sir Ferdinando Gorges had not been, the Earl of Essex had yet been living and a true subject", and adding "The crows will eat his flesh, whatsoever the dogs do with his bones". This was dangerous talk, indeed, of one's commander; and, considering the native caution of the Cornish, a tribute to the potency of that Padstow innkeeper's liquor.

Our little town is reputed at one time to have kept in employment some forty brewers. If this is true, it is evidence enough that the Good Fellowship of Padstow is a barque which sailed for long upon a brown sea of ale. Certainly the town had had many more brewers than mayors, and perhaps it is as well, lest they should have become figures of fun, like "the Mayor of Calenick, who walked two miles to ride one", or "the Mayor of Falmouth, who thanked God when the town gaol was enlarged". Or, having eluded notoriety in such Cornish similes of mockery, a Mayor of Padstow might have figured in an incident which gave him a place in legend if not in history. I am thinking of that Mayor of Truro, who, having presented an address of loyalty to Queen Victoria at Falmouth, withdrew backwards from the royal presence so oblivious of circumstance that he went overboard into the harbour.

Padstow was not incorporated until 1583, and a few years later the Mayor, poor man, figured in a scene the more painful for having the parish church as its setting. Here they had built a new pew for his Worship, an innovation which mightily offended a certain Mistress

Ann Calwoodly. Perhaps the Mayoral pew had been put in front of her own; at any rate, so deep was her resentment that she took a great axe to the church and with it tried to remove the offending thing. This having failed, Mistress Ann resorted to force of another kind, and in 1592 she was cited before the Star Chamber for the use of the axe and also for having "by might and force in the time of Divine service prevented him (the Mayor) from taking his lawful place therein". What personal currents were running so turbulently within Ann Calwoodly's breast one cannot know now; but one may guess that here was an extreme example of Cornish dislike of any departure from "what do belong to be".

In a few years, because of the opposition to them of the lord of the manor, Padstow allowed its corporate rights to lapse, and they have never been restored. In a way, it is a pity. Of the brood which used to send forty-four Members to Parliament from Cornwall—only one fewer than the whole of Scotland was furnishing—there is not a borough remaining which can provide a background more suited to ancient ceremonial, with cocked hats, bright robes and chains, and the mace borne decorously before. And whatever customs might have grown out of mayor choosing at Padstow would have been zealously maintained, just as at Liskeard they still strew the floor of the Guildhall with rushes, and at Saltash the new Mayor, from the Guildhall window, scatters money and fruit and nuts among the eager children below.

Although Padstow has been outside the company of Cornish boroughs these three hundred years and more, and has always been shut in and remote in a sheltering valley of the Camel estuary, the town has had a full part in the life of Cornwall. It was almost wholly on the side of Parliament in the Civil Wars, regarding, as always, the sea and not the land as its special sphere of operations. Among the Cornish who languished in French prisons during the Napoleonic Wars and for whom the county raised a handsome prisoners-of-war fund, the Padstow men were probably sailors whose little ships had been captured by French brigs-of-war or privateers.

Besides celebrating the fall of Napoleon within its own borders, Padstow quite fortuitously assisted in adding variety to the celebrations at Bodmin. There, on a waggon raised between two of the town's two-and-thirty arches, a score of musicians were playing away for dear life, while hundreds of dancers thronged the long, front street. Up Dunmere Hill and down by the Town Wall came "an immensely large pleasure boat being conducted on wheels from Padstow to Fowey". The Bodmin musicians at once swarmed into the boat, and, the crowd following, "Proceeded through the town as in a car of triumph, playing patriotic and loyal tunes, firing pistols, etc.". The remarkable thing about this incident is to find, as in prehistoric times, the overland route from Padstow to Fowey in use, so as to avoid the rounding of Land's End.

I wonder if this was a new boat from the stocks in one of the four or five little shipbuilding yards at Padstow? The schooners built there were among the fleetest and most seaworthy launched from any port in Great Britain. In the yards, generations of skilled shipwrights and apprentices found employment, and few modern regattas have anything to offer more exciting then were the races between the shipyards' six-oared gigs. Only one of the yards remains, with its small dry dock, and its grey stone walls bright in early summer with pink valerian, which we call Padstow Pride and which our sister of the south calls Pride of Fowey. (At St. Mawes and Marazion they know it as Bouncing Bess, elsewhere in Cornwall as Saucy Bet and Ladies' Needlework, and in Kent, I believe, it is Kent Weed.) Even in the remaining shipyard it is a rare joy now to hear the ring of the caulker's mallet—a solo where, in my boyhood, there was a symphony.

Across the years I hear that fuller music faintly still, and wonder sadly whether our best days at Padstow are over. Certainly we shall not hear the caulkers' mallets any more along the estuary, nor shall we revive our ancient trade with Ireland and Brittany. The more modern commerce with Canada and the Baltic States has also long since ended. No more emigration from Padstow, either; and for this we may be thankful. There were times in the nineteenth century when our little streets were thronged with people from the stricken mining districts of the county, waiting for ships to return to port with timber and then to take them to a new life on the prairies or in the mining camps of Canada. The voyage to Quebec in those Padstow sailing-ships took a month in the fastest and a week longer in the best of the others. The nine-hundred-ton *Clio* held the blue riband of the fleet. Sometimes the smaller vessels, after having got far across the Atlantic, were forced to turn back. The passage money was not heavy. Including "head-money" payable at Quebec, the fares from Padstow were thirty shillings for an adult, fifteen shillings for a child under fourteen, and ten shillings for a child under seven. But passengers had to bring their own provisions, and it became a drain on their resources, material and moral, if, after having covered between a thousand and two thousand miles, they had to put back to Padstow and begin all over again. The middle-aged and the younger people might be resilient enough; but what of the older ones?—a couple like Mr. and Mrs. Billing of St. Agnes, for example; he aged seventy-eight and she nearly seventy; a bit late in life, one would have thought, for beginning anew in a far country. Yet some of these old people were wonderfully enterprising and active; in this very year of the set-back to the *Spring Flower*, a field of corn at Padstow was reaped by two persons, a man of eighty-seven and his sister of eighty-one. Elsewhere in Cornwall about the same time, there was a midwife still at work at the age of ninety-seven.

In 1832, when its politicians were celebrating, or bewailing, the Great Reform Act, Padstow was stricken, like many other Cornish towns, with cholera. The next year typhus smote the town, and this, with other diseases, brought the number of deaths for 1833 up to nearly eighty in a population of under eighteen hundred. Yet, for all the appalling conditions, it was only in particular years that Padstow's death rate was very high. Over a long period, its average mortality was low. This the investigating inspector of the Board of Health in 1850 attributed to "the natural advantages of Padstow". Together with the great improvements in the water supply, sanitation, and housing since then, these natural advantages make the town now one of the most pleasant and healthy in Cornwall.

Looking back to the first quarter of my life there, I feel that the place glowed with good fellowship. My family were poor folk. My father and mother brought up four children—there were five for a while—on a not too certain pound a week. My favourite grandmother, from whom I never heard a querulous word about her circumstances, wrested a living from mangling clothes—a box like a broad, low coffin, full of big stones, had to be turned to and fro over wooden rollers like giant rolling-pins—and from kneeling and washing great floors of Cornish slate. But if poverty and affluence created a division at all in our community at Padstow, it was a material one, and no more. Once you descended the hill from the great house of the Prideaux, our society was not in strata; it was a warm and vital medley. Everybody knew everybody else, and the life of the place flowed through or over all the material obstacles.

Home-along, then, to me means this little place of slate and granite on the Camel estuary, which—I know, for I have looked at it long and with the eye of a lover from every point of the compass—is best seen as you sit in a boat in mid-stream between the quayheads and St. Minver sands. There, scores of times, I have shipped the paddles, thrown the gripper overboard, and squatted on the stern-sheet.

From somewhere forrard comes soon one of the loveliest sounds I know: the urgent, excited ripple of the tide in ebb or flow. Sometimes a butterfly passes low over the boat and the eye follows anxiously its adventurous flight towards the soft, warm dunes. Or suddenly a shag will break surface a few yards away, and, with some little distress, you watch the head-shakings and neck-stretchings as this diving-bird deals vigorously with a tiny plaice.

From such distractions my eyes soon turn to the town. About it, like the protecting arm of a lover, is the great arc of the Prideaux trees, hiding from view the embattled house whose foundations they were laying in the year when the beacon fire on Crugmeer Cross spluttered into the darkness to St. Minver Highlands the message that the Armada had been sighted. In the midst of the lovely green arc is the grey church tower, round which are clustered, "as a hen gathereth her chickens", the dwellings of Up-town and Down-town. Abreast of you is the quay, the grey walls and wooden piles of which seem to support the town no less than to stem the tidal waters and gather them into a great pool of quiet. Above the quay are the houses, cheek by jowl under the slow curve of the trees. And quietly dominating all is the tower of the Church of St. Petroc.

It was the Celtic holy man and his followers, in their monastery hidden from hostile eyes at sea, who gave to life in this valley motif and rhythm of which, after fifteen centuries, something still lingers. But long before the coming of the saint, the estuary had had a life and an importance of its own, of which we may dimly guess from the Iron Age cemetery discovered at Harlyn Bay, and the two large crescents of gold found near the fish cellars by an undiscerning farm labourer, who wore those delicate ornaments of the Early Bronze Age to keep up his trousers, as a navvy wears a garter of cord below the knee.

The estuary, thousands of years ago, was a key position on the trade route from the Continent to Ireland and Western Britain. Few places are more surely established than this in antiquity. Why wonder, then, that for all our true zeal for progress and our love of mirth and good cheer, we part so reluctantly with our past? Nature, it would seem, has willed it: this innate conservatism deep in our beings, and this sturdy tradition of radicalism which, on one matchless occasion, found its champion in the heir to the broad acres of Lanhydrock[1]—that leader of Edwardian *jeunesse doré* who, so soon afterwards, was to lose his life in rescuing a wounded comrade in France, and so narrowly to

[1] Captain the Hon. T. C. Agar-Robartes, M.P., Coldstream Guards; killed 1915.

miss, for that gallant exploit, the posthumous award of the Victoria Cross.

As I sit in the stern of the boat, the town, huddled and grey in the valley, seems to me fashioned so that Time itself may like, or be bound, to tarry there. For on three sides the hills enclose us, and high up is that close-ranked regiment of trees. On three sides enclosed: and then the urgent ripple of the tide under the bottom-boards stirs me to observe that on the fourth side the little place lies wide open—and the fourth side is the east, whence the new day comes.

V

THE DAY'S WORK

Fishing claims to be Cornwall's oldest industry and finds proof in the precedence given to it in the former toast, honoured at public dinners and all such gatherings, "Gentlemen, I give you 'Fish, Tin, and Copper'!" For centuries fishing and mining were the twin pillars of our Cornish economy, and nobody can hope to understand us who does not keep this in mind. If we talk more wistfully of the great days of Cornish mining, as though that were the sole industry which has suffered a grievous decline, it is only because fishing has never yielded quite such glittering prizes, or left in Cornish stone so many monuments to its former importance. Yet fishing, too, has decayed; and, in testimony to its old vigour and proportions, has left all round our coast, from Cawsand in the south-east to Port Gaverne in the north, several grey and crumbling buildings, over the portals of each of which the stonemason might well have inscribed a sad and reluctant *Hic jacet.*

In one at least, though with neither sadness nor reluctance, he carved a Latin inscription. If the words had been translated for him, it must have been with a smile that he worked away there, over the entrance to the fish-cellars at Harlyn Bay, a little to the east of the famous Cataclewse Quarry whence so much stone has been taken for church building in Cornwall. Very carefully as a schoolboy I copied that inscription into a little notebook to show our Latin master at Bodmin— a Yorkshireman—as evidence of our culture even in such a common enterprise as fishing. *Dulcis lucri odor.* Profit smells sweet.

Of all aphorisms this was the most apt; for here, among the tamarisk in the lew of the western arm of the bay, used to be brought for curing and storing hundreds of thousands of pilchards. The rank smell of the fish and their oil must have pervaded every nook and cranny of courtyard, salt-stores, and lofts. This was no place, in the old days, for men and women with delicate nostrils and queasy stomachs; though perhaps it was for these that the words had been inscribed, so that they might comfort themselves with the thought of rewards to come.

Only about nine inches long, and very much like a small herring, the pilchard was for centuries the most important fish taken in Cornish waters. Carew, felicitous as ever, wrote of it as "the least fish in bigness, the greatest for gain, and the most in numbers". Norden, still earlier, had observed, "The most commodious fishe and richest fishing is of the least fishe, which is called a pilcharde; which kind of fish infinitely aboundeth upon the sea coast of this countrie between St. James's tide and the Feast of All Saints".

At that time of the year millions of these little migrants came in "schools" (shoals) as far east as our shores, and no farther. "When the corn is in the shock, the fish is on the rock", the old people used to say; and along the coast they used to look for the coming of the pilchard schools as confidently as countrymen look in spring for the return of the swallows. Sometimes the first indication of the presence of the fish would be when a few of them were taken in shrimping nets; sometimes when a section of the fishermen had put out to meet them and had had good hauls from the drift nets let down in deep water. Ashore, on the hills and in huer's houses, careful watch would be kept, and when the pilchards came into the shallows they would be surrounded by big nets, called seines, in which on one occasion at St. Ives some thirty million pilchards were caught in an hour.

Until the late nineteenth century the pilchards were "bulked"— i.e. built up in layers, with salt sprinkled between them. Then the Spanish method was adopted, the fish being salted and left lying in the salt, in vats or tanks, for about three weeks. Treated in this way they looked, and were, more palatable. Not all the pilchards were taken to the cellars for curing, for as soon as they heard that big catches had been taken, the country people who were able to make the journey, hurried to the ports and coves to buy as many as they could take away— sometimes at ten for a penny—for salting down for the winter. With potatoes, a few salt pilchards boiled made a tasty meal in days when for most Cornish people butcher's meat was a luxury. Those who could not go to the fishing-places, awaited the rich tenor or baritone voice of the jowter (travelling salesman) calling, "P-i-l-c-h-e-r, pílcher, pilchér!" a sound as welcome in the inland villages and towns as the huer's "Heva, heva" along the shore.

Familiar in the St. Ives district were the voice and figure of Nancy Humphries, who "was noted for many years as supplying the parishes surrounding that place with fish, and has been known to travel more than twenty miles in a day, carrying upwards of one cwt. of fish on her head". Such was her strength. Her weakness also is recorded, with what seems nowadays graceless candour, in the obituary notice which appeared in 1826, when Nancy was fifty-four. "Her passion for ardent spirits was extreme, and its indulgence is supposed to have hastened her end". Nancy's method of conducting her business was all her own. To a customer who expostulated that she was charging that day a high price for her mackerel, she replied, "No, m' dear, 'tedn' no such thing. I do lose 'pon every one I sell; but thanks be, I do sell a perty lot, else I shudden be able to keep my ole man out of the workhouse!"

It was the export trade that made the pilchard season the crown of the fishing year. For a time Cornish pilchards were sent overseas as far as the West Indies; but our best customers were always the Mediterranean countries, and particularly Italy. In one year Cornwall sent over a hundred million pilchards, sixty millions of them from St. Ives and twenty-five millions from Penzance. No wonder that Cornish people, and in particular fisherfolk and sleeping partners in seining companies—seining nets and other equipment were too expensive for financing except through companies—prayed often and fervently for "long life to the Pope and death to the thousands"; though I think poverty had at least as much to do with the ready sale of the salted pilchard in Italy as the scrupulous observance of the Church's feasts. In the days of bulking, the *salacche*, by the time it reached the Italian townspeople and peasants, must often have been a most unappetizing fish. And in spite of the later improvement in curing, the first publisher of D. H. Lawrence's *Lady Chatterley's Lover*, Pino Orioli, in his *Adventures of a Bookseller*, was writing in 1938 of all Italian-imported salted fish as making "wretched dishes, which even common people in England would not touch".

The first set-back to this profitable Cornish export trade came early in the nineteenth century with the almost simultaneous withdrawal of the home Government's bounty and a steep rise in the import duty in Italy. At once about nine thousand men and women in the fishing-boats and fish-cellars were thrown out of work; but, even so, until quite late in the century and apart from the seining craft, there were six hundred fishing-boats employed in pilchard driving—i.e. using drift nets in deep water.

The last shoal of pilchards seined in Cornwall was taken in 1916 at Porthgwarra, not far from Land's End. It was war-time, when all food was valuable, and the three million pilchards fetched £4,500. Thereafter the fish failed to appear in the seining areas; though right up to the inglorious invasion of Abyssinia by Mussolini's Italy our drift boats were bringing in pilchards for export there. In the meantime, a most interesting experiment was being made at Mevagissey where, until the outbreak of the First World War, pilchard canning had been

South Gate, Launceston

carried on for about forty years. The canning was revived, on modern lines, and was meeting with well-deserved success when war again called a halt to the enterprise. After the war pilchard canning was extended to other Cornish ports, though the local fishermen were deeply dismayed early in 1962 when it was announced that the factory at Looe would no longer can fish but would be used for canning other foods. Said one of the fishermen's leaders, "We must try to maintain our boats, even if it means shark fishing in the summer". There was nothing fanciful in this transition from the smallest to the largest denizens of Cornish waters. For Looe had by then become the centre of the new national sport of shark fishing in summer.

That some such basis should be found is important, for in the years of decay in this branch of the Cornish fisheries there have been in other branches no counter-balancing improvements. Why the pilchards should suddenly have failed to come, as by immemorial custom, close in to the Cornish coast in summer and autumn, I have never seen explained. Perhaps changes in fish migrations are inexplicable. The haddock and hake had already changed their habits when the pilchard changed his, and for a time there was anxiety about the rare or non-appearance of the mackerel in his old numbers. This anxiety lifted, another took its place. The mackerel came again; but price and marketing difficulties came also, and great quantities of the fish had to be thrown back into the sea. Newlyn Harbour was once the base of the largest mackerel fishery in the world; but in the sixteen years up to 1936, the value of the mackerel landed there declined by about six-sevenths. There was nothing sudden or spectacular about it; each succeeding year was marked by a further ominous decline. But Newlyn has maintained its position as the most important of Cornish fishing ports and mackerel once more contribute substantially to the total annual fish landings, which fetch about £300,000.

I am not competent to write of the economics of the fishing industry, and all I can do is to record what has happened in Cornwall. In fifty years the pilchard seine dwindled from three hundred to half-a-dozen. In the same period, one out of every four drift boats was laid up, and one out of every three fisherman ceased to belong to the industry. Between the two World Wars scores of young Cornish fishermen had begun to look, mostly overseas, for other employment. In a year from one small port, eighty men whose ages ranged from eighteen, to forty, went off to America, and others made ready to follow them. Many of these men, who had families to maintain, had that year earned an average of less than ten shillings a week. At St. Ives in the

7

Cornish Cross at Mylor, the tallest in Cornwall

six years before the Second World War, four out of every ten boats, and three out of every ten fishermen, dropped out of this industry which once was first in our traditional Cornish toast. At Padstow and Port Isaac, Newlyn and Mevagissey, one of every four boats was either laid up or sold.

In latter years the herring, like the pilchard, has become estranged from Cornish waters. It is the custom in Cornwall for the owner of a fishing-boat—usually the skipper—to draw two shares of the proceeds of each catch to one share for each of the remainder of the crew, I remember one herring season so lean that all the fishermen "shared and shared alike", the result being that between September and Christmas some of the men earned a *total* of fifteen shillings. Because of the share basis of Cornish fishing, there are no employer and employed, and therefore none of the men was then eligible for State unemployment insurance.

What the men desired most was not that they should be allowed to pay into and draw benefits from unemployment insurance, but that they should be able to earn from their calling a reasonably good livelihood. Failing this, they naturally sought for their families the only other tolerable security against want. For there comes a time when, friendly and constant in kindness though the shopkeepers may be, the fishermen are humiliated to have to add another penny to the accounts which are to be settled from the takings of their first good catches. Some of them may have recalled with a wry smile, the statement once made by Howard Dunn: that Cornwall, with its fish, had once been to Southern England and some Continental countries "what the Argentine, with its beef, is to Europe today".

There is a sad symbolism, then, in the scores of old fish-cellers, crumbling and deserted, which are scattered round the Cornish coast. One of these cellars stands athwart the beach-head at tiny Polkerris, which nestles under the long arm of the Gribbin as it thrusts southwards to the English Channel from the grounds and grotto of the old Rashleigh home at Menabilly. Across St. Austell Bay is Porthpean, with its bathers and pleasure-boats, and beyond are the trees of Penrice. This "seine house", as they called Polkerris cellar in Tudor times, was one of the longest in Cornwall, as befitted a bay "where great store of Pilchardes are taken at the time of the yeare". Here, Norden saw "at one draught, 15 boats loden into Foy, besides a great companie carried away by the countrie". One can picture the scene: the country people's mules climbing away inland with their fish-laden panniers, the poor miners and cottagers toiling homeward with all the pilchards they could pack into whatever receptacles they could provide, and still those fifteen boats, the water lapping their gunwales, rounding the Griggin with cheap food for Fowey.

The courtyard of Polkerris Cellar is now empty and silent; and under the ridge roof, once straight and true upon its stone piers and granite pillars, the air is as sweet as though millions of pilchards had never been "bulked" within those walls, or gallons of oil had never oozed out from the barrels under the presses. (Pilchard oil was a profitable side-line of seining; and Cornish women who were occupied about it were noted for the purity of their complexions and the lustre of their hair. Vitamin A?) From May to October fuchsias bloom outside nearly every cottage in Polkerris, and I wonder, as I leave the grey cellar and come upon this brilliance—remarkable even for Cornwall—whether these are fires in remembrance of the great days when "profit smelled sweet".

Padstow has never been wholly dependent upon fishing. Its own little fleet has virtually disappeared and not one of the fifty or sixty dashing drifters from Grimsby and Lowestoft now lands its lucrative catches. Of all the Cornish fishing-places, except Newquay, where they have beaten their fish-cellars into promenades, Padstow has least of the symbolism of the industry's change and decay. But people of my generation know that at Padstow, too, a fine, independent race has been slowly dying out since they began laying-up the brown lug-and-mizzen boats in Dinas Cove, to keep company with mouldering relics of the shipyard days, when here upon the stocks took shape the lovely vessels which, under full canvas, were so fleet that their cargoes, loaded one day in Southern Ireland, were being discharged the next day at Penzance. It is long since the last echo of the smiths' hammers and the caulkers' mallets died away under Dinas Hill; and seldom is the quiet broken save by the lapping of the tide, the wind in the elms, a blackbird's fluting over the meadows, and the ripple of the stream which flows down the valley and under the greystone arch into the estuary.

To the south, Dinas (the fortified) Hill slopes to a creek which winds past Sunny Corner and Salt Water Mill, Creddis and Costis-lost, to Little Petherick where once St. Petroc's bell was heard among the trees, and where, through medieval times and almost to our own day, the millwheel roared and flashed beside the bridge which carries the Padstow road steeply to St. Issey Churchtown. Hundreds of times I have moored my boat at Little Petherick beside the crumbling lime-kiln, and walked slowly in the green shade to the little Early English church, upon the interior of which Viscount Molesworth and his family and Athelstan Riley lavished so much loving care.

It is odd to recall with what resentment I first went in that stuggy old boat under Dinas Hill and up the creek towards Little Petherick. That was on one of many Saturday afternoons in summer when, instead of joining, as I wanted to, the boys who were sailing their model yachts at St. George's Well, my mother made me go with Grandfather Helbren on blackberry-picking trips to Creddis. These were the most silent expeditions of boyhood, partly because of my resentment, but also because "Granfer", who was so essentially friendly and attracted to crowds on high days and holidays, was walled in, poor man, by deafness. With sadness I have since remembered how pathetic and baffled the old man looked, in his bowler hat and blue reefer jacket, among the crowd at the parish church bazaar, standing at the foot of the steps outside the library window of Prideaux Place, where the son of his brother Hodge, drowned years before in the ferry, was reciting, with quite remarkable feeling and style, passages from "The Idylls of the King", or "Henry V", or the more hempen, homespun stuff of our Cornish tales. But boys can be callous creatures, and on those trips to Creddis Granfer's deafness seemed an affliction far less irksome for him to bear than, for me, was this submission to the inflexible will of his daughter, my mother.

If Granfer and I had talked more, while we filled our baskets on those still, blue afternoons, he might have told me about Creddis Mine, which was already one of Cornwall's "knackt bals". There are few districts in the county which, at one time or another, the "old men", seeking minerals, have not tunnelled, teased, and torn. In North Cornwall miles from the granite and the mineral zone, we have yet, in our slate, lodes (veins) of lead and antimony (in which the Romans were interested), and, at Creddis, copper with a little silver. The mine was a small-scale venture, its shaft no deeper than thirty fathoms, and I doubt whether there were ever at work above or below grass more than fifty men. There are two or three such mines in the district; and one, Wheal Paynter, showed a fine course of lead at twelve fathoms depth.

Along the coast, too, the search for minerals was pursued. I am amused to observe how romantic strangers still ascribe to smugglers the tunnels driven into the cliffs, a mile or two from Padstow, at Tregudda Gorge, that chasm hundreds of feet deep with a castellated island as outpost—a spectacle as memorable as anything along the Cornish coast. Our smugglers were daring and ingenious fellows, but they had a sea-sense which would have told them that landing "moon-shine" at Tregudda Gorge was an enterprise of the kind that men do not live to repeat. The truth is that the cliff face has been hewn and blasted not by smugglers but by miners, who have also left their traces for some little distance inland. The five acres of Gudder Common, as it used to be called, once abounded in minerals, and in the early nineteenth century Gudder Mine was in full working.

It was probably a lead mine like Pentire Glaze, a mile or two further up the coast, where for at least two centuries they were producing this mineral and some antimony quite profitably, the ore being shipped in barges from Trebetherick to Padstow. The passage across the estuary was often risky, and one January night in 1819 a barge which had put off from the landing-stage was soon "struck by a heavy sea, and in consequence of being heavily laden, she instantly foundered". Of the nine men on board, only three were saved. A wild, winter night; yet it is characteristic of Cornwall that a day or two later, in the same neighbourhood, "some gentlemen who were sporting at St. Minver" should have come upon an adder basking in the sun!

For St. Minver parish and St. Minver "smoothers", as we call our neighbours across the water, I have a special place in my affections. In the highlands at Trevanger, not far from the old Quaker burial ground, was the tiny home of my father's forbears, the Tremaines, and in the lowlands, nearer the waterside, the Helbrens, my mother's forbears, were reared. One of the Tremaine girls married a miner, who had returned from Australia and was busy for a time with silver-lead above the St. Minver sand-hills. I know very little of that great-uncle, the only man in our family directly connected with Cornish mining. While he was at St. Minver he probably looked upon his work as "scratching about", for he came from West Cornwall, the home of deep mining, and thither before long he returned, to the shafts and levels (galleries) of Tresavean, once the richest copper mine in the country and employing about twelve hundred men, women, and boys. Looking south-east from Carn Marth, you can see how the mine scarred the broad shoulders of the hill under which the neat stone village of Lanner, built largely with remittances from Cornish miners on the Rand, stretches along the Redruth to Falmouth road.

The shaft of Tresavean, when my great-uncle went back, was nearly two thousand feet deep; and, not many years before, he would have had to go to his work down ladders almost sheer and climb them again at the end of the day. This dangerous and exhausting business occupied about two hours, and its effects on the miners were the worse because of one of their time-honoured practices. After the laborious eight hours underground in a high temperature, they were accustomed to take their pace in scaling the ladders from the two most active of their number. One reason was that they wished to keep together, but they did it also "to avoid a certain disgrace or slur, which they attached to any who should fall in the rear". The miners' temperaments being what they were, it was useless, I fear, for men like Dr. Richard Wise, of Nansloe, Helston, to point out that "this imprudent pace" gave rise to the most serious diseases of heart and lungs. Deaths from respiratory diseases among Cornish miners, about the time of Dr. Wise's warning, were ten per cent higher than among the coal miners of Staffordshire and Northumberland, and Sir Charles Lemon attributed this to the fact that miners in other counties were brought to surface in buckets, while our men had to endure the strain of climbing hundreds of feet of ladders.

It was not a question only of the physical energy expended, though the ladders, it was estimated, took one-third of a man's total energy. On their way to the surface in buckets, the coal miners had a chance to cool down. Our tin and copper miners, working in temperatures so high that they were known to lose five or six pounds in weight in a single shift, came hot and exhausted to the cold air above grass, and so fell ready victims to colds and chills. From its first meeting in 1833 the Royal Cornwall Polytechnic Society—child of the seventeen-year-old Anna Maria Fox, and christened by her sister, the adorable Caroline—encouraged plans for bringing miners to surface by machinery, and premiums offered by the Society at length resulted in the introduction at Tresavean of "man-raising machinery", designed by Captain Michael Loam. The machinery was neither complicated nor elaborate and its wooden rods, unfortunately, did not reach the bottom of the shaft, so that there were still twenty fathoms of ladder and eleven of rope to be used by those whose work took them that deep. But the "man-engine" was a vast improvement and one can appreciate the fervour with which an ex-mine captain at Tresavean—the superintendent of a Cornish mine or clayworks is always a "cap'n"—spoke at the luncheon to celebrate the completion of the man-raising machinery. He regretted, he said, that it had not been installed a year and a half earlier; "if it had been, he believed he should have been in good health that day. It was in climbing this mine that he broke a blood vessel, and there were twenty other men on his club similar to him, *broken down by that deep mine*".

In the history of Cornish mining, then, Tresavean, as the pioneer of this machinery, has a place all its own. It has other claims to distinction. Nearby, at Redruth, William Murdoch, an Ayrshire man, who was employed by the famous engineering partners, Boulton and Watt, first put to practical use in 1792 the discovery of coal gas by the Rev. Mr. Clayton, half a century earlier. Murdoch used a gas lamp when he was moving about the mining district at night, and his house and office at Redruth—still known as Murdoch House—were the first ever to be lit by gas. The first Cornish mine to use gas lighting may well have been Tresavean.

It is a good example, too, of a mine which was abandoned by its discoverer—a member of the Williams family, the foundations of whose fortunes were solidly laid in Cornish mining—when the tin which had been so profitably worked gave place to copper. The Tresavean miners must have been dismayed when they first came to what they contemptuously called "the yellows"; and they also rejected as valueless the black copper ore. It was, in fact, one of the richest of ores, as a man in the Goldsithney neighbourhood found when he sold a field hedge, built entirely of black copper, for a large sum of money.

Had the early Tresavean miners lived until the middle of the nineteenth century, when Cornwall was widely known as The Copper Kingdom, they would have learned that their mine in forty years had produced copper to the value of about one and a half million pounds. Altogether, in tin and copper sales, Tresavean must have made three million pounds, and it is fair to assume that three-quarters of a million, or more, of this was paid in dividends. No wonder the barren countryside on and around our mines was described by an old writer as being "like the shabby mien of a miser; its aspect does not correspond with its hoards".

Still easier to understand is the eighteenth-century Cornish miners' concern above all else for tin. For this was the foundation of the industry. In the early days there was no need to sink deep shafts. Tin of the finest quality was present, in abundance, in the alluvial deposits of our valleys, notably the Red River Valley, near Redruth; the Pentewan Valley, running down to the sea from St. Austell; and the Carnon Valley, which opens out to the main Truro-Falmouth road and the Devoran River. The alluvial deposits, which had been exposed by the action of the sea upon the foot of the granite hills, when these were really islands and much of Cornwall was submerged, were attributed by the ancient tinners to Noah's Flood. With their horn picks and wooden shovels, some of which have been found, together with "certaine little tooles heads of Brasse, which some terme Thunderaxes", the stream-workers persevered until lumps of tin-stone were uncovered. After the lumps had been crushed finely, the ore was washed in sloping water-ways. By the fifteenth century there were signs that our alluvial tin was becoming exhausted, though tin-streaming has continued down to our own day.

Early in the seventeenth century, following the search for the lodes from which the alluvial deposits had come, some of our tin mines were fifty fathoms deep, and Carew has described the miners' toil as so "extreame as they cannot endure it above five hours in a day", the remainder of which "they wear out at coytes (quoits), kayles (ninepins), and the like idle exercises". It was about a hundred years later that Cornwall was found to have plenty of copper as well as tin, but this was at first so little esteemed that the annual output at the end of the eighteenth century was only about four thousand tons. By the middle of last century fifty times as much was being produced, or three-quarters of the world's output.

It was tin, however, which had given the Cornish miners their special place in the community. Early in the thirteenth century they were, by charter, given law courts, a prison, and even a Parliament of their own (the last Tinners' Parliament was held at Truro in August, 1752, and continued with adjourments until September, 1753). Only in matters of land, life, and limb were tinners subject to the ordinary law courts, and they had the right of appeal from these direct to the Duke of Cornwall, or to the King in Council. The tinners had also complete freedom from fair and market dues, and they paid no tithes. Only the Lord Warden of the Stannaries (the four mining areas) could order them to undertake military service.

The quest for tin and copper has taken men and boys deeper and deeper into the earth and under the great seas rolling in upon our north-western shores. Sea-water above his head the Cornish miner has not regarded as any special difficulty or danger, and I have heard of one mine where the threatened entry of the Atlantic was successfully blocked by the use of oakum. Water presented much more difficulty and danger in the inland mines, until Newcomen and Watt came down in the late eighteenth century with the new pumping-engines. These were improved by our own brilliant school of engineers, headed by Richard Trevithick, "the Cornish giant" and father of the locomotive. So came into use the Cornish beam engine, one of the few mechanical inventions which it has been unnecessary, or impossible, to improve. At one time there were three hundred of these Cornish engines at work in the county. Of the last two that still functioned in recent years, one had started working during the Crimean War and had been running almost incessantly since.

Many lives were lost in Cornish mines when, in blasting, goose quill and rush were used as fuse; and the invention of the safety-fuse by William Bickford, of Tuckingmill, near Camborne, was a boon not only to our own, but to miners all over the world. In its first year (1830) Bickford's little factory at Tuckingmill, near Camborne, produced forty-five miles of fuse, which, in 1947, from a greatly enlarged establishment, was being turned out at the rate of three hundred miles a day. The factory, by that time owned by Imperial Chemical Industries, closed down at the end of 1961. Fuse-making was then succeeded by the manufacture of agricultural machinery.

Another revolutionary mining invention was the safety-lamp, and Cornish people are proud that its inventor was a native of Penzance. Sir Humphry Davy's lamp, though it did not benefit our own miners, who have never had to contend with fire-damp, armed their comrades in the coal mines effectively against a most formidable adversary. Except for premature and retarded explosions in the days before Bickford's safety-fuse came into use, falls of stone and falls from ladders were the cause of most fatalities in Cornish mines, and one in every five miners in the former industrial parish of Gwennap met a violent death.

A vivid description of the Gwennap mines, as seen from the summit of Carn Marth, appeared in the *Edinburgh Review*, a century ago. I find it particularly interesting, because scores of times in the past ten years I have looked down upon the countryside from the windy height where Captain Head, the writer of the article, then stood. There still, though greatly diminished since the American troops got to work with bull-dozers in 1944, are "the heaps of 'deads' which rise among the green fields and the grazing cattle, like the workings of a mole"; and there still, though fewer alas, are the "small, whitewashed, miners' cottages which, being neither on a road, nor near a road, wear to the eye of a stranger the appearance of having been dropped down, apropos of nothing". Mining has ceased for many years in this district, which, for about a century, was the richest copper-producing area in the Old World. But through the Captain's observant eyes we can still see the hundreds of men, women, and children, in the early morning sunshine, "converging like bees towards the small holes at which they are to enter the mine".

With the girls, and the boys under ten, the women remained on the surface in rough sheds, where they dressed and washed the ore sent up from below. The men and the bigger boys—but how small they must have looked!—stripped off their surface clothes and put on underground garments of coarse flannel. Then, with candles stuck into lumps of clay on their hard hats, one after another they went down "the several shafts of the mine by the perpendicular ladders". In the deep levels the temperature was sometimes as high as 115 degrees Fahrenheit, and the men worked practically naked; though, even so, three of them could do only as much work as a single miner performed in other mines where the air and water were not so hot. I don't think Captain Head can have known this, or gone underground; and I feel uneasy about his description of the scene at the end of the core (shift), when the crowd we have seen through his eyes in the morning are returning from work.

Unlike coal miners, the Cornish miners did not wait to reach home for baths in front of the kitchen fires. They bathed in the warm water of the engine cistern before they put on their surface clothes, and Captain Head saw them "so clean and fresh, and seeming so happy, that one would scarcely fancy they had worked all day in darkness and confinement". Then follows an idyllic picture of the boys hopping and skipping and leap-frogging on the way home, and the girls, "as the circumstances require", laughing or screaming. There is something incontrovertibly Cornish in the description of the young miners talking and laughing and so full of high spirits that, wherever they find a suitable strip of grass, they turn aside from the track to enjoy a "hitch" or two of our ancient sport of wrestling.

It is the *Edinburgh Review*'s reference to "the old men, tired with their work and plodding their way home in sober silence", that disturbs me. Did Captain Head, I wonder, have an opportunity to ask any of these "old men" their ages? I doubt whether half-a-dozen of them were past forty, and many were probably in their early thirties, or younger. Few other industries have aged men so prematurely as Cornish mining. It was a good old age if a miner lived to be fifty; and if he was able to work underground at thirty-five he was exceptionally robust and exceptionally lucky. In the middle of last century, chest diseases carried off nearly twice as many miners as people in other occupations in Cornwall; and if Captain Head had called at some of the whitewashed cottages he had seen from the granite boulders of the carn, he would probably have found, outside the doors, men with sallow, wasted faces, and eyes preternaturally bright, sitting in the warm sunshine—and in the shadow of death.

Meanwhile, in the mine, their sons, whom once they had carried on their shoulders down the hundreds of feet of ladders, were wresting copper from the slate and granite. All too soon these youngsters, going home-along after core, would cease to enjoy a spirited hitch on the green sward; and, in the manner of their fathers before them, would plod their way home in sober silence.

Far be it from me to suggest that romance has been lacking from the long and hazardous search for the minerals which Nature has provided in such variety and abundance under the rolling surface of the Cornish countryside. There is romance of a kind in the immense rewards: some the results of persistent endeavour, others as gratifying in their promptitude as in their proportions. (I think of Captain Josiah Thomas's tireless advocacy of "Go deeper" at Dolcoath and the triumphant sequel; and the Godolphin tin streamers who, while cutting a leat, came upon a rich copper lode.) But against these rewards may fairly be set for remembrance also the poverty and squalor which were the lot of thousands of working miners.

A salutary corrective to the hill-top exuberance of Captain Head are the almost contemporaneous observations of Stockdale, whose *Excursions Through Cornwall*, though here and there its note may be pitched too high, has the genuine ring of fidelity. The former Assistant to the East India Company's Military Secretary, in his description of our mines, wrote, "The hardships many of them (the miners) endure is beyond belief; particularly such as have large families, and who, in most cases, live in little huts in the immediate vicinity of the mines. Their mode of living is very hard, as they seldom taste animal food; indeed, the reduced scale of their wages is such as scarcely to allow bread, and that in many instances composed of ground barley only. In some cases, many of the miners work like slaves, and are obliged to wheel barrows a considerable distance filled with ore to the extent of four cwt., while, on the other hand, those who are employed underground, have a wretched, emaciated appearance and mostly die at an early age, in pulmonary consumptions."

As the nineteenth century advanced, the lot of the miner improved; but even after the First World War the average wage was not much more than two pounds a week. Working conditions also were better; but as recently as 1938 the Registrar-General's Report on Occupational Mortality showed that the death rate from consumption and silicosis was highest among tin and copper miners.

From this point of view it was fortunate that there were by then no copper miners and fewer than two thousand tin miners at work in a county where once sixty thousand people were employed in the mines, over three hundred of which were in production in the 1860s.

Our population, then at its peak, had nearly doubled in sixty years. Soon came signs of exhaustion of copper, new supplies of which, as well as of tin, were being produced more cheaply overseas. So the great days of Cornish mining began to wane, and by the end of the nineteenth century this industry, which had reared its engine-houses and chimney-stacks from Kit Hill and Caradon, not far from Tamarside, to Levant and Botallack, on the edge of the western cliffs, had become constricted to the foot of Carn Brea and St. Agnes Beacon.

The First World War, with its demand for tin and wolfram, revived mining in Cornwall, though in a way most unsatisfactory to the industry. With little or no development work, there was a heterodox scramble to produce for the war effort the greatest quantities of minerals in the shortest time. "The eyes of the mines were picked out", and soon after the war had ended darkness fell upon the industry.

But that was not the end of mining. A million pounds' worth of tin was produced in Cornwall in 1926, and although the Census of 1931 revealed that our tin and copper mines were employing fewer than seven hundred men, this number was doubled when the Second World War came, with its pressing needs for tin and wolfram (which hardens steel). From 1939 onwards, however, there were never more than five Cornish mines at work, and one of these, a wolfram cliff-working, between St. Agnes and Perranporth, had closed down before the war ended.

Those competent to give an opinion have never doubted that beneath Cornwall's crust of granite lies the most varied concentration of metal ores in Europe. When therefore in 1964 a world shortage of tin came to be regarded as a distinct possibility and its price rose to £1,500 a ton, Cornwall again attained some of its eminence as an area of mineral wealth. By early 1965 some half-a-dozen of the world's most powerful mining combines became closely interested in the county and before long their diamond drills were at work both in the east and the west.

Meantime, from this county, which has supplied the world with so much of its tin and copper, men have gone to the ends of the earth to take part in deep mining. There is a story that "way back-along" a Cornish miner, who had committed a murder, escaped to Bohemia, where he discovered tin for the Germans. It may well be true. Cornishmen, the great Trevithick among them, played their part centuries latter in the re-opening of the flooded gold and silver mines of South America, and early in the nineteenth century others were busy in Colombia. Soon afterwards they were deep in the earth in Norway and Cuba. When iron lodes were found in Durham a century ago, off went a hundred Cornish miners to work them, sailing from Falmouth Harbour, where lay that week at anchor—lovely sight!—"upwards of two hundred sail of merchantmen, some of a thousand to twelve hundred tons burthen, chiefly corn-laden, and waiting for orders".

Then came the gold rush to California, and from half-a-dozen Cornish ports the miners set out upon the three to six months' harassing and detested voyage to the diggings of the Far West. Gold called from Australia, too, and off went our miners in droves. Diamonds and gold lured them to South Africa where, by the time of Dame Fanny Moody's visit, the "Cousin Jackies" were a solid colony. They have been so ever since. Indeed, the saying has long been true, that wherever in the wide world a deep hole has been dug for minerals, you will find in it a Cornishman: highly-skilled, self-reliant, with the tradition of centuries of mining enriching all his work, and most probably with the teachings and tunes of Methodism giving direction and rhythm to his life.

It is this tradition that nourishes our reluctance to part with the roofless engine-houses and broken chimney-stacks which stand in solitude upon wave-swept headlands, or cluster at the feet of boulder-strewn hills. Even if the buildings were ugly memorials of an industry which dominated Cornish life for so long—and ugly they certainly are not—we should still like their removal to be left to time and "the inevitability of gradualness". For they are, in a sense, family history in stone; even to people like myself, whose links with the industry are slender. Directly, mine are through the great-uncle who quitted the dunes of St. Minver for the depths of Tresavean; indirectly, through my Great-Grandfather Berry, master of a little vessel which used to beat down Channel and round the land, with Welsh coal for the mines of Gwennap.

I wonder whether, as a change from pacing the deck, or sitting aft in his tiny cabin poring over his Bible, he sometimes went ashore at Devoran and wandered through the ochreous Carnon Valley to Gwennap Downs. His great-grandson is often attracted to this mining country, not least because, when he looks across the valley from the high ground above Twelveheads, he is reminded of the cliffs of his native North Cornwall and the sailor's daymark high on Stepper Point. From the engine-house of Wheal Clifford, the old arsenic track, like a dove-grey stream cascading through the heath, descends to a valley which once was full of the roar of ore-stamping machinery and where one hears now only the murmur of running water. Over the downs, broad paths and narrow, steep and flat, mark where the miners moved above ground; and a score of shafts, with crumbling walls scaled here and there by bramble, mark where they entered the underworld.

All about are heaps of "deads", which were once part of that world. The scars of the patient earth are hidden by heath and bracken and stunted grasses, and here and there is the flame of gorse and broom. One rocky tract, *mirabile dictu,* is crowned with a crab apple tree, "with blossoms brave bedeckèd daintily". Not far away, among rotting woodwork at the top of a shaft, the nesting daws sometimes dislodge small pieces of stone which, as they fall, rumble like boulders down to the dark depths and the still water. Nearby, was a miner's cottage, of which a jagged wall and a heap of stones are all that remain. Through what was once a fireplace a fuchsia has spread, its bells the brighter beside the pallor of over-running and intertwining bramble blossom. All around the impudent ragwort has opened its yellow parasols; and nettles, as their way is, flourish where formerly man had his home and little garden.

My thoughts wander from this poor miner's cottage to the fine Georgian town houses a mile or two away, over the hills at Truro. The foundations of those grey and gracious buildings, too, rested, though not entirely, upon tin and copper; for there must have been a shining stream of dues and profits for landlords and merchants flowing from this mining country into eighteenth- and early nineteenth-century Truro, where "all the modes of polished life were visible in genteel houses, elegant hospitality, fashionable apparel, and cautious manners". (Cautious manners—the pride of Truro!) Awaiting coinage, blocks of tin used to lie about in the streets as though they were common paving stones. Thousands of tons of minerals were shipped from the riverside, whence were carted away for use in the neighbouring mines great quantities of timber—in one year, some thirty thousand pieces of imported fir. With such an economic background, no wonder there was a quality, a style, about life in Truro that was matched nowhere else in Cornwall.

It is not likely that the miner who lived on these bleak Gwennap Downs ever saw the interior of Truro's Assembly Rooms on an evening after the races when "the beauty and fashion of this and the neighbouring towns" had assembled for a ball, led off by the Mayoress, in silks and jewels, and a Yeomanry officer, in the gay uniform of the time, and still flushed with the day's excitements; or when rose-cushioned and curtained sedan chairs, stately landaus, and barouches and fours, brought the nobility and gentry to see a comedy by Mr. Moon and his players: that talented company who had performed on one memorable occasion "before their Majesties and the Royal Family at the King's Lodge at Weymouth, where His Majesty was very condescendingly pleased to say that it excelled every performance of the kind he had ever witnessed".

The Assembly Rooms no longer grace the Truro scene; but there still, at the west end of the Cathedral and looking out upon High Cross, is the free-stone front of that select rendezvous, with its charming Wedgwood plaques of Shakespeare and Garrick, and of Thalia in exquisite gesture with mirror and mask. As I pass in the quiet of an autumn evening, I fancy I hear echoes of the laughter that once greeted some racily declaimed lines, or the ghostly voice of the violins in that "numerous and respectable orchestra".

And what of this miner who, after his labours deep below grass, came panting and sweating to surface from the foolish, high-spirited struggle on the interminable ladders? Where, in his hours of leisure, did he turn? Perhaps he was one of "the people called Methodists", like the effervescent and evangelizing Billy Bray, the Twelveheads miner, who styled himself the "King's son", and who built chapels as nets for souls. But this miner may have been commoner clay, gathering with this kind, not in the Methodist class-meeting "up to Kerley" or "over to Great Deliverance", but on the edge of the downs, towards Falmouth, under the thatched roof of the Miners' Arms.

The inn is no longer there. It must have been, I think, that farm-house, screened from boisterous north winds by the clustered elms, remarkable and not unpleasing for having the half of its front directly under the thatch in warm and alien brick. If this was the Miners' Arms, the change is as symbolic as the gradual extension of tiny fields over ground once laid waste by mining. This slow and arduous re-covery of land to agriculture explains why, from Carn Marth, the countryside looks so much like an array of coloured handkerchiefs. Captain Head saw that undulating landscape in terms of the battlefield, "the farmer and the miner occupying the country in something like the confusion of warfare". The fortunes of war were then ranged with the miner.

So, almost insolently, they were when Dr. Paris was writing of the mines that "in a narrow slip of barren country, where the purposes of agriculture would not employ above a few thousand people, they alone support a population estimated at nearly sixty thousand, exclusive of artisans, tradesmen, and merchants in the towns". But in the end the battle has gone decisively, overwhelmingly, in favour of the farmer.

If the ghost of Dr. Paris ever wanders from the Mount's Bay district that he loved, it must find strange indeed a Cornish land in which, for every man employed in the mines (only two were worked in the opening years of the present decade) there are probably thirty men serving "the purpose of agriculture". Had not the inn on Gwennap Downs become a farmhouse, it might well be displaying now to travellers along that exposed high road to Falmouth the sign of the Farmers' Arms.

Just as the mainstay of our fishing industry in its most prosperous days was "the least fishe", so the mainstay of Cornish agriculture has been the small farm. A walk of a mile or so from where I live near Truro takes me past eight farms, the largest of about a hundred acres, the others ranging from forty to twenty.

Of the thirteen or fourteen thousand holdings in the county in 1962, one in every five was of five acres or under, and roughly three out of every four were of fifty acres and under. There are obvious disadvantages to this small-farm economy; but it does ensure in normal times intensive cultivation and cropping, and probably more is produced to the acre in Cornwall—certainly in the area round Penzance and towards Gwinear—than anywhere else in the country.

This is the more satisfactory because the Cornish record in agriculture up to Tudor times was shocking. So complete was our neglect that Devon and Somerset farmers used to hire our pastures and store them with their cattle. Upon those neighbouring counties we were also dependent for the bulk of our corn, and even for bread. Such was then the dominating position of mining in the Cornish economy. But there came a time when the tin works began temporarily to fail, and our population had greatly increased—a double necessity "that drave people to play the good husbands, and to provide corne of their owne". Once they turned to this new task, the Cornish, as their way is, made a "bra'e job o' it", and by the end of Elizabeth's reign the county was not only self-sufficient in corn, but was able for the first time to export it.

We have little or no limestone in Cornwall; but our sea-sand is remarkably rich in carbonate of lime, and about nine out of every ten tons of lime used on Cornish farms are sand. For hundreds of years our farmers have had a legal right to take what sand they require for their work, and the only part of the county where the right has not been much exercised is in the south-east, where are available cheap supplies of lime from Plymouth.

The Cornish coast has provided the land with another valuable

St. Michael's Mount

manure: sea-weed, or ore-weed as we call it, tons of which used to be taken inland by donkeys, whose tracks may still be seen along the coast—and are often attributed to the ubiquitous smugglers! Sea-weed is particularly rich in potash, and the use of it in large quantities is one reason for the success of horticulture in the Mount's Bay district, which can produce three crops in a year.

The mild climate and humidity have much to do with this market-gardening *par excellence*. Besides supplying England with the earliest home-grown potatoes, the first outdoor-grown strawberries, and the first spring cabbages, Cornwall sends beyond the Tamar spring flowers weeks ahead of those grown elsewhere. The Scilly Isles were pioneers in this flower trade, which in peacetime every year involves for the islanders and growers on the Cornish mainland the export of some five thousand tons (or 250 millions) of blooms, which grow three times as thickly here as in the Fens. The trade began in a small way. When the Bristol merchants put an end to dealing with the Scillies in kelp (sea-weed calcined and used for its carbonate of soda, iodine, and so on), the islanders turned reluctantly to fishing as a livelihood. This having failed, they began to cultivate early potatoes; but frosts and storms made returns so uncertain that Augustus Smith, the Lord Proprietor of the Isles, advised the Scillonians to make a start with the commercial cultivation of flowers.

One day, William Trevellick, of St. Mary's, having read in the market notices that good prices were being offered for flowers, packed into a hat-box some of the narcissi which were growing wild in the hedges. So handsomely was this tiny consignment received at the market that Trevellick sent more, and soon it began to leak out that he was doing quite a profitable trade in blooms. Before long bulbs were being planted in all parts of the islands. The mainland of Cornwall, particularly the Penzance district, has also been transformed into lucrative flower gardens, and it is from this remote corner of the British Isles, on days bleak and bitter in London and the industrial towns of the North, that the golden trumpets, whose silence is more arresting than any sound, make their first triumphant appearance.

During the Second World War this traffic in beauty was necessarily small, for the flower growers had to give over much of their land to cultivating food. There was little space on trains for packages of flowers, and the regulations governing their carriage resulted in the creation of a new smuggler—an enterprising fellow from up the country who came down to the flower farms, bought what blooms he could, and exercised much ingenuity in getting them to the distant

8

Roche Rock and the ruins of St. Michael's Chapel

market, where fabulous prices were paid for them. At first the flower smuggler used trunks and suitcases, and when these became liable to search by railway officials, he concealed the anemones, irises, violets, and daffodils underneath lettuce in sacks, and among broccoli in crates. Defying the ban on the use of petrol for flower transport, he hid the blooms in lorries, empty petrol tanks, and even, on one occasion, in a coffin. A legal, but arduous, method of taking boxes of flowers from Cornwall to London was the use of relays of pedal cyclists.

Normally, this is a county of mixed farming: chiefly dairying, pig-raising, and poultry-keeping. A cow to the acre is common on many small farms, and Cornwall's pig population has at times been larger than that of any other county. A magnificent war-time achievement changed the face of the Cornish countryside. One hundred and forty thousand acres were taken from the pig and the cow and put under the plough. In the late summer, shocks of corn stood where corn had never stood before: I saw them in one valley meadow that could not have been more than a single acre.

The war, which had brought all this remarkable activity to the countryside, slowed down our biggest exporting trade. While china clay workers in Mid Cornwall were hard at it in a number of ways, they were busy least of all about their customary tasks. By the irony of circumstance, some of them were directed from this important industry into the comparatively tiny tin-mining industry; and little they liked it, too. For there is a world of difference between working in a clay-pit even at its deepest and working a thousand feet or more underground in a tin mine. Our china clay deposits are fairly close to the surface, over large areas, and are therefore neither dear nor difficult to work. The sky above the worker's head is always spacious. No wonder these clay-pit men disliked so much following a war-time occupation in which, it may well be, their grandfathers or great-grandfathers would have felt at home. True, the old men would have found the swift cages taking them to and from the deep levels a strange experience, and they would have been new to the use of the pneumatic drill. But the winning of tin ore from the rock in darkness and confinement would have been second nature to them.

It was fortunate for the St. Austell district that by the time it no longer paid to mine tin, copper and iron, around the granite mass of Hensbarrow, the china clay industry had become fairly well established. This mineral was first worked in China, in the mountain of *Kao Lin*—the other name now given to china clay—and it was next discovered in Tregonning Hill, not far from Helston, where the disused quarries may still be seen. Kaolin is the decomposed felspar of granite, and the job of clay workers is to separate this from the other two constituents, quartz (sand) and mica. This is done by what is technically called "lavation". The older method is to remove the earth from over the decomposed granite, and then to direct streams of water down channels, the sides of which are constantly falling, and being assisted to fall, into the water. There the lumps are broken up, and at the bottom of the pit the quartz is trapped and carted, or trammed, to the surface, where in time it makes the great white pyramids, which are a feature of the Mid Cornwall scene and which are made up of millions of tons of clay waste.

The mica and clay are pumped to the surface, where they flow slowly through wide launders, in which the heavier mica sinks while the clay goes on to settle in pits as a pure white mud. Thence it is carried away to long drying-sheds, near roadsides or railway lines, and spread on tiled floors under which flues run. When dry, the clay is ready for dispatch to many parts of the world, chiefly America. The newer method of winning clay, instead of guiding streams from the surface downwards, is to work from below with nozzles which direct water at high pressure against the exposed sides of the weathered granite. The pressure not only dislodges lumps, but breaks them up as they descend towards the sand-pits.

I wonder if people realize in how may forms Cornish granite, so massive and stolid in its native setting, insinuates itself, as china clay, into their lives and homes. Three-quarters of the china clay produced goes to the making of paper, and about ten per cent to the potteries for manufacture into china, porcelain, and other wares. But this Cornish product is nowadays incorporated in an ever-increasing number of articles, coming to the home and the person in such things as textile fabrics, linoleum, and *papiermâché*; cosmetics, rubber articles, and toilet and dental powders. China stone, which is granite in another form, is used chiefly by the potters, and is the biggest constituent of enamel.

A use, or misuse, of china clay to which nobody has called attention since *The West Briton* recorded it in 1814, was in the adulteration of bread during the Napoleonic Wars. Some millers in the Truro district managed, in the course of two years, to mix two hundred tons of china clay with their flour, thus making for themselves a profit of about £5,000—which would be a very large sum of money in the 1960s, allowing for the depreciation of the £. The adulterated flour caused much illness among miners in the neighbourhood, but it went farther afield: to our soldiers in the Peninsula, our naval men of the high seas and the French prisoners-of-war on Dartmoor. The chief offender was sent to prison for two years and his accomplices were fined. So inflamed was feeling about their anti-social conduct that they were burnt in effigy in the streets of Truro.

Much of our china clay, of course, goes to the home market, but in 1961 well over a million tons were also shipped abroad, thus earning between eight and nine million pounds in foreign currencies, a million pounds more than in 1960.

This is an industry which, like the seasonal tourist industry—though in this respect only—creates new records year after year. It has been estimated that during 1962 over 300,000 holiday-makers came to Cornwall from beyond the Tamar between the months of May and October—a figure which approximates to that of the county's normal population.

Granite quarrying had been until late years another industry of great importance to Cornwall. For a century or more this native stone, much of it a lovely silver-grey, was sent to all parts of the country and far overseas, its export bringing in not less than a million pounds a year. When I lived in London, it used to comfort me to know that while I was crossing the Old Waterloo Bridge, and the bridges at Blackfriars, Westminster, and the Tower, or when I was walking along the Thames Embankment, there beside me or beneath me was Cornwall, in the form of her granite. The first Eddystone Lighthouse was of Cornish granite, a solid block of which, thirty feet high, makes the shaft of the Strathsfieldspaye monument to the great Duke of Wellington. The sarcophagus of the Duke in St. Paul's Cathedral is of a special kind of Cornish granite: Luxulyanite, a surface stone, which is mostly big crystals of black tourmaline and felspar, embedded in grey quartz.

There were complaints some years ago that the granite in the old Waterloo Bridge was decomposing. Even if this were true, it was by no means a criticism of Cornish granite, for the stone used in the bridge was not quarried, but simply surface boulders squared up on the moors. The remarkable thing is that this soft stone should have stood up to the weather so well for over a century. Of our moorstone Norden had a high opinion, and he considered it "in building most firm and lasting". That was several centuries before the Cornish were quarrying their hard granite, which also "hath a glittering hue, as if it were sett with the sparkes of Diamondes".

Norden was complimentary, too, about Cornish slate, "the best to cover houses that is within this Region, and (for the most part) of the colour of lead; they are thin, beautiful, and light, and continue very long without prejudice, unless by violence. They are in great request, and very vendable, as well in foreign parts as at home". The quarry at Delabole has been worked for the past four centuries and is about a mile in circumference and five hundred feet deep. In its heyday the industry in North Cornwall provided employment for about six hundred men, but in 1962 the number had dwindled to about one hundred and fifty. The slate-quarrying industry, in fact, has changed with the times. The old traditional industry, producing thousands of tons of roofing slate every year, was a heavy employer of labour, but modern applications do not need so many men. Today at Delabole roofing slates are still supplied for "high class" building, but there is a heavy output of slate in another form—slate powder (filler for bituminous products, insecticides, plastics, and fertilizers) and slate granules (for roofing felt). And, in keeping with modern building techniques, a section of the labour force is devoted to concrete block-making. I wish that more slate was used instead of roughcast over the concrete blocks for the outsides of new houses and bungalows. I like slate for headstones, too; even though we have nowadays no youthful Neville Burnard to embellish them with those blithe cherubs born of his genius and a borrowed nail.

This chapter has been mainly about Cornwall at work. To our forbears work was of two kinds: "schemey" and "louster". Even to this day in the country districts there is in circulation an old saying as fresh as on the day it was minted: "If you can't schemey, you must louster", i.e. if you cannot earn a living by planning, by brain work, you must earn it by labouring long and hard. "Aw, he'll never be nothin' no more than a lousterer," sighs a mother regretfully of her son, or raps it out disapprovingly of a young fellow whose claims to be considered a prospective son-in-law have been advanced by her too susceptible daughter. Although it may be convenient at times, I do not like this arbitrary division of mankind; particularly if on the one side, among the favoured, is the host of clerical workers, admirable though they may be, and on the other, the less favoured, first-class craftsmen like the best of our land workers.

In the altar painting by Ann Walke, in the Jesus Chapel of Truro Cathedral, of Christ blessing Cornish industry, our land workers are in the foreground. Although the treatment is new, the subject is one which has inspired artists from very early times, and their paintings may still be seen on the old walls of some of our Cornish churches.

The dominating Figure of the central panel is our Lord, regal on the Cross, which, following the long tradition of religious art, is planted in the globe. He is being adored by two angels who, in the side panels, are depicted alighting in Cornish meadows, with their hedges of granite boulders and their familiar flocks of hens, one of which is being snatched away in the mouth of a fox. Nearest to the Figure which has its arm outstretched in blessing, are the men and women of the farms, market-gardens, and flower fields; in middle distance and background are miners moving towards the still tenanted engine-house and stack, and a broad stream of water, beside which is a fishing village with its Norman tower and its little fleet. Elsewhere along the bank a ship is being loaded with china clay. Ann Walke has contrived to impart to the humble, purposeful figures of these Cornish workers, bent over the bountiful earth, striding to the distant mine, or loading the pure white clay, something of the essence of that benign central Figure.

It was a happy inspiration of Bishop Frere to choose this west end of the north aisle for the Jesus Chapel, with its theme of the blessedness of everyday work. For one thing, the chapel is near the window in which figure groups of miners at work in Dolcoath, deepest and richest of Cornish mines, and above them their guardian angels. For another, the Jesus Chapel is in the Statesmen's Corner of the Cathedral. As you turn away from it, you are aware of three of the great ones of Cornwall looking gravely from medallions in the memorial on the north wall: Sir John Eliot, of Port Eliot, the seventeenth-century champion of Parliamentary government; Sidney, Earl of Godolphin, friend of Marlborough and Lord High Treasurer for eight years in the reign of Queen Anne; and Sir William Molesworth, of Pencarrow, nineteenth-century Colonial Secretary—a son each of East, West, and Mid Cornwall. It seems to me most fitting that the memorial to these statesmen, whose labours were in high places far from their homes, should be close to that west window and to Ann Walke's painting of lowly fellow Cornish men and women, working in the common places of their homeland, with Christ's blessing upon them all.

VI

"MAIT AND DRINK"

I forget why I soon abandoned my *History of England*, the composition of which occupied a few Saturday mornings when I was about nine. This monumental work I proposed not only to write but to print—a single copy, which was to bring me fame and to make my grandmother's three-roomed cottage in Commercial Terrace, Padstow, a place at least as important as the bakehouse, just opposite, or the tinsmith's, at the far end of the terrace.

Possibly the boy from whom I borrowed Dickens's *Child's History of England* as the basis (a euphemism for quite shameless plagiarism) of my contribution to historical literature, suddenly made up his mind that I had had the book long enough. Or possibly the setting-up of rubber type from the cheap toy printing-set, with tweezers which persistently extracted the wrong letters, proved too tedious for one who by nature was coltishly impatient and wished to make an end of a job almost before it was begun. Come to think of it—though without being at all a braggart—I was not unlike that Cornish wrestler, who, strutting into the ring at St. Merryn once, shouted to his supporters, "What's going to be done today, boys, is going to be done quick!"— and was clean thrown in the first ten seconds.

Cornwall having since produced a historian of the calibre of Dr. Rowse, it does not matter, I suppose, that my *History of England* came to no more than two or three shockingly misprinted and purple smudged sheets of notepaper which were soon lost. But on those few Saturday mornings I was so engrossed in my work as historian and publisher, that I was annoyed when my grandmother, in mid-morning, turned from the creaking and wheezing mangle at which she had been labouring, with the confession familiar at that hour: "My dear sawl, I'm feelin' so weak as a robin." (On the strength of this old Cornish phrase, I regarded the robin, until I was well into adolescence, as the valetudinarian of wild birds, instead of the hardy and pugnacious little fellow that he is.) My annoyance was not due to my grandmother's confession, but to what I knew would be its sequel: a suspension of work by both of us, so that we might have either a cup of tea and a slice of saffron cake out of the brown earthenware "stug", or a small basin of "Kiddley broth".

In cooking, only the Cornish and the Swiss, I believe, have retained their constancy to saffron, the dried stamens of the crocus. We use it in making cake and buns. I was always pleased to run to the chemist's or the grocer's for a drachm of saffron for my mother, and interested in watching her put the delicate strands in their clean, white paper on top of the Cornish range to dry thoroughly. Then the strands would go into a tea-cup, lukewarm water was poured on them, and thus they were left for the night to steep. I liked to watch the orange-red from the strands first streak and then permeate the water, which next day would be poured into the mixing bowl, colouring the dough a deep yellow, and giving it a distinctive flavour and fragrance.

If "saffern caake" is not the favourite with me still that it is with so many of my fellow Cornish, it is because of the surfeit I once foolishly indulged in during the First World War. A parcel from home containing two or three large saffron cakes, with plenty of currants and lemon peel, reached me just as I was leaving our base in France to rejoin my unit "up the line", and I ate nothing else during the thirty-six hours' journey in a cattle truck. It was easier and cheaper to buy saffron during that war than the more recent one when the price made it prohibitive for most Cornish people. But our old saying, "dear as saffern", proves that if we have always used it as one of the necessaries of life, we have regarded its price as that of a luxury. In the Second World War a substitute was available; but it was a colouring only, and the Cornish showed little interest in it.

More than once during the war, when we had to use coal sparingly, I thought what a boon it would have been if there had survived in Cornwall the old bakehouses of which in my boyhood there were four at Padstow. To the bakehouses in the course of a year were brought many thousands of saffron cakes and "sheets" of saffron buns. The bakehouse cooked other things too: Cornish splits, pasties, under-roasts, pies, and fruit tarts; and I can still see Bess, who used to manage the bakehouse opposite my grandmother's cottage, plying her broad-faced shovel with its long handle, and carefully depositing cake tins and dishes among the glowing embers in the great oven, or extracting them—how *did* she remember which belonged to whom?—when the housewives called for them. Dear Bess, of the flushed face and flying hair, the rash tongue, robustious nature, and kindly heart, sweet sleep to you, into which may drift, as in a dream, the good smell of faggots from the distant wood, and the fragrance of saffron cakes browned, as you knew how, to perfection.

Much as I liked saffron cake, I always hoped, when my grandmother made her avowal of a weakness like unto the robin's, that she would make "kiddley broth". There is nothing Cornish about the word "kiddley" here; though Kiddle Rock, at Padstow, off which are the good mussel beds, is probably a corruption of *Guidal* (the tide-net) Rock. "Kiddley" comes from kettle, which we call kiddle, and kiddley broth is made by pouring boiling water upon pieces of bread which have been put into a basin, with pepper, salt, and a tiny lump of butter as seasoning. The broth is tasty, and had long been in Cornwall a stay-stomach of the poor—we often had it for breakfast—and a light meal for those recovering from an illness. Grandmother's kiddley broth was delicious and soon dispelled my annoyance at being interrupted in the throes of mal-paraphrasing Dickens, or fixing elusive type into the narrow groove provided for it. In any case, nobody could for long have been annoyed in my grandmother's presence. I think she could have "slocked" sweet responsiveness from a stick or stone.

Certainly, she could make a very good pasty; but find me the Cornishwoman, worthy of the name, who cannot. Nobody knows through how many centuries the pasty has been the staple dish of the Cornish, so that it would be a reproach beyond bearing for one of our womenfolk—maids and matrons from fifteen to ninety—not to be able to make pasties "crimped" delicately and quickly, and cooked to a turn. A good pasty means different things to different families and individuals. We get a laugh from our story of the young miner who had just married and who went off to work one morning with the first pasty made for him by his bride. She had been a cook in service and had made the pastry very light, confident that this would count to her for righteousness at "crowst" (lunch) time in the depths of the mine. But after the day's work the young miner came home with no word of praise; indeed, no mention of the pasty. When the girl inquired timorously whether he had enjoyed it, he replied, glumly, that he supposed it "wadden bad"; but his mother's pasties were much better, because "you could l'ave they fall from top o' shaft to bottom level (say, a thousand feet), and when you picked 'em up they was jus' like when you dropped 'em—the crust wadden brawk nowhe'er!"

Evidently that miner's mother made pasties as thickly encased as those baked by the wife of Old Joe, at Padstow. Old Joe was not Cornish, and he used to boast, in his younger days, we were told, that he was "the son of a Lincoln Yellow-belly". If his wife was Cornish, she certainly belonged to the old school, whose pastry was heavy. When we saw Old Joe, with his bright blue eyes and his bushy whiskers which almost hid the stump of a pipe he called his "nose-warmer", we boys used to shout, in mimicry of his "foreign" speech, something that he was supposed to have said to his eldest son: "David, bring me that mallet, an' I'll break off a little piece of pasty for Baby!" Then we ran.

My mother's pasties were delicious, and so were my aunt's: and yet, although they were made in the same way and cooked in similar ovens, we could always distinguish between them. The truth is that no two Cornishwomen's pasties are alike; the difference may be subtle, but there it is. Mother had often to make pasties: in my elementary school days, for my father to take, or for me to carry out to him, for his dinner at some farmhouse, a mile or two from home, where he was carpentering; and, in my secondary school days, so that I might take one each day in my schoolbag; until at length a hot meal was provided every day at Bodmin County School, and my parents somehow scraped together the money for me to benefit by this.

The usual Cornish pasty is "beef and tetty" (potato), with, or without, onion, and very often with a little turnip. When I was growing up, I liked to watch Mother rolling out the pastry until it was about a quarter of an inch thick, then putting a plate on it and cutting round the edge, so that she had as many circles of pastry as she intended to make pasties. Half the circle would be laid over a rolling-pin, while the beef, potatoes, and onion, cut into small pieces, were placed on the other half. Then the edges of the pastry were damped—I believe Mother used milk—and the filling was enclosed between the two semi-circles. With forefingers and thumbs mother would neatly crimp the edges—so that there was a wavy effect—and make a slit in the top to let the steam out. Into a quick oven the four or five pasties would go, and in about three-quarters of an hour out they came, smelling as good as they looked. In summer as in winter, I prefer meat and vegetable pasties hot; but, hot or cold, they make savoury and satisfying meals.

At one time, it is said, we Cornish were addicted to the use of every likely and unlikely thing as fillings for our pasties; and generations of Cornish children have grown up believing for a while that the Devil never dared to cross the Tamar from the English side lest some enterprising Cornishwomen should put him into a pasty. It is perfectly true that we like variety in our pasties, but we never rate that quality above tradition and commonsense, both of which would tell the Cornish housewife that even baked, and for a long time, in a pasty, the Devil would be tough.

I doubt if I can remember the full range of my mother's versatility in pasty-making; but certainly, besides beef and potato pasties, I used to take on various occasions to Father, or carry in my schoolbag, pasties made of turnip and bacon (seasoned turnip alone is a good filling, but it must be eaten hot, the pasty being split and the contents spread with Cornish cream); dates or figs (as we call raisins); egg and currants, or egg and bacon; rabbit, pork, or hogspudding (a special type of sausage usually eaten cold and in round slices), herbs ("herby" pasty), leeks ("licky"), apples, or jam. Some Cornish people like fish, especially mackerel or herring, in a pasty, but Mother evidently considered that wherever else fish might be with propriety, it was out of place in a pasty.

When Father was working in the country, Mother on one or two mornings a week, would write a note, in the stylish hand of her generation, asking my headmaster if I might leave a bit early, so that I could be back from my dinner-carrying in time for afternoon school. As I was supposed to be "a good scholar", the request was always granted, and soon I would be climbing Place Hill under the great oaks and elms, with a basket containing for myself and Father a bottle of hot tea and two hot pasties, each carefully wrapped in grease-proof paper and a napkin. Proud and happy I used to be, swinging along the lanes between old stone hedges covered with flowering pennywort and dainty, ivy-leafed toadflax, and crossing the fields by paths which had been dedicated to public use since our forbears of the Middle Ages walked thither to the chapels and wells. As I neared the farm where Father was at work, I kept an eager look-out for the familiar figure coming to meet me, with his carpenter's apron caught up for ease in walking.

No matter how many times during the late spring and early summer I went on those trips, there was always a thrill when I first saw Father rounding a bend in the lane or field-path; for we were an affectionate family, and I had an enormous admiration for him, particularly as a craftsman. He could do anything, I think, with wood, except make it talk; and, in its own way, it even talked in some of the things he made: for example, my model of a Padstow-built schooner, which said, as plainly as any lady should, that she could "sail like a witch".

Sitting on a sunny bank, with the larks singing overhead and a blackbird fluting among the foam of May-blossom, with the bare, broad uplands of St. Wenn and St. Breock in front of us, and behind us, the length of two or three fields, High Cliffs and Tregudda Gorge and the deep roar of the ground sea, Father and I ate our pasties and "gaddled" our tea. We ate properly; that is to say, we held the pasties upright in our hands and munched our way, with gradually flagging gusto, from corner to corner. Many years later, one of my boyhood friends who had won a scholarship to the secondary school when I did came back to Cornwall. He had had a distinguished record in the First World War, and had deservedly become, in his own sphere after the war, an important person. As I had not seen him for many years, I invited him to lunch, and at my suggestion, my wife, though she herself was all for a more elaborate meal, made pasties.

We used to have pasties for lunch at least once a week, and on Pasty Day, as we called it, our little maid did not lay knives and forks. For this meal, however, knives and forks glittered in the sunshine of our dining-room looking due south to the valley where big crowds used to gather of old for the Fair of St. Lawrence. (How the great fairs have declined since my boyhood, when Summercourt Fair was one of the events of the year in Mid Cornwall, and now but a trace of its former prestige remains.) As we sat down to lunch, I wondered whether I should start on my pasty Cornish fashion or make a concession to the occasion and use knife and fork. My wife had evidently made up her mind and was about to do this when our guest caught up his pasty in his napkin and bit deep into the corner. "I'd almost forgotten how good a pasty tastes," he said; "but at least I haven't forgotten how a good pasty ought to be eaten." After that, the luncheon went with a swing.

Next to pasty, the Cornish like pies. At a most humiliating moment in his early life, Richard Trevithick found a pie irresistible. He had just been served with an injunction, which he had long managed to evade, and simultaneously cannon were roaring out in celebration of the victory of Boulton and Watt over those who were infringing in Cornwall the patent of Watt's steam engine. The giant Cornishman, whose exuberant genius was to make such vast and varied contributions to the Industrial Revolution, "walked backwards and forwards in the house like a madman, and firmly resisted all temptation to dinner; till the smell of a hot pye overcame his powers, on which he set to and did handsomely, but in such a manner as showed him not quiet in mind".

The pie I have known from boyhood is "mait and tetty", for which the meat and potatoes are cut up as in pasty-making, put into a pie-dish with water and seasoning, and given a roof of pastry. Potatoes and turnips often share the same roof, and some Cornish people like turnip only with the meat. Mother used also to make "herby" pie, putting chopped, scalded, and well mixed herbs into a dish lined with bacon; but my favourite was "squab" pie, with sliced apples, onions, and fat mutton, a little sugar, and perhaps a few currants. Squab pie is supposed to be a legacy to the Cornish from the Phoenicians when they were here in the dim ages for tin; and I am prepared to be as grateful to the Phoenicians as to anybody else. Another dish which my family liked was pig's leg pie, which is called in West Cornwall knuckle pie, a name that more precisely describes it, since only the lower part of the leg is used. I find no reference to pig's leg pie in Mrs. Alfred Martin's admirable *Cornish Recipes*; but I have never heard of it outside the county.

We were too poor to enjoy giblet pie more than once in a while, and I regretted the Methodist tradition in our family when at Christmas-time I heard the Parish Church choirboys boasting about the big helpings of this pie they had been given at the choir supper at Prideaux Place. Since Mother favoured fish in pie as little as in pastry, the famous "star-gazy" pie, with the heads of pilchards, mackerel, or herrings protruding through the pastry, never came my way; and I think it was seldom made in my part of Cornwall. Likewise unknown to me are conger, and eel, pies.

In the far west of the county they used to put curlew into pies. It is probably a good dish; but only the worst pangs of hunger would drive me to eat it. For the flight and call of the curlew are associated with some of the loneliest and loveliest moments of my life—in a boat in the Little Petherick River as twilight falls and the only sounds are the drippings from my paddles and the faraway barking of a farm dog; on the dunes and moors, where the curlew's cry deepens rather than breaks an eerie silence; or at St. Saviour's on a night of magic, with the moon rising above the St. Minver sand-hills, and a curlew flying low out to sea over the rippling and sighing waters of the Town Bar.

As when a boy, I still feel slightly sick when I hear people talk reminiscently of pies made of wild birds. Some of the bigger boys at my elementary school used to go "bird baiting", as we called it. They did not bait the birds; they went out on winter nights, with cheap and stinking bull's-eye lanterns, and with sticks which beat the roosting birds to death. The bigger birds were the victims, chiefly blackbirds and thrushes. They were probably killed instantly, but the practice seemed to me none the less revolting. It has long since died out in Cornwall; and it must, I think, have been a survival into better times of the "good old days", when poor people could not afford butcher's meat, except for festivals and other rare occasions, and "birdy pie" was a change from the monotonous recurrence of "fish and tetties". It was the greybird (our name for the thrush) that was most commonly put into pies—a thing I found particularly hard to credit a few years ago, when day after day for months, a thrush used to hop briskly from our garden, through the kitchen, into the dining-room, where he perched on the leg of the table, near our tolerant cocker spaniel, and had his breakfast or lunch of cake, made specially for him, with flour, lard, sugar, and currants.

This was, in fact, a Cornish heavy cake, though not so rich as those for our own use and for our visitors. The thing for strangers to remember about heavy cake is that it is not in the least heavy. It is a round, flat cake, about an inch thick, its surface criss-crossed with a knife before baking, which takes about twenty minutes. For fat some people use Cornish cream or butter, others suet, beef dripping, or lard. I like plenty of currants, and very little lemon peel. As a boy I used to stuff a lump of heavy cake hurriedly into my pocket when I heard the rockets summoning the life-boat on service, and I have spent a whole day on the cliffs with nothing else to eat—for sometimes the life-boat had to go a long way, in foul weather, to reach the vessel in distress, and it was a point of honour with us not to go home until we had seen the boat coming home-along round Stepper Point and suddenly plunging from the heavy seas and the furious nor'-wester into the still waters and the lew of The Narrows.

Only a little lower than heavy cake do I rate our potato cake, which I prefer plain, as Mother made it. She used mashed boiled potatoes, flour, grated suet, and a pinch of salt; and the surface was criss-crossed like that of heavy cake which potato cake resembles, though it is only about half as thick. There are richer variants, with bacon or sliced meat in hollows pressed into the pastry; or the cake may be made sweet with sugar and currants. The cooking takes a very short time— and so, in my experience, does the eating. As a boy I ate cold potato cake left over from a former meal, but wisdom grows with the years, and to suit me now it must be piping hot. Many Cornish people like cream or butter on potato cake, but my digestion will not cope easily with such rich fare.

Does one still have to emphasize that when a Cornishman talks about cream he *means* cream, and not the "milky trade" which up-country people pour from little jugs over their fruit, puddings, and jellies? Devonshire people are much more knowledgeable about cream than any other English folk; indeed, they entertain the curious notion that, in this matter of cream, they *are* the people, and that

Devonshire cream, instead of being the sincerest form of flattery, is the real thing. It is too late in the day to hope that this question will ever be settled to our mutual satisfaction, so I will merely affirm that while we have, in the Devonians, the best neighbours Providence could have given us, we have also the best cream.

Truly, "this 'ere Progress, it do go on", but I am saddened by several new-fangled notions ("new vangs", Mother used to call them), and not least by the notion that Cornish cream separated by machinery from the milk is as good as clotted cream. In the fragment of auto-biography which "Q" left, and which is full of his old grace and mastery, there is an expostulatory footnote on this subject, which I hope has been read by zealots of separated cream. Nobody can deny that this is pleasant, and I consider it markedly superior to any cream I have tasted outside Cornwall (Devonshire excepted); but it lacks the richness of clotted cream made in the old-fashioned way. As soon as the milk was taken from the cow, it was strained and put aside to stand for twenty-four hours in winter and twelve in summer. Then the pan was heated slowly on the stove until the cream began to rise on the edges, and there followed a long cooling in the dairy. There was then a "crust" over the top, the colour of wet sand, and a portion of this was carefully removed to cover every dish of cream taken from the pan.

One of my boyhood's delights was the trip on Sunday mornings half-way up School Board Hill to old Mrs. Carlyle's dairy, from the slate floor of which I would readily have eaten all the cream she might have dropped—but never did—from the big pan surrounded by scores of customers' glass dishes and cups. Instead, on the way home I used to dip a forefinger naughtily into the dish, lick it hurriedly, and smooth the surface of the cream so that Mother would never suspect. When we could afford a whole quarter of a pound of cream instead of the customary twopenn'orth (two ounces), I dipped and licked with an easier, though never a quiescent, conscience; for among six of us even a quarter did not go far. With our apple, or blackberry and apple tart at tea on Sundays, our ration of cream was a teaspoonful each; and I shall never forget the gaping astonishment with which I first saw well-to-do people heaping cream upon their plates as it should be heaped. I felt very much as I should now if I came upon people drinking tumblerfuls of liqueur.

If we had used raw milk, instead of skimmed, which was cheaper, Mother could have made her own little dish of cream, as many Cornish housewives still do. She did the next best thing, and sometimes made "splits", with which we ate Mrs. Carlyle's cream. Devon women have long practised the art of making splits, "toughs" or "cut-rounds" —which, I must admit, are very well made. Flour, butter or lard, yeast, sugar, milk slightly warmed, and a good pinch of salt are the ingredients of splits. These figure on most Cornish tea-tables, especially at the public teas which are such a feature of community life in the county. Their name is derived from our splitting the small, round cakes in half before buttering them, or eating them with jam and cream, or treacle and cream. The latter combination we call "thunder and lightning", and with a clear conscience I can, for once, describe a storm as delectable.

Cornwall has been called the Land of Pilchards and Cream, but strangers think more gratefully of the county for its cream than its pilchards. This must be because they have never tasted our marinated pilchard, an *hors-d'oeuvre* of the first order. We eat pilchards served in other ways: salted and boiled, or "scrowled" on a gridiron over a clear fire; but give me the pilchard marinated, for that is a fish *par excellence*. My weekly pocket money in boyhood was a ha'penny or two, and those were the days when one could buy something for a ha'penny. Indeed, in shopwindows along the quayside and in the Market Square, there were so many competitors for mine, that I had to make repeated tours, which only left me the more confused and undecided—"mizzy-mazed", as we say.

But if, through the little bow window of Mrs. Lucas's shop in Duke Street, I saw on a chair a big, brown earthenware pan (a bussa, as we call it), my mind was instantly made up, and home-along I would run for a deep saucer to buy a marinated pilchard. Nobody could have feasted more royally on a ha'penny, and my satisfaction was the deeper because you can enjoy marinated pilchard, bones and all.

This was how Mrs. Lucas marinated her pilchards. After she had cleaned them, she split each one not quite open and inside, where she had sprinkled pepper and salt, she placed a bay leaf. She almost filled the bussa with fish and poured in vinegar enough to cover them. I think she put in a few peppercorns, too; but most people are satisfied with the pepper inside the pilchards. When she had tied paper over the top of the bussa, Mrs. Lucas put it in a slow oven and left it there all night. If the bones were not soft when she came down next morning, the fish had to be baked a little longer. I have known people to eat marinated pilchards warm, but only, I think, out of curiosity. From childhood every Cornish man and woman knows " 'tes ridi'cless to ate pilchers onless they'm cold as paddicks. 'Tedden fair to yerself to

Truro Cathedral

ate 'em hot, and 'tedden fair to the pilchers". We have a great regard for fair play all round.

Except sweets, the only close competitors with the pilchard for my ha'penny were "scollops" from Mr. Tom's pork shop. Scollops are cut-up portions of the dried, brown residue after pork fat has been "run down" for lard and dripping, and they are delicious with a slice of bread. Minced scollops, and cooked pig's heart are ingredients in gurty (groats) meat puddings, which I have never tasted, but which are well known in parts of East and Mid Cornwall. In the west of the county scollops, with barley flour and salt, go to the making of grovey cake, which is a good hot savoury. Until I came to the borders of West Cornwall to live, I had never even heard of "figgy 'obbin", but now my wife often bakes one. She spreads on rolled-out, light pastry either figs or raisins, and rolls it as if it were a roly-poly jam pudding, and she cuts grooves in the top. Then she brushes it with milk and sprinkles a little sugar on top, but Cornish housewives rarely do this.

What is called figgy 'obbin in some parts of West Cornwall I knew, and much enjoyed, at my North Cornwall home, as figgy duff. Members of Perranporth Women's Institute, who contributed the recipe for this to Mrs. Martin's admirable little book, also record having seen in a Cornish shopwindow the notice: "FIGGY DUFF, 4d. LB. MORE FIGGIER, 5d."

A West Cornwall dish which I have yet to sample is "pudden skins", made of flour, suet, oatmeal, raisins, and an egg, mixed as in a batter, put into pigs' skins which we also use in making hogspudding, and lightly browned. Hogspudding is popular in all parts of Cornwall, and the remarkable thing is how it varies in quality. It is either very good, good, or not so good—even in the most restrictive period of the Second World War I did not come upon hogspudding which was bad. Mr. Tom's was very good; I think he must have had one of the recipes which are handed down in some Cornish pork butchers' families from generation to generation. The method we all know is to boil pigs' skins stuffed with minced pork, lean and fat, bread crumbs, thyme, salt, and pepper. I must have eaten hundreds of pasties filled with hogspudding, which some people like sliced and fried. Until I came to Truro I had never seen so many recumbent ranks of hogspuddings, nor did I realize that any Cornish town had so many pork butchers. It shows what a power is the pig in our normal farming economy.

The Cornish use pickles freely. I have not tasted pickled samphire, which, although by no means peculiar to the county, has long been used here. Mrs. Martin has recorded a Cornish recipe, more than two

9

Bench end, Padstow Church:
Fox preaching to the Geese

hundred years old, which may not be much known in the Southern Counties where common samphire grows. (At Padstow we have, along the cliffs, the rarer, golden samphire.) Shakespeare in *King Lear* speaks of the gathering of this cliff flower, sometimes called St. Peter's herb, as a "dreadful trade". It has had its fatalities even in recent years outside Cornwall. The truth of Shakespeare's phrase was shown in our county on a June evening in 1813, when a poor St. Agnes man and his wife left their four little children at home while they went to gather samphire on the cliffs near Perranporth.

"Whilst engaged in their hazardous employment," *The West Briton* reported, "the man stood on a projecting part of the cliff. With one hand he held part of the rock above him, and with the other he pulled the samphire, which he handed to his wife, who stood a few yards below him. Unfortunately, the part upon which he stood gave way, and he fell upon the woman, both being precipitated down a tremendous precipice, about one hundred feet from the spot where they stood, and they fell within about three yards of each other." Man and wife were terribly injured, and he tried in vain to crawl to her. In a few hours she was dead. With nearly every bone in his body broken, the husband lay for twelve hours before he was found by anxious neighbours. Soon afterwards he died.

The double fatality illustrates not only the perils of the quest for samphire, but also the passionate independence of the Cornish "These poor creatures," says *The West Briton*, "were compelled by extreme poverty to resort to this dangerous occupation, in order to provide the means of support for their children, and . . . they did so in order to avoid the necessity of applying to the parish for relief." I have never heard of another case so painful; but I have memories of the shamed reluctance with which men and women, in my boyhood, even though they were too old or too frail to earn a living, cleared a little channel for the thin trickle into their homes of what was called "parish pay". It was almost as though they were conniving at the inflow of a corrosive acid among their poor, cherished possessions.

With the trickle of "parish pay" came, from mysterious sources not unconnected, I suspect, with the Good Fellowship of Padstow, little gifts, among which the most welcome were the packets of tea. If the Cornish have a national drink, it is tea; and although nine out of ten of us may never have heard of the great Dr. Johnson, we should, on being told of his "swallowing his tea in oceans" at once conclude that this was a man after our own hearts—a man, indeed, who deserved to have been born at Truro or Bodmin rather than at Lichfield, and to have spent his days within reach of the teapot never long absent from the Cornish hob.

In Dr. Johnson's day, and for long afterwards, tea was too dear for most Cornish people, and even a century ago at seven shillings a lb—the farm workers' wage being then about seven shillings a week—it was, like champagne or port today, kept for the great occasions: christenings, weddings, and buryings. Between times, the poor counted themselves lucky if they could drink tea made from the dried leaves of mugwort, or from burnt scraps of cake and wheaten bread.

So far as we know, the subject of tea drinking was mentioned to Dr. Johnson neither by Mrs. Boscawen, who was the widow of the famous Cornish Admiral ("Old Dreadnought"), and of whose manners and conversation Boswell wrote in the superlative; nor by Mr. Eliot, descendant of the great Sir John, who, however, brought to the Doctor's notice "a curious liquor peculiar to his country, which the Cornish fishermen drink". This was "Mahogany", made of two parts gin and one part treacle, well beaten together. Boswell "begged to have some of it made, which was done by proper skill by Mr. Eliot". The drink pleased Boswell, who greeted it as the counterpart of "Athol Porridge", a Highland mixture of whisky and honey. "That must be a better drink than the Cornish," adjudged the Doctor, "for both its component parts are better," and he also observed that "Mahogany" must have been a name given to the fisherfolk's drink no great time before, the wood called mahogany not having been known long in England then.

The drink is mentioned in Mrs. Martin's *Cornish Recipes*, and "Q" added a note calling attention to Boswell's reference to "Mahogany", but patriotically refrained from recording Dr. Johnson's preference for "Athol Porridge", with which, as with so many other of the Doctor's judgements, I completely concur. Until I first read Boswell, I had never heard of this Cornish fishermen's drink, and I doubt whether much of it has been made in our coves and ports since the first half of the last century.

Even nowadays, when motor lorries laden with cases of factory-made soft drinks thrust their insensitive snouts down most of our byways, and quiver and stutter impatiently while their drivers call upon lonely cottagers, the Cornish are great hands for home-made wines. My favourite aunt is so given, at irregular intervals, to following tradition and making experiments of her own, that I conclude Cornish women are as catholic in their choice of things to bottle as of things to put into pasties. Mostly my aunt follows tradition, which means that she makes blackberry, sloe, elder, and sometimes cowslip wines, and by no means disdains incursion into the vegetable garden, in particular for potato, parsnip, and beetroot. Nettle beer has many devotees, and I like it because it is the reverse of most things that are "good for you", in being pleasant as well. This is true also of our "herby beer", made with young nettles, yarrow, wild sage, and centuary.

But blackberry wine is my favourite, especially if "a little something" has been mixed with it. Until a few years ago, I looked upon blackberry wine as being among our "teetotal drinks"—a phrase of most accommodating elasticity—but one Christmas I had a salutary lesson. Like every other sensible Cornishman in London who was able to do so, I used to come home-along for Christmas—I wonder if Paddington and Waterloo will ever again be so beautifully festive as when the Cornish exiles sang their carols there? On the morning of my return to London towards the end of my tour of leave-taking, I was lured to the home of an old friend, who gave me a wide choice of drinks, but pushed to the fore a bottle of blackberry wine. Anxious not to miss my train, I gulped the drink less graciously than it deserved, but not so ungraciously that its excellence was lost upon my palate.

This was the best blackberry wine I had ever tasted, and I was about to ask my host to give me the recipe when I found myself confronted by another glass and being pressed to "drink hearty" and be quick about it. I did so, with the result that of the many journeys between Cornwall and London I remember less of this one than any other. There was still a pleasant buzzing in my head when I went to find a taxi at Waterloo, and I felt an elation altogether improper— almost disloyal, indeed—in a Cornishman returned to exile from the far western land of his fathers. Too late, alas, I afterwards sought the recipe for that blackberry wine, as delectable as this Duchy itself.

On the whole, we Cornish are a temperate race, and if we go to extremes in this matter of drinking, quite often it is to teetotalism. Nothing would induce my father to touch alcohol, though never once have I heard him say anything to suggest that he accounted this to himself as a virtue. Great-Uncle Gilbert was a teetotaller also, as might have been expected of a devout Methodist who had originally been a Bible Christian, and who must have tramped hundreds of miles to preaching appointments in wayside chapels. But there was a refreshing quality of unexpectedness about the old man. Staunch Methodist though he was, he was a no less staunch Tory, a most unusual combination in Cornwall. And although he was a teetotaller, he never departed from the tolerant view that another man had as much right to his pint of beer as he himself had to his cup of tea. If a man who liked his drink knew when he had "had enough" that was all Great-Uncle Gilbert required—and the test he applied seems to me the true test of temperance.

What county can say of sons and daughters that they are all strictly temperate? Certainly, I make no such claim for Cornwall. How could I, when one of the best stories that have come down to us is of a country-man who, having been to market and had a good many drinks, "fell asleep" when he was driving home in his pony trap. A friend found the vehicle at a standstill by the hedge; and, thinking this a good opportunity to point a moral, took the pony out of the shafts and along the road with him. Some hours later the sleeper awoke, stretched himself, scratched his head, and solemnly surveyed the scene. "Now which *is* it?" he asked himself aloud, at length. "If I'm Jan Trewhiddle I've been an' lost a pony; but if I baint Jan Trewhiddle I've been an' found a trap!"

VII

AS IT DO BELONG

IT IS highly unlikely that the Artist who lived in the tall, stucco house not far from where, as a boy, I dwelt on the quayside, was ever heard of outside of Cornwall, or even our little town. To me he was immensely important. His white hair and long beard were beautifully silky, and he would have made a fine figure, at one of the great festivals, in the gorgeous apparel of a Prince of the Church.

He was, in fact, a Wesleyan; but I thought of him as the high priest of Art, and his prestige increased the more I saw of the carelessly, and sometimes oddly, dressed men and women who came from nowhere, with their stools and easels, daubed or washed at the canvas or paper for an hour or two on the quayside, loudly proclaimed their dislike of small boys who timorously ventured near them, and then departed whence they had come. How could one, to their advantage, compare these ruffled birds of passage with the silken keeper of the temple of Art across the way from Market Circus?

Sometimes I had to enter the house—always in fear and trembling lest the Artist should become aware of the presence of a creature so small and uncouth within the precincts. Never since have I opened and shut a door so quietly, or tiptoed so furtively along a passage. Up to the last moment there was danger, for just as I was nearing the warm security of the kitchen, I might be confronted at the foot of the big staircase by the Master, descending from the holy of holies, the studio.

How good it was, after the apprehensive moments in that preternaturally solemn and silent house, to be out again among the common sights and sounds. I used to stand on the pavement for a few moments, surveying the scene as though it might somehow have undergone a desolating change. But no; everything was most comfortingly the same: the little, weathered stone figure of a man on horseback high on the roof of the Post Office; the big carboys of amber and green and red liquid in the windows of the chemist's shop; Blind Charlie, with his unsold packets of tea in a bag slung on a stick over his shoulder, tap-tapping his way into the barber's shop; a gull, perched on the topmast of a vessel in the quay, bill and breast to the wind; the bent figure

134

of Old Harriet passing along the Market, gesticulating and incessantly voluble without a sound issuing from her lips; the dust cart piled high with rubbish rumbling on its way to the precarious tip at High Cliff; winches screeching and rattling, and men shouting warnings, as huge baskets of coal swayed upwards from the hold of a schooner, discharging her cargo outside Bray's yard; "Granfer" J. (he was Granfer to everybody) emerging, with a list to starboard, from the sinister gloom of Mumpers' Inn—a jovial giant, whose blue eyes were boyish and sunny, for all the dark things they had seen; and there, toddling ahead of Granfer, my young brother, making for the slipway and the water, with Mother in pursuit, astonished as ever that offspring so small should have been able to scale the door-board which Father had made to keep his little ones in and the high tides out.

This was *my* world; it was "mait and drink" to me. Into it I plunged with the same zest as Padstow boys dive from the Tortoise Rock, marvellously balanced above the alternating sand and shingle of Chidley Pumps, or as they strain at the oar in the last few yards of the rowing races on regatta day. While I knew the Artist was slightly interested in my world, it never occurred to me that he was part of it. To me he was aloof, remote, withdrawn; but for all that, I should have been puzzled and shocked had I known then how intensely he disliked and disapproved of one feature of our world which, to us, was part of its very axis. This was our May Day celebrations, like no others in the country except an attenuated form of them at Minehead in Somerset. For us, as for our forefathers, May Day meant Hobby "Hoss" festivities, to be present at which I have known old Sam Fielding, the perfect ship's cook but for his freedom with the pepper-pot, to tramp home-along from ports as far away as the North of England. Next to Christmas Day, May Day is the festival of the year.

As a boy I could not afford to buy the Artist's little book about Padstow, and I am afraid I had forgotten its existence until the other day, when I came upon a long passage from it quoted by Lewis Hind in his charming *Days in Cornwall*. Hind apparently accepted the little essay on "Padstow Saturnalia" as uncritically as Leland's bad guess about the relation of St. Petroc to Padstow. The Artist's description of the Hobby Horse festival is accurate enough; but his comments showed that he looked upon it with the deepest distaste. To him it was "a very rough and coarse pastime", a "relic of barbarism", which had survived only because "the principal actors get a little money out of it, and the youngsters, who follow, an abundance of fun and frolic". To our May Song he conceded the "merit of antiquity"; and then, lest this faint praise should insufficiently damn it, he described it downrightly as "doggerel without rhyme or reason". As proof, he quoted three stanzas, the last the chorus:

> With the merry singing and the joyful Spring—
>   For summer is acome in to-day—
> How happy are those little birds that merrily do sing
>   In the merry morning of May!
>
> Young men and maidens, I bid you every one—
>   For summer is acome in to-day—
> To go into the green woods, and bring the May home,
>   In the merry morning of May.
>
> Unite, all unite! Let us all unite!—
>   For summer is acome in to-day—
> And whither we are going, let us all unite,
>   In the merry morning of May!

Although the Artist did not mention it, these and several more stanzas are sung to one of the loveliest of folk tunes.

The classical description of the Hobby Horse itself, in days when its antics were familiar in other parts of the country, is Scott's in *The Abbot*. "One fellow, with a horse's head painted before him, and a tail behind, and the whole covered with a long footcloth which was supposed to hide the body of the animal, ambled, carolled, pranced, and plunged, as he performed the celebrated part of the Hobby Horse." But this gives no real notion of the grotesqueness of the Padstow figure, with its protruding snappers, and headgear of black and white and brilliant red, tapering to a tuft of horse-hair; or of the physical endurance involved in carrying the Hobby Horse during several hours of a warm May Day. The man who carries the Padstow horse leaves all the carolling to others, for his lungs and limbs are sufficiently tried by the tossing and dancing required of him; and, anyhow, nobody would hear his song from under the tall, heavy headgear. There are always a few little Hobby Horses, exact replicas of "the Old Original", prancing about the streets on May Day, and one of these I was rash enough, as a boy, to carry. After half an hour of it I was nearly stifled, and more exhausted than I had ever been before. In following years I was content among the singers.

Although the Hobby Horse itself is the principal figure in the festivities, scarcely less important is the man who, with mask and club, "dances before" the horse the long day through, except in those solemn moments when horse and dancer sink to the ground as the musicians and singers reach the *pianissimo* portion of the May Song:

> O where is St. George? O where is he, O?
> He's out in the long boat, all on the salt sea.

The club rests lightly then upon the motionless snappers of the horse, which the dancer has been teasing unmercifully throughout the rest of the song. Then suddenly, singers and concertina-players, in gay apparel and bedecked with flowers, come to a livelier verse, and up leaps the horse, the dancer trips and teases once more, and the crowd moves, singing gaily, through the narrow streets, or gathers round the Maypole, crowned with furze and draped with sycamore leaves, at the foot of School Board Hill. Now and then the Hobby Horse darts towards a girl or woman and bumps against her, or, taking her under the black-painted sailcloth gown, touches her face lightly with a hand which in former days was grimy with lamp-black. It is all part of the fun, and such is our innocence, that whole generations of Padstow people have had their share in it and gone to their graves without having recognized in this exciting by-play the survival of an ancient fertility rite. No doubt its pagan significance was not lost upon the Artist; but he was so proper as to record only that the horse "pretends to hit at or push someone near".

Nobody in Padstow can have been more relieved than he when, for the last time, towards evening, the Hobby Horse singers came to the end of the song:

> Now, fare you well, and we bid you all Good Cheer—
> For summer is acome in to-day—
> We call no more unto your house before another year,
> In the merry morning of May,

and there was a general withdrawal to the Golden Lion, outside of which at midnight, the festivities had begun. When he was writing his essay on "Padstow Saturnalia", the Artist must have been greatly pleased to have had within himself assurance of the impending doom of the celebrations. "The whole affair," he concluded, "is gradually dying out, to the honour of the town, and ere long may be consigned to the limbo of the past."

But so far from having died in the intervening years, the Padstow

Hobby Horse may still be seen on a May morning prancing with much spirit through the streets and round the flame-capped Maypole, the drum beating imperatively, musicians playing and singing as merrily as ever, and the dancer, waving aloft his brightly coloured club, no less than of old "a proper teaser". And still the boughs of sycamore are hung from the houses, and in their headgear men and boys sport gay little bunches of primroses and cowslips culled from shady hedgerows and sunny headlands, with a tulip or two from town gardens to keep company with their sweet country cousins. Since the Artist wrote, moreover, the Hobby Horse has taken part in international folk-dancing at the Royal Albert Hall, and more than once the British Broadcasting Corporation has given a place in its programmes to the singing and descriptions of the scene on May Day at Padstow.

A century ago the celebrations survived a more potent antagonism than the Artist's. The spirit of Thomas Tregaskis, a West Cornwall "praicher" and temperance leader, was so vexed by our revels that he essayed to put an end to them by bribery. He had announced to "the patrons of the Hobby Horse" that if they would allow him to throw overboard the paraphernalia of the festival he would provide for the poor of the town, seven years in succession, a fat bullock weighing not less than four hundredweight. "It is for you to consult," he wrote, "whether you will give up your vain practice of the Hobby for the more rational amusement of eating Roast Beef." This was a tempting offer to a poor community who seldom saw roast beef, and the townsfolk were immensely excited about it. Through the streets all the cry was, "Who is for Roast Beef, and who is for the Hobby?"

In the closing days of April, Tregaskis chose the finest beast on his farm and drove it from the sparse pastures behind the dreary, industrialized Carnon Valley, through Truro and St. Columb past Winnard's Perch, solitary and grey amid the bright fires of furze on the downs, and on past Highlanes and Four Turnings to Padstow. With Tregaskis was his wife, like himself a preacher but much more fluent and retentive of memory, so that from the rostrum he would sometimes appeal to her to supplement or substantiate portions of his sermons. They purposed holding a temperance meeting in front of the Market House, culminating presumably in the gift of the bullock should the townsfolk have agreed to abandon the morrow's May Day festivities. But from the first the crowd was restive; soon the meeting was broken up, and Tregaskis and his bullock were driven from the town. As the clock in the tower of St. Petroc's Church struck midnight the Hobby Horse emerged as by custom from his quarters in the Golden Lion, and later the crowd was singing

> Rise up, Richard Nance, and your bride by your side—
> For summer is acome in to-day.

Tregaskis was a good, homely Cornishman, with plenty of moral courage and commonsense, and I am surprised that he should have treated his fellow-Cornishmen as though they could readily be bribed into breaking with an old custom. But I daresay the heart of a staunch teetotaller was chilled and his intuition faulty because of his revulsion from May Day merrymaking associated with strong drink. Until the middle forties when first Tregaskis came to Padstow, I have been able to trace no adverse comments upon the conduct of our Hobby Horse day. True, for long before this, "the ancient and favourite amusement" had been "kept up with great spirit", and in 1830—the only occasion when this was recorded—"the amusements concluded with 'ram-riding', which afforded much sport".

This was not at all genteel. On the contrary, it had often led in Cornwall to "much riotous behaviour". Ram-riding is not related to the Hobby Horse festivities, and must have taken place on this occasion because a Padstow husband or wife had been unfaithful. When such a thing became known in a Cornish town, and more particularly a village, there was a procession—men and boys astride donkeys and blowing horns, being headed by a cart "in which were seated burlesque representatives of the erring pair". No doubt this made May Day, 1830, a rowdy festival at Padstow, but in the following year, when the Hobby Horse parade was over, the young people "formed parties and went into the country to take tea, cream, and syllabubs, and in the evening joined in a dance, which was kept up to a late hour". Could anything have been more pastoral and innocent?

If, in later years, the proceedings had more vitality than decorum, it was futile to have tried to put an end to the whole thing by offering in their place "the more rational amusement of eating Roast Beef". No people cling more tenaciously than the Cornish to the things that custom has ordained "do belong to be", and when they have loosened their hold, as great numbers of our people did in the eighteenth century, it has been the result neither of bribes nor processes, however brief and salutary, of ratiocination. What the "foreigner" John Wesley understood, and the rugged old Cornishman Tregaskis, in this instance, did not, was that if we are to be turned away from amusements regarded as sinful or undesirable, we are to be led by our hearts. The savour of a bribe and the dry light of reason will fail again and again; but the leaping fires of a great revival will achieve remarkable success. Or so it has been.

No other individual in our history has left such an impress upon Cornwall as Wesley, and if beneath that impress something of our old spontaneity and naïvety was lost, much was buried that was brutal and depraved and did not deserve to survive. Some who desire still further to accentuate Wesley's triumph have said or implied that Cornwall in the middle of the eighteenth century was the blackest spot in the country. I do not believe it. Our miners and the people generally were probably a rough lot who, during that nadir of the Church's influence and ministry,[1] had "got into heathen ways". It must be remembered, however, that Wesley was preaching to a people who, for all their wildness and debasement, were by temperament and tradition passionately religious. Living arduously and dangerously by fishing and mining, and often ill-rewarded by these chancy occupations, is it any wonder that men abandoned or ill-served by their pastors, in that period of "the fat slumbers of the Church", should have turned in their squalor and spiritual neglect to the strong drink of the "kiddleywinks", and to practices and amusements which we regard with disgust or dismay? With these Methodism was bound to come into conflict.

While other customs and festivals may have lost their hold thenceforth, the Padstow Hobby Horse and the Helston Furry (Cornish *fer*, a fair) buoyantly survived the Great Revival and the years that followed, during which Methodism rooted itself in Cornwall more deeply and fruitfully than anywhere else in the country. Wesley did not visit Padstow, and that may explain the survival there; for direct contact with his personality might have made all the difference to Methodism in its beginnings in the town. Anyhow, it is not without significance that, more than a century after Wesley's first visit to Cornwall, Tregaskis, a lay preacher who had seen remarkable "ingatherings of souls" in his own chapel of Hicks Mill, should have come to Padstow to put an end to our "relic of barbarism" as a rationalist offering plates of roast beef, rather than as a revivalist proclaiming the love of God and the wrath to come.

But if Wesley's absence from Padstow explains the survival of the Hobby Horse, so that it troubled the spirit of his follower, the Artist, less than half a century ago, some other explanation must be sought of

---

[1] But "the Bishop of Exeter in 1764-65 confirmed 41,642 in Cornwall and Devon alone".—Trevelyan, *English Social History*, p. 361.

the apparently unbroken sequence of Furry Dances at Helston on May the Eighth; for Wesley preached there more than once, finding the town on his early visits a turbulent place. The simple, perhaps too simple, explanation may be that the Furry Dance, which is said to have had its origins in the successful struggle of St. Michael with the Devil for possession of Helston, was even then so sober, decorous, and civic as not to challenge opposition from the Methodists or any other religious people. When the Hal-an-Tow, sung through the streets in the early morning to the accompaniment of fifes and drums, got out of hand much later than Wesley's time, it lost its place in the Furry Day proceedings, until its revival between the two World Wars at the instance of the local Old Cornwall Society. That was a piece of good work, for the Hal-an-Tow, which begins

> Robin Hood and Little John,
> They both are gone to fair, O,

is, like the Padstow Song, which it somewhat resembles, the very thing for a May morning.

Those who have seen the May festivals at Padstow and Helston must have been struck by the contrast. If the Furry ages ago was robust and spontaneous, it has since been turned to "prettiness and favour". The dance is as charming a thing as you could wish to see. People flock to Helston on May the Eighth from all over Cornwall and much farther afield, to watch the scores of couples of children at their appointed time, and the formally apparelled men and women, in proper precedence, at theirs, dancing faultless steps through the hilly streets and in and out of the houses, led by the one band in the world that can "play the tune proper".

With dismay and regret I should contemplate any future Eighth of May when this delightful spectacle should have vanished from the Cornish scene. Yet I cannot help wishing that the Furry Dance had more vitality and spontaneity and less formality. We at Padstow are quite unselfconscious and informal in our festivity. Anybody and everybody can join in. Well we know that crowds will not come from elsewhere to watch our revels; and we are neither sad nor glad therefor. Ours is not a "show piece" to be staged with elegance and precision for the satisfaction of the formal or the delectation of strangers. Ours is a happy-go-lucky affair, with a few unwritten rules, but offering within the slender framework of the customary scope for inspiration and improvisation. By comparison with the Furry, the prancings of the Hobby Horse and its teaser are crude, and there is always present an element of the grotesque. Yet beauty is there, too: in the flowers and the sycamore leaves, and in the May Song which has preserved the simple joy of men and women, long since dust, who once rejoiced together when the time of the gales and rains was over and gone, and to the earth had come back the lights and colours and scents of early summer.

It was our eighteenth-century savants, with their delight in the classical, who attributed to the festival at Helston a Roman origin and called the dance the Flora. Outside of Helston, it has been known as such ever since, and has been a familiar feature of times of rejoicing in many parts of the county. On the downfall of Napoleon, as on the downfall of Adolf Hitler, the Flora Dance formed part of the celebrations in places widely separated in Cornwall. Ever since I can remember sports, regattas, "tay fights", and the greater occasions like Coronations and the return of peace, have been marked at Padstow by the Flora through the streets, though never in and out of the houses. I could hum the tune of the Flora as soon as that of our own May Song. I think it quite likely that the dance is peculiar neither to Helston nor to Cornwall, but is, or was, well known to our Celtic cousins, the Welsh and the Bretons.

There was probably a time when the steps of the dance as well as the tune were really well known throughout the county. The tune has lingered, but the steps have been forgotten, except at Helston, and except by children taught them in the schools, where also on evenings from October to April between the two wars, grown-ups could learn them at classes held by the Cornwall branch of the English Folk Dance Society. But as a dance of the people the Flora is no more. Readers of Dr. Rowse's *A Cornish Childhood* will remember his description of the scene on Armistice Night, 1918, at St. Austell, where they celebrated with the Flora. "There was something instinctive, pathetic, about it, like a gesture remembered from a former existence, which had no meaning any more. Hardly anybody knew how to dance it by now: we just crowded the narrow, tortuous Fore-street of St. Austell town, treading on each other's heels in a snake-walk, for we had forgotten the steps, though all of us knew the tune." That might have been written of the victory celebrations in several Cornish places in the summer of 1945. Only Helston did it "proper". The first V-Day was also Helston Furry Day. There was never a Furry Day like that one.

Much else of what once "belonged to be" besides the steps of the Flora Dance the Cornish have forgotten or allowed to become only a name in the memory. There is hurling, for example; one of the two great pastimes of our forbears, as of the Celts in general. Parishes all over Cornwall used to meet as rivals in strenuous out-hurling, which took the players over miles of rolling countryside. Hurling lingers now only at St. Columb, where there are two games a year (war or no war) on Shrove Tuesday and the Saturday next but one to it; and at St. Ives on Feast Mondays (except during the Second World War) over the sands of Porthminster. The Puritans are blamed, in part, for the decline of the game; and theirs, it is held, was the "devout and godly error" which led to the Hurlers, the famous stone circles near St. Cleer, having been proclaimed "men sometime transformed into stones, for profaning the Lord's Day with hurling the ball".

The St. Columb hurling gives the curious spectator a real notion of the pace and vigour of the game as it was played in Old Cornwall. In preparation for it the shopkeepers and the more prudent private residents in the main street board up their windows with wood or galvanized iron as against a siege. For the wooden ball, encased in silver, can do much damage after it has been tossed into play, with proper ceremony, in the Square, and the hundreds of players have been incited, according to the inscription on the ball:

> Town and country, do your best,
> For in this parish I must rest.

St. Columb's is a parish, not an inter-parish hurl; the contestants being Townsmen and Countrymen. There was nearly a free fight once in the Square at St. Columb, when a countryman, who had taken the ball successfully to his goal and had come to the town to be "called" the winner at the customary public ceremony, was found not to belong to the parish. The goals are some two miles apart, and the object of the players is to get the silver ball to their own goal. In the old days the hurlers on one side wore different attire from that of their opponents, but nowadays they have to tell by instinct who are friends and who are foes. Everybody turns out in his oldest clothes—a wise precaution at any time but particularly so during the Second World War when clothes were severely rationed.

"The ball in this game," wrote Carew, in his long description of hurling in Elizabethan times, "may be compared to an infernal spirit; for whosoever catcheth it fareth straightways like a madman, struggling and fighting with those about to hold him; and no sooner is the ball gone from him, but he resigneth this fury to the next receiver, and himself becometh peaceable as before." The Squire of Antony professed himself uncertain whether he should "more commend this game for manhood an exercise, or condemn it for boisterousness and harms which it begetteth". In this—dare I say?—more gentle age, I am in no such quandary. Hurling is still boisterous enough; but no more than a Rugby player can take in his stride. Indeed, the game has a faint resemblance to Rugby; and our long tradition in hurling may have helped us to produce in Cornwall a Rugby Fifteen of good county standard and a few international players. (Rugby is, roughly speaking, a West Cornwall game; Soccer is the favourite east of Truro.)

If the hurling at St. Columb is still fast and robust, it is yet a shadow of the game of three centuries ago, when the stars looked down upon players "retyring home as from a pitched battaille, with bloody pates, bones broken and out of joint, and such bruises as serve to shorten their days". The players, no doubt, did their best to bear in mind the ancient motto of the game, "Fair play is good play"; but in inter-parish hurls, in particular, deep-seated rivalries must have found plenty of opportunities for full expression and temporary satisfaction.

On other occasions, too, these rivalries and antagonisms of Cornish parishes have found vent—sometimes in what *The West Briton* in 1816 described as "disgraceful broils, which were formerly so prevalent in Cornwall; but against the recurrence of which it was hoped the improved moral feelings of the lower classes had erected an effectual barrier". With a curious mixture of relish and repugnance, the county newspaper was recording disturbances at what we should now call Lanivet Feast—celebrations of much importance in Cornish parishes still, usually beginning on the day of the saint to whom the church is dedicated, and uniting families severed the rest of the year by sometimes very considerable distances. The disturbers of the peace at Lanivet were visitors from Bodmin, a mile or two to the east, and from Roche and Luxulyan, two granite villages not far away to the south and southwest, Roche being famed for its great rock and ruins of the old chapel of St. Michael on the summit, and Luxulyan for a special kind of granite and its beautiful setting high above the woods of Prideaux.

"On Sunday last," *The West Briton* reported, "the commencement of the annual revel at Lanivet drew to the parish churchtown a number of the inhabitants of Bodmin. As soon as the service of the Church was concluded, the younger part of the congregation adjourned to the adjoining public-house, to qualify themselves for commencing their amusements with proper spirit. Here, it seems, the lads of Roach and Luxillian showed some jealousy of the youths of Bodmin, whom they

Tregudda Gorge, near Padstow

were disposed to regard as intruders. From jeers, the parties proceeded to blows; but after a short skirmish the Bodmin men were overpowered by numbers and forced to make a precipitate retreat.

"The sports of Monday passed without any serious disturbance, but on Tuesday the attraction of the wrestling brought out a number of young persons from Bodmin, one of whom entered the ring and threw two Roach men. This success was immediately followed by an attack on the Bodmin men, and a general battle commenced. After having, for some time, contended in the pugilistic style, the combatants armed themselves with bludgeons from a large wood rick in the Churchtown. Thus equipped, the fight was renewed with fury. Heads were laid open, teeth knocked out, and the field of battle was quickly strewn with the maimed. After the contest had continued about two hours, and when twilight had commenced, victory still hung doubtful; but about this time the Roach and Luxillian men were reinforced by a considerable detachment from the neighbouring mines. The fresh body of forces soon decided the fate of the day. The Bodmin men were forced to fly in disorder, pursued by the shouting victors, being unable to cover the retreat of their wounded, who were forced to limp off as well as they could."

It must not be assumed from this that Cornish wrestling "belonged to be" attended by such ferocious disturbances; though sometimes there were unpleasant scenes, and the Methodists, who had been mainly responsible for "the improved moral feelings of the lower classes" during the eighteenth century and the early nineteenth, did their utmost to expunge both wrestling and hurling matches from the Cornish calendar of sport. Sometimes they tried to do this by direct intervention; more often, I should say, by the general influence of their teaching and example. Of direct intervention two instances were recorded by *The West Briton*—in 1823 and 1844. By the former year, Germoe—a parish famed for its mining and notorious, like Breage, for "wrecking"—was the only parish in the county whose feast celebrations included hurling. This distinction attracted thither "a body of Brianites, a sect lately sprung up from amongst the Wesleyan Methodists", who made their appearance as the hurling was to begin, "and attempted to put a stop to the diversion by commencing their devotional exercises". But they had no success, and hurling at Germoe on Feast Monday lingered on for six or seven decades.

Another mining parish famous for its hurling was St. Just-in-Penwith, that grey, rather bleak town, not far from Land's End, where wrestling also was as popular as anywhere else in Cornwall. For two or

10

The Deserted Mine

three weeks in May, 1844, a wrestling tournament had been in progress to decide who among the "standards" should contest the finals. On the day when these were to be held, for the customary prize of a gold-laced hat—which afforded so much protection from unwelcome attentions in press gang days—the wrestlers had no sooner gathered in the ring than two Wesleyan ministers, with several of their friends, came on the scene. The ministers "immediately addressed the ring-leaders of the games, kindly offering to pay them the value of the prize, to be divided between the standards, and so to stop the practice of wrestling in future; but their proposal being declined, they commenced singing and prayer, and were soon left by the wrestlers in possession of the ring".

This looks like a clear victory for the Methodists, though it is quite possible that the wrestlers, in their coarse canvas jackets, went off to find another ring. Any fairly level piece of meadow would have served, provided there was room for all the spectators. Not that it was likely, at St. Just, and in 1844 when wrestling was approaching a long period of decline and even disrepute, that the crowd was nearly as large as that at Penzance a dozen years or so before, when the sport was at its zenith. On the first day of the Penzance Wrestling there were five thousand spectators; on the second day, twice that number. And this crowd enjoyed a rare diversion.

At a parish church not far from the town there should that morning have been a wedding. Parson, bride, and friends were there for the ceremony; only the bridegroom was missing. Inquiries revealed that this naughty fellow had set off early for the Penzance Games, and before long the angry and mortified bride was also on her way to the town. Peering through the ranks of the crowd at the "wrastling", she espied the truant blissfully absorbed in the play; and, pushing her way through to the ringside, she darted towards him. He turned quickly to escape; but the crowd, instead of making way, closed its ranks, and he had to dash into the ring. Soon the wrestling was suspended while, to the roars of delight of ten thousand voices, the girl chased her errant lover round and round and across the ring, until at last, either from lack of breath or grace restored, he gave in and sheepishly consented to be led away by his fair pursuer.

The inference to be drawn from this is not that Cornishmen are laggards in love, or capricious and undutiful bridegrooms; but rather, that wrestling has been so much in our blood since the olden times that it is apt to be, with some of us, an irresistible attraction. I have heard of a Cornish wrestler who, after long and painful heart searchings, decided to enter the ring no more, because his bride either downrightly dis-liked the sport and its followers, or feared that her husband might be badly injured. A good man had apparently been lost to the game. But there came a time when the scent of crushed grass on a summer day would stir in him poignant memories of the ring—the tense, patient play for a fall; the roars of the crowd as two shoulders and a pin (thigh) or two pins and a shoulder, or both pins and both shoulders, met the turf in a "fair back"; the brief conference of the three "stick-lers" (umpires), who, with the eyes of former leading wrestlers, had been watching every move of every "hitch".

So here and there, at long intervals, this young husband would turn up at the ringside and delight the crowd with his prowess at the "fore-heep" and the "flying mare"; always playing his old, immaculate game; stimulated by an opponent's strength and skill, rejoicing in his own when the opponent was down fair back. For an afternoon in blue trunks and loose, crumpled jacket, he was a man among men. But very late at night, when sleep, he hoped, must surely have come even to a loving wife anxious about his occasional absences upon urgent business, he would steal into his cottage like a naughty child for whom a whipping might be in store.

Every Cornishman who talks or writes of wrestling does so with a wistful glance over his shoulder into what he regards as the Golden Age of the sport. When *was* that Golden Age? Was it in the Celtic Cornwall of Roman or pre-Roman days; or centuries later, during the Hundred Years War, when the Cornish contingent marched into battle under the banner into which was woven the figures of two wrestlers in a hitch; or in the Eighth Henry's time, when Godolphin received the Royal command to send Cornish wrestlers to the great sporting tourney at Calais; or when Charles the Second, knowing that "the Cornish are masters in the art of wrestling", watched our cham-pion, Weynorth, exhibiting his mastery of the hug and heave? Or was the Golden Age that which followed the Napoleonic Wars?—when inter-county wrestling in the Westcountry style produced memorable matches not only in Devon and Cornwall, but in London, on the Wellington Cricket Ground at Chelsea, where it was graced by the presence of "over a hundred Noblemen of the first distinction", or at the Eagle Tavern in City Road, where "the amateurs of Devon and Cornwall were warm in behalf of their respective men"—some of them weighing eighteen stone!—and where, by the time of the last fall, not a little money had changed hands round the ring.

It was easy enough to tell the Devon men from our own. The

Cornishmen were in stocking feet, while the Devonians wore specially hardened shoes, with which at time they "kicked furiously". Theirs indeed was mostly leg and foot play; while ours brought more into use the whole body. This was the period of the great Polkinghorne, who was born in St. Keverne Parish down towards The Lizard and died as mine host of the Red Lion Inn, at St. Columb, where a plaque commemorates him. The Devon champion at this time was Abraham Cann, with whom Polkinghorne had memorable matches. The two were sticklers in 1846—Polkinghorne, in blue swallow-tail coat and yellow breeches, by that time "a martyr to gout" (a malicious St. Columb man described him as "a big bustguts"). The old rivals umpired at the Camden Town contests, from which Gundry, of Helston, then thirty-one, emerged champion of Devon and Cornwall. Great names in Cornish wrestling are those of Polkinghorne and Gundry; but for a quarter of a century before the former took to the ring, our champion was Parkyn, the mighty smith of Lower St. Columb, whose lustre would have made his period, whenever that had been, a Golden Age of wrestling.

In mid and late Victorian times the sport declined so steeply that one who remembered the great days of the early eighteen-hundreds was constrained to ask whether wrestling had not been "civilized off the face of the earth". It had not; but it had become heavy and slow and tedious. From the shadows into which it had thus ponderously receded, it emerged in my boyhood with the gay promise of a May morning. Those were the days of the Chapman brothers, of Rosenannon, in St. Wenn Parish, into which roll the St. Breock Downs that overlook the northern cliffs and the wide expanse of sea beyond. Was it that clear, bright air that gave such vitality to the play of Reub, Sid, Jim, and the youngest brother, Charlie? At sixty I have few enthusiasms —who has?—but as I look back upon the Cornish scene of the decade before the First World War I recapture something of the boyish delight with which I followed the fortunes of the Chapmans in tournaments marked no less by their loyalty to our motto, "Fair play is good play", than by their remarkable skill and prestige.

Into the ring where versatility and resourcefulness had long been strangers, the Chapmans brought these qualities in such measure that, while they wrestled, there was never a dull moment. People who for years had not been to a tournament flocked to watch the brothers, and talked about them for weeks afterwards. Reub, dark and sallow, a wisp of grass in the corner of his mouth, and Sid, taller and heavier, were the more consistently successful. Sid was a Cavalier of the ring, with all the fire and dash of the Cornishmen who fought for King Charles. All four Chapmans knew the game from A to Z, but whereas Reub, the muscles rippling in his broad back, wrestled with changes of style and regard for the finer points of the game that made him a wrestler's wrestler, the play of Charlie and Sid was fast and dazzling as when the blade of an oar, in being feathered, catches the eye of the sun.

But that there were other good men in the ring, wrestling tournaments would have been a series of walk-overs for the Chapmans. It was they who inspired Cornish boys to wrestle as they had never wrestled before. The vigorous hitches in my old school playground, or at St. Saviour's Field, where we pretended to be the Chapmans, produced years later at least two wrestlers of repute. With one, when we were boys, I had a few hitches, and, for the only time in my life, disputed a fair back after I had been thrown. I deserved what came to me in the fisticuffs that followed: one eye closed, the other bleared from a blow, and what seemed an endless succession of punches out of the dark, while I sagged against the moorstone front of the school. I forget which of the Chapmans I had pretended to be. It would have been well for me had I remembered that no Chapman disputed a verdict.

The outbreak of the First World War put an end to that remarkable renaissance of Cornish wrestling, but there was a revival during the years between the two World Wars when I, like so many other ex-soldiers, was too busy with wrestling of another kind, and too far away from Cornwall, to enjoy the revival. It was not until the eve of the Second World War that I went to the "wrastling" again: on this occasion having as fellow spectators a noble duke and hundreds of other less august holiday-makers from all parts of the country. It was the first time I had ever seen women at the wrestling. They, too, were "foreigners". Some inscrutable delicacy still keeps our own women away. They "don't belong" to go.

As I sat there, in the meadow behind the Cornish Arms, just across the road from the old parish church, with its beautiful font of Cataclewse stone, the shadow of impending war was in my heart. Yet, for a few hours in the bright sunshine, with the ground sea thundering half-a-mile or so away over the towans, and the faint smell of salt water mingling with the scent of the trodden grasses, it was almost like having recaptured a bit of one's lost boyhood. And the illusion was the more comforting and complete because among the wrestlers no fewer than four were Chapmans. Not, of course, the Chapmans of my youth. Years before, Reub had at last been thrown, two pins and two shoulders, by the Dark Wrestler whose victory puts an end to all joys and prowess of the flesh. Charlie was in America—like so many other Cornishmen. Sid was still living at St. Wenn, where these four boys, like their fathers before them, had been wrestling in spare moments almost from the time they could stand upright. So there, at St. Merryn Churchtown, strong, supple, and shapely, were the new generation of Chapmans: Bernard, Reub's son, the middle-weight champion of Cornwall; William and Charlie, Sid's boys, the former at the age of sixteen, the all-weights champion; and John, who succeeded his cousin Bernard to the middle-weight belt.

It is no disparagement of the other young wrestlers to say that the Chapmans, as of old, dominated the play. The thing spoke for itself: no Chapman was thrown save by another Chapman. It would have been worth walking a dozen miles to have seen the prolonged struggle between Bernard and William, which excited the admiration of the "foreigners" no less than the Cornishmen. There could have been nothing like it since the boys' fathers "wrastled it out" in their best days. It was not simply an exhibition of virtuosity; though even as that it would have been satisfying. It was clean, spirited, unsparing play for a fair back, in the course of which both youngsters drew upon the wide range of their ringcraft. In the end Bernard "gave his back" to his cousin. Such play as we then saw ought, one felt, to have summoned from the shades Parkyn and Polkinghorne and all their fellow-champions through the centuries to pat the backs of the youngsters and to seal their approval with a "Good boys both!"

Like so much else of what "do belong to be" in peacetime, Cornish wrestling during the six years that followed was a sport of the memory only. In its long history the twenty years between the World Wars had been as a day, and for me that day had been crowned with a sunset as glorious as the one I saw above and beyond the western cliffs as I sped home-along from St. Merryn. Once more war scattered the wrestlers over the world on active service, or bound them by new and closer ties to the Cornish earth. What would the new day bring? Its promise was but fair, and there has been no heart-warming revival, but I still hope that for generations to come—no matter what fast, new-fangled counter-attractions may be provided—this ancient Cornish sport will survive, and even flourish again. Reasonably flexible and not unreceptive, I am yet unashamedly traditionalist; and I would rather see the lads wrestling on the village green or in the croft than racing off to the towns on motor-cycles to join the crowds of sightseers at some "up-to-the-minute sport of a thousand thrills", and particularly the alien and loathsome all-in wrestling.

But I know that neither evocation nor exhortation will restore wrestling to its old place in the Cornish calendar. It will survive, if at all, on its merits, and on the appeal, to the people themselves, of a people's sport which has outlived many wars and innumerable changes. As to its merits, nobody will persuade me that a pastime which can produce such wrestlers as took the ring again the year the1939-45 War ended deserves to perish from our midst. It is indigenous, clean, skilful, and, in the best sense of the word—though not in the very letter—amateur. Its merits the wrestlers themselves will have to expound in their play; but they should be fostered and encouraged by all who cherish, in sport as in other things, the Cornish tradition and the Cornish spirit.

Of these we heard much in the years that followed the First World War. There was then a memorable re-creation of interest in and devotion to the things that remain of our Cornish past. Old Cornwall Societies, their members pledged to gather up these fragments from the days of our forebears, came into existence in all parts of the county. And in 1928, in the stone circle of Boscawen Un, four miles from Penzance, there was a revival of the Gorsedd of the Cornish Bards, a ceremony in which the Archdruid, ex-Archdruid, and several other office-bearers and members of the Welsh Gorsedd took part. Except during the Second World War an open Gorsedd has since been held every year in various parts of Cornwall chiefly at spots where, in long bygone days, our ancestors gathered for some such ceremonies.

Only by pretending that the lapse of a thousand years or two is of no great consequence may the Gorsedd be included among the things that "do belong to be". It has neither the unbroken tradition nor the popular support of kindred ceremonies in Wales and Brittany, and there was still something artificial and novel about an open Gorsedd when the war caused its suspension. Several of the initial Bards have died, including that massive old Celtic scholar, Henry Jenner, who was, I believe, the real inspiration of the revival. Other Bards have been initiated, some as a result of examination, and good work has been done among children in encouraging them to read and write about Cornwall and its history. With the remarkable exception of Dr. Rowse, who has done more as poet, scholar, and essayist to celebrate Cornwall and its past than any other living Cornishman, the Bardic circle has included all who have, in one way and another, devoted their gifts and energies to maintaining clear and bright the Cornish tradition. But whether the Gorsedd will last long to continue this function, with robes and trumpet, harp and sword, and the semblance of tribal ritual, is a question I should not care to answer. Nor do I think it matters much. The important thing is that the Federation of Old Cornwall Societies, which one may fairly describe as the Gorsedd without robes or ritual, should continue its work, preferably in ever closer relations with the three learned societies of Cornwall.

The late Grand Bard of the Cornish Gorsedd, Mr. Morton Nance, was our leading authority on the Cornish language. I have already referred to his invaluable dictionaries which I hope will continue to be reprinted so as to serve young people who may like to talk and write the language of their forbears. But I am convinced that Cornish will never again be spoken or written outside of a small group of devout lovers of Cornwall, and I am equally convinced that it is a profound mistake and a disservice to Cornwall to make a knowledge of the language a test of such devotion. I am much more concerned about the decay of the dialect, which has been going on since the eighteen-seventies and more particularly during the past quarter of a century. Nobody, from my speech, would put me down as Cornish; and an expert in such matters once concluded, after a talk we had had, that I was either (I forget which) an Edinburgh man who had lived in London, or a Londoner who had lived in Edinburgh.

When I am with old friends of the quayside and the coves, I find myself, after a while, talking away in the dialect as in the old days. But even then there were influences at work to make me "talk proper". The headmaster of my elementary school, a well-educated "foreigner" was one. Two others were maiden ladies, also "foreigners", with one of whom I began at eight or nine to learn French, and with the other, who founded a lending library in a room which was also her private chapel, to read Henty and Ballantyne, Dickens and Scott. Then I won third place in the county in the first of the minor scholarship examinations for places in secondary schools, and the process of making me "talk proper" was accelerated. If we had beeen able to afford it, I should have gone on at seventeen or eighteen to a teachers' training college; but at sixteen I crossed the Tamar and went on to Hampshire in search of a living. Until the First World War came to rescue my pupils from the inexpert cultivation of their minds by a very junior master, I was talking more and more like a little gentleman of England. It was akin to protective coloration in Nature. One mustn't appear odd, or by one's pronunciation and phraseology, draw attention to one's self. I had to get a living out of this world to which I did not, in essence, "belong", and to get along comfortably with the big family of conformities of which economic necessity is the mother, or foster-mother. I was agreeably surprised sometimes to find what healthy and comely children some of them were. But a lapse into dialect in their presence would (or so I thought) have upset the family party. How young and foolish I was!

For the purposes of dialect the whole of Cornwall has been divided into two parts: East and West. It is a familiar and convenient division; but I am sure the parts should be at least three—based roughly upon the three great granite masses round which our people have lived and toiled. Instead of dividing the county by a line drawn from Perran Bay through Truro to the Roseland coast, I would have another drawn to follow the ancient track from Padstow through Lanivet to Fowey, and the portion west of this to the Perran–Roseland line I would call Mid Cornwall. I do not profess to have such a sensitive ear as Tregellas, whose sketches and stories in the dialect used to delight a former generation of Cornish people. He could distinguish a St. Agnes from a Perranzabuloe man—who lived in adjoining parishes—by the single note higher of the Perran man's speech. But, sitting in a restaurant in Truro, or listening to the talk in the streets on a market day, I think I can tell fairly quickly and accurately who comes from West, and from Mid and East Cornwall.

The mark of the West Cornwall man is his expressive sing-song, which is probably how our Celtic ancestors talked, or chanted. Most of all, I think, I like about the West Cornwall people their charming, "Please?" rising to a sweet crescendo, when they have not heard a remark addressed to them—so much more expressive than the conventional "Pardon". Our old saying, "East of Truro, out of Cornwall", although far from true, does emphasize an essential truth; namely, that the area west of the city is where the most distinctive characteristics of Cornish life have lingered on. Successive waves of English influence, rolling over East Cornwall, lost much of their power as they went westwards, and it was long before their spent wash made any perceptible difference to the life of the West Penwith peninsula. When, as a small boy playing on the quayside at Padstow, I first heard the crabbers and fishermen of Sennen and Porthleven talking among themselves, I could follow them only with difficulty. It used to be great fun, out of earshot, to mimic them mockingly. It wasn't the phraseology so much that amused and excited us, as the intonation, the sing-song— which differed even in men who came from these two West Cornwall fishing-places.

As you go eastwards from the Land's End peninsula, the sing-song becomes gradually less noticeable, and beyond Truro it is absent. Not until you reach the other side of Lostwithiel do you hear the East Cornwall dialect, faintly at first and then taking on, more and more, the qualities of the speech of South-West Devon. Its most marked characteristic, I suppose, is the u sound for oo, so that noon becomes nune; and there is the tendency to substitute her for she, and us for we; so that "She said to him" becomes " 'Er zayed t' une", and "We are coming soon", "Us be cummin zune". (The use of z for s begins in Mid Cornwall and becomes more marked as you go east.) But I must echo what has been said many times by others since 1870: popular education and the revolution in transport are leading to a period when a dialect that was as rich and racy as the English of Chaucer's and Spenser's time will be heard no more in this far south-western land. I comfort myself with the knowledge that in the coves and the heart of the countryside it is still putting up a brave fight for survival.

Not much of the old Cornish language, it seems, passed into the dialect; but many Cornish words, some of them most pleasing to the ear, will continue in use as long as our hills and other natural features endure. "Mountains and rivers still murmur the voice of nations long denationalized or extirpated"—and not mountains and rivers alone. Scores of Cornish people, who speak English without a trace of their Cornish origin, will yet carry to their headstones, and pass on to their children, names as Cornish as the earth that Matthew Arnold's grandmother, when she set off for England, left her coach to kiss "in tender farewell to the land she loved".

Some words and phrases which were familiar to Mary Penrose in her Cornish parish a century and a half ago are with us still; though not in such common use as they were even in my youth. It is years, for example, since I last heard the half-pleased, half-regretful exclamation, after a hearty meal, "My dear sawl, I'm blawed up like a wilky!" ("Wilky" is from the Cornish *quilkin*, a frog; and we have preserved the word uncorrupted in our saying, "You'm so cold as a quilkin".) Nobody says now, as my grandmother used to say, that So-and-So has broken his arm-wrist, or injured the spine of his back. Grandmother never had a wash. She always "washed her skin". But away from the towns, and even there among some of the older generation, one is sure to hear, now and again, some of the familiar expressions used in Grandmother's kitchen, or the bakehouse across the way:

You must scat'n abroad.—You must break it open.
I dun't feel very clever.—I'm not feeling well.
She scritched like a whitneck.—She screamed like a weasel.

He's a proper gate bufflehead.—He's a real duffer.

Do 'ee give'n a dinky bit, co!—Do give him a tiny piece there's a dear.

You shudden mind 'e, my dear; the poor shamick edden 'zackly.— Don't take any notice of him; the poor creature has a weak intellect.

Dun't 'ee be so clubbish; or I'll scat 'ee across the chacks.—Don't be so rough, or brutal; or I'll smack your face.

I'm scat.—I haven't any money.

I'm some leary, you!—I'm very hungry, or empty. The "you" is for emphasis, like the "some".

It doan't zeem fitty to me.—It doesn't seem right, or proper, to me.

Better fit 'e'd 'old 'is gab.—He ought to keep quiet.

You must chow it, and not clunk it.—You must chew it, not simply swallow it. (There is a story of a High Sheriff at Cornwall Assizes offering the Judge, who was suffering from a bad cold, a cough drop, with the advice, "You mus'n chow en, me lord; you must l'ave en conjale." By congeal he meant, I suppose, dissolve.)

You've got the lurgies.—You are lazy.

He d' do everything clicky.—He does everything left-handed. (Cornish, *cledhec*.)

He's a handsome praicher!—Handsome doesn't mean good-looking. It means very good. So a book, or a play, or a pasty, may be handsome.

I shudden be frightened to hear he's married.—Frightened often means, with us, no more than surprised.

Tez a wisht ole job o' it.— It's a great pity. (Wisht is a most expressive word. To look wisht is to look ill or very down in the mouth.)

Sometimes at bedtime even now I hear across the years my father or mother saying to me, as I sat in the lamplight trying sleepily to spell out some passage in a book, "Come on, now, boy; 'tis time to go auver Timberen Hill!" I have always thought that a lovely way of talking about climbing the stairs. One of Mother's sayings still puzzles me. When I was crouched over the fire, on one of our few really cold days, she would exclaim, "Why dun't ye sit up, boy? You'm rumped up like a winnard." We call the redwing a winnard—there is an exposed crossroads called Winnard's Perch near St. Columb—and I suppose Mother's expression, which was widely used in the county, came from the fact that the redwing, being so largely an insect eater, fares badly in a spell of cold weather, and is "rumped up" from cold and hunger. We have our names for other birds than the redwing, among them the missel thrush (holmscritch—holm is holly), blue-tit (hekkymowl), pied wagtail (dishwasher), song thrush (greybird), and redstart (firetail, but I believe this name is found in other counties). We use our own names, too, for trees, flowers, insects, and fish. Hawthorn berries we call aglets, and the young hawthorn leaves, bread-and-cheese; broom is bannel; narcissus, butter-and-eggs; daffodil, Lent lily; bluebell, gookoo (cuckoo) flower; columbine, boots-and-shoes; southernwood, boy's love (Grandmother used to say, "Boy's love, girl's ruin"—or was it rueing?) wood sorrel is hare's meat, and the wild arum adder's meat. The bat is our airy-mouse; the earthworm angle-twitch, and the cockchafer dumbledory. None of our dialect experts seems to have listed the word emmett for ant, though it is common both in Mid and West Cornwall. What we call the bishop is the little *cottus scorpius*, and when I was a boy, setting off for St. George's Well or Chidley Pumps to paddle, or to fish with a piece of thread and a bent pin, Mother used to warn me to be careful or I might be "stung by a bishop!"

In my part of Cornwall we have no special name for the snail, but down West the older people call it the bull-horn. If the miners came upon a snail in their path as they were going to the mine, they carefully put down beside it a few crumbs from their "crowst" bag, or a spot of grease from their candles; thus ensuring for themselves good luck for the day. In West Cornwall, too, they call the blue scabious the devil's bit or button. Nobody picked it in the old days, for fear the Devil should appear at their bedsides that night. This is what my mother would have called "an old 'umman's widdle" (an old woman's nonsense), to be classed with the belief that if any member of the crow family sat cawing on or near the house, it meant a death in the family. Some such melancholy event is foreshadowed by a single magpie:

> One for sorrow, two for mirth,
> Three for a wedding, four for a birth.

From politeness (if you will) I raise my hat to a solitary magpie, and if a lady is with me I like her to curtsey. Many Cornish people still become agitated if a bird, particularly a robin, should hop or fly into the house; for this also is supposed to portend a death in the family. Perhaps it was this superstition that accounted for the country people's dislike—not yet vanished—of opening their windows wide even on a summer day.

If he saw a water wagtail, which he called a "tinner", perched on his window sill, a Cornish miner would expect a stranger to call on him. It would be rash to declare that the men in the two mines still at work do not share the "ole men's" superstitions. None of them, it may be, would care to encounter a white rabbit near the workings, since that foretells an accident. The miners may sing, and swear a bit, as their forbears did; but I doubt whether even now they whistle underground. For whistling is intensely disliked by the "knackers", or "knockers"—the Little People who were as real and sometimes as near to the miners of the old days as their own comrades. These tiny creatures, with the big heads and dried faces of old men and the bodies of year-old children, were often heard tap-tapping in the galleries underground. The wise miner always worked in the direction of that sound, for there the mineral vein was sure to be rich. The Little People were hungry sometimes; and woe betide the miner who did not leave for them a few crumbs from his "crowst", as he had done for the snail on the way to work. The knockers were believed to be Jews, accursed for their part in the Crucifixion; and no Cornishman would make on the side of the mine a mark that had any resemblance to a cross. Properly treated, the Little People were friendly and helpful.

What has become of them now that so few are left of our former three hundred mines? Are they still, where they "do belong to be", somewhere behind the slate and granite faces of the flooded shafts and galleries? I do not know; but I think not. Perhaps if you sit in the sunshine near one of the old shafts you will see ants scurrying about in a hollow; and these "murrians", it may be, are the knockers from the deserted mine—for that is the last state of the Little People. When I have been enjoying a meal among the heath and ling, I like to leave the ants a few tiny crumbs.

I was grown up before I ever heard of the knockers, or of the Jack o' Lanterns who signalled above ground at night to miners whom they liked, indicating the spot from which to drive down to strike a rich lode of tin. But the name of the Piskies has been familiar since childhood. If, of an evening, I had been absent a long time on an errand that should have taken me only a few minutes, Mother would ask, "Wherever have ye been, boy? Anybody'd think ye'd been pisky-led." It was probably true that I had been upon my errand by devious ways, but led astray by a boy's will and not by piskies. These Little People were a mischievous lot, sitting some of their time upon mushrooms (pisky-stools), thinking out pranks to play upon human creatures. Their favourite mischief was to lead the lonely traveller at night miles from his appointed path, and the only way to make sure that you were not pisky-led was to wear one of your garments—a stocking or a sock being the most convenient—inside out. The piskies were up to all sorts of tricks; but they were not deeply malicious like the spriggans, the Little People dwelling near the ancient barrows, stone-circles, and rock-strewn carns. If infants in nearby cottages were left unguarded, the spriggans were given to taking them away and substituting for them their own brats. They were a mirthless, hateful branch of the family of Little People; whereas with the piskies there was always plenty of amusement and merriment, and to this day I hear it said often of a perosn who has very obviously enjoyed a joke, that he "laughed like a pisky". And we still have our own version of the well-known nursery rhyme:—

> See-saw, Margery Daw,
> Sold her bed and lay upon straw,
> Sold her bed and lay upon hay,
> Pisky came and took her away.

If I am asked whether piskies may still be found in Cornwall, I am bound to say that I have never seen one, and that none, to my knowledge, has ever led me astray over the moors and hills. But I shall not say flatly that they are no longer here. Many a time along the cliff-tops, not far from an old stone hedge with its thick, cool tamarisk and clustered sea-pinks, I have come upon a ring marked by a green darker than that of the dwarf grass surrounding and enclosed by it. There one night when the moon is high and the roar of the sea enables me to approach unheard, I may yet through the screen of tamarisk see the laughing piskies, "as they do belong", dancing round the ring to their hearts' delight—and mine.

VIII

THE PEOPLE NEXT DOOR.

IT IS CURIOUS that Robert Louis Stevenson, who took so much trouble with genealogy in the hope of establishing himself among the Celts, should have been so baffled and exasperated by the Cornish miners whom he met when he made the arduous journey by emigrant ship and train to California, whither Mrs. Osbourne had preceded him. When he wrote of the miners in *Fellow Passengers* it was with some antipathy. They were men who "kept grimly to themselves, one reading the New Testament all day long through steel spectacles, the rest discussing privately the secrets of their old-world mysterious race".

There is, no doubt, something disconcerting about this way we have of "keeping ourselves to ourselves". It is less noticeable at home than abroad, and far less noticeable anywhere since Stevenson's time. But we are still clannish. Scattered all over the world are scores of Cornish Associations, formed many years ago when groups of Cornish emigrants —of whom, between 1850 and 1900, when mining declined, there were nearly a quarter of a million—first resolved to meet together to exchange news and memories of their distant Duchy, and to sing the songs of Zion in a strange land.

Individualists though they are, the Cornish are drawn together in exile as instinctively as the swallows when the time for migration has come. In the centre of Johannesburg, on ground which came to be known as "Cousin Jack's Corner", the Cornish miners used to gather on Saturday nights just as they had crowded the hilly front street of Redruth and The Grizzle at Camborne, or as they had talked in groups outside the cottages of a gusty little churchtown. Though some of them did not return from the new lands into which they had ventured, they were never completely absorbed or assimilated there.

For the group of miners whom Stevenson encountered, the process of partial absorption or assimilation had not even begun. It was perfectly natural, in this period of transition in particular, that they should keep together; for they had much in common, and not least the calling which they and their ancestors had followed for centuries. A pity that R.L.S. could not have overheard the talk among those uprooted men instead of having had to make a guess about its nature. More than likely it consisted not at all of "the secrets of their old-world mysterious race"—unless these be construed as the technicalities and adventures of tin and copper mining—but of simple and wistful evocations of the Cornish scene, which had become for them a precious memory since they had seen through the darkness far astern the last faint gleam of The Lizard Light.

The fact remains that Stevenson was not favourably impressed. "Lady Hester Stanhope", he wrote, "believed that she could make something great of the Cornish; for my part, I can make nothing of them at all. A division of races, older and more original than that of Babel, keeps this close, esoteric family apart from neighbouring Englishmen. Not even a Red Indian seems more foreign in my eyes. This is one of the lessons of travel—that some of the strangest races dwell next door to you at home."

So far as I know, Stevenson was the only man of his times, or any other, to have left on record a flat confession of failure to make anything at all of the Cornish; and I cannot help thinking that the Cornish may have been less responsible for Stevenson's failure than he was himself, with his preconceived notion of race division—real enough in its way, it is true, but easily bridged by a person with that imaginative sympathy which is among the predominant characteristics of the Celtic peoples and which, in much of his life and writing, Stevenson displayed.

A very different impression might have been left upon him if his contacts with Cornish miners had been in circumstances which brought out their qualities; if, for example, he had sailed fifty years earlier from Falmouth in the brig *Cambria* and had had as fellow passengers Cornish miners bound for the Mexican mines. On a boisterous March afternoon in 1825, the *Cambria* was rolling and pitching across the Bay of Biscay when one of her crew sighted a larger vessel from which was being blown over the waters a cloud of smoke lit here and there by jets of flame. The ship in trouble was the Indiaman *Kent*, of 1,400 tons, which had on board many soldiers of the 31st Regiment, with their wives and children, and some one hundred and forty tons of ammunition.

Just before midday the mate had gone below to ascertain whether the heavy seas had displaced any of the *Kent*'s stores. During his inspection the ship had given "a terrible lurch", and a cask of spirits had been stove in. The mate's lantern had been jerked from his grasp and the flame had set the spirits alight. The fire spread quickly, and soon passengers and crew were fearful lest at any moment the ammunition should explode. Already "the lower guns were firing with the heat". In the early afternoon the *Cambria* was sighted, and

A China Clay Pit

before long she had got as close to the doomed ship as her master deemed prudent. Soon the *Kent*'s boats, six of them, filled with women and children, were lowered. The crew of the first boat to reach the *Cambria* refused to return to the burning ship, the coxswain protesting that his craft could not live in such seas.

Among the Cornish miners who had been assisting the women and children into the *Cambria* was one more agile and powerfully built than his comrades. This was James Warren, a famous Cornish wrestler, whose home was at St. Just-in-Penwith. Pushing his way towards the boat's coxswain, Warren seized him "in a lion's grasp" and gave him the choice of going back to the *Kent* for more passengers or being thrown into the sea. The boat was soon making her return. It was dangerous work, and of the six boats only three survived, one of these kept afloat by soldiers' jackets stuffed in a hole in her side. But before the *Kent* was lost more than five hundred people had been brought to safety. "Of the many drowned only one was a sailor, and he had plundered three or four hundred sovereigns, tied up in a handkerchief round his waist. As he attempted a leap into the boat he fell over and sank."

Meantime, the Cornish miners, men quite unaccustomed to the sea and with a deep dislike of it and its ways, had engaged in the rescue work with exemplary courage and devotion. Warren, in particular, had distinguished himself. He was not the man to "force others into dangers he would not face himself, for he placed himself in the main chains, at the imminent peril of his life, and by the muscular strength of his arms, when tackle could not be used, lifted into safety in the *Cambria* the women and children, who were half dead with fear and incapable of any exertion". To commemorate his work that afternoon a medal was later struck for Warren who, however, now nearly forty and with a wife and ten children dependent upon him, must have found even more welcome the gift of £150 from a major of the 31st, whose wife was among those the wrestler had hoisted to safety. From this lady Warren received a small pension until his death in 1842, for in his rescue exertions he strained himself so severely that he never quite recovered from the effects.

Before setting sail in the *Cambria* the miners had had to save hard and long to purchase (as was required of emigrants) stores and provisions for the journey. All these, with "their cabins and every comfort", they handed over to the survivors of the *Kent*, and thus exemplified the Cornish motto, "One and All!" It is not to be doubted for a moment that if the passengers in the *Cambria* had been Englishmen, or

11

Zennor Church Town

Scots, or Welsh, they would have behaved in the same way as the Cornishmen; and all that this incident suggests to me—though naturally I am proud of the miners concerned—is that the Cornish are no whit less comprehensible than anybody else in these islands when their qualities are put to the test rather than obscured by a theory about race divisions.

The stranger in distress, for example, will find that the Cornish are as swift as any others to succour and comfort. This was illustrated on the return of the *Cambria* to Falmouth. Conrad's dictum of the port, that it has thriven on the casualties of the sea, is true. But if Falmouth has profited by the damaged ships which have crept in across the bay, it has treated with conspicuous tenderness and generosity the human casualties. On that early morning when the *Cambria* reached the port with "the half-naked and suffering beings from the *Kent*", almost at once "every hand was offering apparel, and every house was open, from the mansion to the cottage, affording rest, refreshment, and consolation. It having been impossible to save any stores, not even clothing, from the wreck, a more than ample subscription soon poured in to replenish those who stood in need".

The commanding officer of the 31st Regiment later addressed a long and glowing letter to the people of Falmouth and neighbouring places. "You have created between us and our beloved country", he wrote, "an additional bond of affection and gratitude that will animate our future zeal, and enable us, amid all the vicissitudes of our professional life, to point gratefully our companions in arms to Falmouth, as one of the bright spots in our happy land where the friendless shall find many friends and the afflicted receive abundant consolation."

But while the Cornish open wide their hearts to the stranger in distress, they are more reserved and cautious with the stranger who comes in normal circumstances to dwell among them. Courtesy from the outset he will find, and kindness, too. But he must win his way to their hearts; and once there he will find that he can do no wrong. "It do take years with we to treat a stranger like one of our own," declares Mrs. Pengilly in Mrs. Havelock Ellis's *My Cornish Neighbours*: and there, I think, speaks still the authentic voice of the Cornish people in the smaller communities. But much depends upon the stranger; I have known him to become a member of the family, or next to it in intimacy in quite a short time. And in Mrs. Pengilly's further confidence to Mrs. Havelock Ellis, "We've been reared to look upon all up-alongs (strangers) as natural foes", there is a spirit alien to anything I have known in Cornwall in my sixty years.

No such hostility was engendered in me by my parents or grandparents, whom I regard as typical Cornish people, and members of a community which was as self-contained as a small Cornish port can be. What is true, I think, is that some "foreigners", egregiously obtuse and impulsive, provoke hostility in a Cornish community here and there by trying, in the name of progress, or some such thing, to turn the place upside down "in forty minutes". Not so is the way of life to be drastically changed in Cornwall, where the people, as our old saying goes, "will be slocked (persuaded) but won't be drove". Happy is the stranger who remembers this saying, and who links with it the more widely known *Festina lente*.

To the courtesy of the people of this peninsula there is testimony from as long ago as 8 B.C., or thereabouts, when, "They that inhabit the British Promontory of Bolerium," wrote Diodorus, the Sicilian, "by reason of their Converse with Merchants, are more civilized and courteous to strangers than the rest. These are the People that make the Tin." On a dark February night eighteen centuries after that was written, a stranger knocked at the door of a poor miner's cottage in the then dreary and mine-pocked parish of Gwennap. He had lost his way, and desired to be directed to Truro. The miner might easily have given a few verbal directions and returned to the comfort of his fire of furze and dried turf. Instead, he accompanied the stranger for some distance on his way. Once the traveller was set right, the miner turned homewards through the darkness—himself to suffer the fate, which, he may have feared, would befall the stranger. Stumbling into one of the many mine-shafts, the miner was killed, "leaving a wife and eight children to lament his loss".

Queen Elizabeth used to say of her Cornish gentlemen that they were "all born courtiers, with a becoming confidence". Carew, superbly placed by class and gifts to appraise their qualities, noted first among these "their kind entertainment to strangers", going on, in a characteristically delightful passage, to describe their rounds of visits among themselves. "A gentleman and his wife will ride to make merry with his next neighbour, and after a day or twain, these two couple go to a third, on which progress they increase like snowballs, till through their burdensome weight they break again." They were then bound by a stronger tie than neighbourliness. "All Cornish gentlemen are cousins," wrote the felicitous one in his study at Antony; and only hinted at the feuds and squabbles which none the less persisted, aggravated at times by differences on national questions. But Carew admitted of the gentry, as Norden had declared of "the baser sort", that they were a litigious lot; and so we have been down to modern times. Neighbours' quarrels still lend a piquancy to proceedings in our magistrates' courts; but for all I know there may be quite as many of these summonses and cross-summonses in any other county. Not in Cornwall alone, I fancy, is propinquity the mother of dissension.

In the Caroline Age the Gloucester man, John Taylor, who liked to be called the Water-Poet, and who was proud of having travelled from London to Land's End, described the Cornish as "affable, courteous people . . . loving to requite a kindness, placable to remit a wrong, and hardy to retort injuries". From a man whose progress through the county—warmed and cushioned though it had been by seven days in the home of the Godolphins under the slope of that western hill—had not lacked unpleasant and occasionally ugly moments, Taylor's is a handsome testimony. Excessively handsome, perhaps. For the Cornish are not, I think, notably "placable to remit a wrong", though we are so individualistic, and wrongs are of so many kinds and degrees, that to generalize too much is dangerous. But I believe we are more sensitive, and therefore more deeply hurt by slights and injuries, than English people generally, and we are given to brooding over wrongs until they assume unwarranted, sometimes even fantastic, proportions. A slight or an injury swiftly acknowledged and regretted by the offender we are no less swift to forgive and forget; but the wrong followed by no sign of contrition we nurse passionately, and "I'll pay'n out for this" is a resolve which sometimes waits so long upon opportunity that the offender may have forgotten for what he has been "paid out".

This disposition of ours—not indeed "greatly to find quarrel in a straw", but to store up resentment by brooding over wrongs, real or imagined, is not nowadays so pronounced as in former times, when our outside contacts were fewer and the range of our interests was altogether narrower. Earlier I have referred briefly to the hanging of a St. Merryn girl of twenty years—poor, crazy, vindictive Elizabeth— who had set fire to the wheat mow of her former employer "over to Trevisca". I think she was, as we say politely, "not exactly"; but several witnesses at her trial declined to admit that she was mentally deranged, and she was not treated as such by the judge. If she was "all there", the crime for which she paid with her life looks like the outcome of brooding upon a wrong which she probably magnified immeasurably.

Elizabeth had for seven or eight years lived with the farmer as a parish apprentice. Three years before the May night when she set fire to his wheat with steel and brimstone borrowed from her lodging, she had been discharged for some sort of misconduct. Clearly, she deeply resented her dismissal, and the farmer several times "heard her use expressions by which he thought she bore malice to him". She had threatened, for example, to burn his house. Having decided upon his wheat mow instead, she had not long set fire to it before she was knocking up the innkeeper at Churchtown to tell him what she had done. He did not believe her, but said angrily that he would "horse-whip her for going about the country at that hour at night". A little later, in a lane, Elizabeth caught up with a labourer who was about to climb the stile leading to his cottage. Had he not seen a light? she asked, and on his replying that he had not, she told him, too, that she had set fire to farmer's wheat mow. "With all appearance of exultation", the Judge commented at her trial, she "had needlessly informed several persons of the act". If this was not the exultation of a mad girl, what else can it have been but the fleeting triumph of one who, having for so long brooded over the farmer's treatment of her, and perhaps awaited a chance which seemed never to present itself, had at last "paid'n out" with steel and brimstone?

Rarely does nursing an injury have consequences so serious, but the results are occasionally distasteful and embarrassing. In his auto-biography *My Life of Music*, the late Sir Henry Wood recorded a "beastly prank" by a gifted Cornish musician whose pupil he was for violin and organ. After some years as organist of Westminster Chapel, Buckingham Gate, the Cornishman was dismissed. Sir Henry knew nothing of this when, one Sunday morning, the other called for him and the two drove to the chapel. "We went to the upper gallery from which we watched the new organist about to begin a quiet voluntary. He drew the correct stops, but instead of a quiet diapason tone, the heaviest reeds (both eight and sixteen feet) blazed out, complete with the three and five rank mixtures." The Cornishman was convulsed with merriment at his successor's humiliation, and in delight told Sir Henry that the previous night he had changed the loud and soft draw-knobs. Sir Henry was disgusted at the trick, and left his companion there and then, never to see him again.

Since first I came upon it in an issue of *The West Briton* of a century or so ago, I have wondered what story lay behind this brief paragraph: "A man residing not a hundred miles from Chacewater, being asked, at the time his sister lay dead, whether he was going to the funeral, answered very coolly, 'I don't think I shall, because I've got some oats that ought to be saved immediately'." Nobody who knows the Cornish and the trouble and inconvenience to which they will put themselves in order to attend the funeral of even a distant relative, can fail to detect in that cool, brisk response an implacable hostility—the outcome no doubt of brooding over a slight or injury received years before in some family upheaval.

There was a Cornish husband, also a farmer, in another part of the county, who, about the same time, felt slighted because his wife "allowed of a salute from a relative who was taking leave on going abroad". That farewell kiss led to husband and wife parting, and to the most eccentric conduct by the man, including a quarrel with a clergyman which led him to resolve not be be buried in his parish churchyard. Forthwith he enclosed a small space near some castle ruins on a hill overlooking both the Channels. On the enclosing wall he had two tablets fixed, one engraved, "Custom is the idol of fools"; the other, "Virtue only consecrates the ground". There he was interred, and over five thousand people were present at the ceremony.

It may be objected that I have chosen some remarkable cases to illustrate a characteristic of the Cornish which rarely nowadays provides an incident or a saying worth recording. And I hope I have not given the impression that Cornish life is in constant tension because of our disposition to smart and quiver at the smallest slight and to brood interminably over a wrong. For that is a false picture. While we are peculiarly sensitive, we are not less so in our giving than in our receiving, so that a Cornishman is most unlikely to wound blunderingly and unintentionally as, in my experience, do so many less imaginatively sympathetic people. To put it bluntly, we are thin-skinned and we know it; and this knowledge smooths and softens our relations wonderfully. No doubt our intercourse loses in spontaneity and directness; but it is enriched (or so I think) by sympathy and subtlety.

Are we prone to over-subtlety? Charles Lee, among "foreigners" by far and away the best writer of Cornish stories and sketches—*The Widow Woman* and *Our Little Town* I regard as Cornish classics—thought we were. It all depends upon one's own temperament: I find our subtlety stimulating and often amusing, but then I am Cornish. And Lee himself would never have accomplished a delicate task with such signal success unless he had found real enjoyment in accepting and portraying us as we are; "loving . . . the circuitous, shunning ever the direct statement, dealing much in qualifications and cautious ambiguities". He did not see at the root of this—one of several fibres—something Celtic rather than peculiarly Cornish: rebelliousness against fact, and a certain wariness and delicacy in handling a thing so crude and often so painful.

We know that, in the end, we have to get a grip with it; but instead of the direct approach we weave ourselves in, as do our wrestlers with opponents whom they deem formidable. That is why, as Lee remarked, we hedge about—with "it do seem to me", "a-believe", "a-spoas", "they do say" and suchlike—"the simplest, most indubitable statement of fact". But these phrases and others so familiar to former generations are now less commonly used; and this trait, as Lee perceived, is often a mechanical habit only.

Intercourse, though it may be impoverished, is greatly simplified by directness, and many strangers to Cornwall must have wished fervently that we were given to the more ready use of a plain yea or nay. Some allowance should be made because our Cornish-speaking forbears through long centuries had no choice but to manage without the direct affirmative and negative; and it has been suggested to me that the first English-speaking Cornish people used the alien Yes and No merely as intimations that they had heard or not heard. Not so summarily were they to be committed to agreement with what they had heard. Even today the note of finality is often absent from our soft, meditative, almost reluctant "Ais" or "No"; and there are still numbers of Cornish people who aschew "Ais", and whose assent must be deduced from a sharp indrawing of the breath like that occasioned by a sudden stab of pain.

From this the philologist may, or may not, be able to draw some interesting conclusions. The layman, I hope, will not have been led by it into regarding us, in the general business of life, as woolly-headed and vacillating. The Cornish, in fact, are shrewd and decisive enough in all dealings in which the purely human element is not predominant. It is when their feelings, and the feelings of others, are concerned that they shy at sudden decisions and carefully wrap up in verbal cotton-wool hard facts which may seem to them hurtful. Then, above all, they tend to be oblique and ambiguous; motivated in this realm of feelings by a delicacy which baffles and dismays the stranger, and leads even us to wonder sometimes whether this or that one among us is not "two-faacëd". For with this natural delicacy goes often an almost uncanny insight, enabling the Cornish to detect motives deeply hidden, and to associate deeds and words which appear to have no relationship whatever.

We are blessed (or accursed), in great numbers, with the ability and impulse to put ourselves in other people's places, and in consequence to implicate ourselves emotionally when no more is required than cool, detached judgement. In judicial qualities, indeed, we do not shine; and it is worth remarking that there had been no Cornish-born judge for six hundred years before the appointment of Sir James Anthony Hawke, who, alas, graced the Bench for so short a time between the two World Wars. Mr. Justice Hawke's solitary Cornish predecessor was a favourite at the Court of Richard II, but immensely unpopular in the country. From a secret haunt he rashly emerged to see some great event that was taking place at Westminster, and there he was recognized by the crowd, who seized him, carried him through the streets on a hurdle, and then hanged, drew, and quartered him. His body, they found, was covered with pictures of the saints to avert evil.

The kind of thing that has sometimes happened in court with a Cornish jury was shown at the Epiphany Quarter Sessions some years ago, when the proprietress of one of those dark and dubious haunts of former days, the mumpers' inns, was indicted by the parish authorities with having kept a disorderly house. A constable, who described mumpers' inns as "receptacles of poverty and crime", declared that in this one there had been many and various disturbances "to the great injury of public morals". The evidence showed that he was not exaggerating. But the foreman of the jury, although his colleagues had found the woman guilty, was, when he came to announce the verdict to the court, full of ifs and buts. "We find her guilty of a breach of the law, you know," he grudgingly admitted, after much prompting by the chairman, and then went on hopefully, "And we will say to her as was said to the woman of old, that she should go away and sin no more."

Quick as lightning, the solicitor for the defence leapt to his feet, claiming, on the strength of this, his client's acquittal; but he was more astute than successful, and the woman was sent for six months, hard labour. She must have been what plain-spoken members of the older generation would have called a "brassy bitch". On hearing that hard work would be expected of her in Bodmin Gaol, she protested vigorously that she could not do it, "for she had never been able to labour hard all her life". Her indignation somewhat subsiding, she proceeded to make a concession to the foolishness of men and the rigours of justice. With a show of sweet reasonableness, though still in the very accents of outraged gentility, she informed the court that *she should have no objection to doing some needlework for the county!*"

The story of this offer, almost in the voice in which it was made, probably went the rounds for many a day after that trial. For the Cornish, although they do not much exercise this talent nowadays, are good mimics. My father's mimicry was one of the family's delights, and through it I got to know the idiosyncrasies of scores of people whom at that time I had not met. A special joy, I remember, was his version of a Cornish parish council in session; every member a distinct personality: this one "gaakin' in the fire", that one "zookin' his pipe", and all giving the impression that for the despatch of the parish business specified on the agenda an eternity stretched before them. And was it my father, or some other, who mimicked so well the chairman of that other parish council of bygone days, rebuking a persistent and loquacious member thus: "What do 'ee mane by it? You keep us here till nine o'clock at night and then cast the town drains in our teeth. You keep us here ploughin' the sands, and then, at nine o'clock at night, you drag in that everlastin' red herrin' and expect us to swalla it. You rake up a motion that was carried *non com* at the last mittin', and away you go into the public drains, causin' onnecessary friction. I tell 'ee 'twon't do, my friend. 'Tes too bare-faced to hold water!"

The greatest mimic Cornwall ever produced was Samuel Foote, with the broad fat face and the sparkling eyes, that gifted, extravagant, thriftless son of Truro, of whom Dr. Johnson, for all the brusque things he had earlier said about the so-called "English Aristophanes" of the eighteenth century, was moved in the end to remark, "He was a fine fellow in his way, and the world is really impoverished by his sinking glories. I would have his life written with diligence." Macaulay, in his essay on Madame D'Arblay, concedes that Foote's mimicry was "exquisitely ludicrous", but declares that it was all caricature, and leaves one with the impression that, by comparison with Garrick, Foote was woefully deficient in polish and subtlety—both of which qualities one would expect to find, above all, in a Cornishman. "Foote, we have no doubt," says Macaulay, "could have made the Haymarket Theatre shake with laughter by imitating a conversation between a Scotchman and a Somersetshireman. But Garrick could have imitated a conversation between two fashionable men, both models of the best breeding . . . so that no person could doubt which was which."

The fact remains that Foote, as caricaturist, was the rage and fear of the town, and if his effects were broad they were, as Garrick himself testified, first-class entertainment. It is deplorable and un-Cornish that Foote should ever have deigned to employ his mimicry upon one whom Nature had delivered so easily into the hands of unscrupulous mimics: and, Cornishman though I am, it warms me pleasantly to think of Dr. Johnson contemplating with gusto the purchase of an extra thick oaken cudgel with which to belabour Foote should he "take off" the Doctor in *The Orators*. But no less warming I find the good Doctor's tribute to his Cornish contemporary: "Sir, the dog was so very comical that he was irresistible." If I were a wit and a mimic I should ask no better epitaph; though it would comfort me if I knew there would be another beside it, like that in St. Mary's, Dover, to Foote,

> Who had a Tear for a Friend
> And a Hand and Heart ever ready
> To Relieve the Distressed.

For all his mordant wit, and his sometimes unscrupulous use of it, Foote, like Mr. Shaw's Doolittle, was "very tender 'earted". In that he was thoroughly Cornish. Not many people are so easily lost or won through their feelings. It may be difficult nowadays for the stranger to believe that we are so essentially emotional. Why this is less apparent than it used to be, I do not pretend to know; though I suppose that education and two World Wars have, in their different ways, had profound effects in this as in other springs of our character. It was because John Wesley preached and practised a gospel of love that he found, after the first antagonisms and suspicions had been withered by the fire of his message, such a remarkable response among the miners and fishermen of Cornwall. But Wesley had something of the restraint of his Age. In many of the long-forgotten evangelists who followed him restraint was lacking.

I was born a few years too late to have experienced the famous Cornish revivals in all their clamour and confusion; though the one revival I witnessed as a boy filled me with astonishment and fear. With antagonism, also. My days and nights for a week were made utterly miserable by the appeals, admonitions, and scenes in our little chapel. A child, especially a highly-strung, imaginative child, should never have been subjected to the almost unbearable tension these revivals created. Chiefly what the emotional appeals and the even more emotional responses did in me was to kindle a spirit of resistance. I felt that I was thoroughly bad and needed salvation; but I was determined not to be saved in that electrified atmosphere and that demonstrative way. Looking back now, I think there was for me in that revival a gust of the great and strong wind that rent the mountains while Elijah lodged in the cave on Mount Horeb, and something of the earthquake and the fire also. But there was no still small voice which would have evoked an instant response from the heart of a miserable child.

Yet this revival was sober and decorous by comparison with those of the early nineteenth century, when meetings of from thirty-six hours' duration to three days, were by no means uncommon, and one, at Mount Hawke, went on without intermission for eight days. All the pent-up emotions of an emotional people burst their bounds in the tiny Bethels of the countryside and the bigger chapels of the towns. Nor were the almost hysterical scenes entirely confined to the dissenters. Anybody interested in this subject should read—I found it an unpleasant task—*From Death Unto Life* by the Rev. W. Haslam, once the incumbent of Curzon Chapel, Mayfair, and previously curate of Perranzabuloe and vicar of Baldhu—*bal dhu*, the black mine.

Of the beginning of his revival services at Baldhu, Haslam recorded that he had not been preaching long "when someone in the congregation gave a shriek, and then began to cry aloud for mercy. This was quickly followed by cries from another and another, until preaching was altogether hopeless . . . I cannot tell how many people cried for mercy, or how many found peace that night, but there was great rejoicing." The noise in his newly built church made the vicar uneasy, and thenceforth the schoolroom was used; though when Mr. Aitken came over from his parish at Pendeen he preached in the church—built to hold six hundred people—to a congregation of fifteen hundred, "and at times it seemed as if he was imbued with power whereby he could make them shout for joy, or howl for misery, or cry aloud for mercy".

These "tremendous scenes" were not confined to grown men and women. "Sometimes," wrote Haslam, "I have known the children of the school to commence crying for no ostensible reason; when a few words about the love of God in giving His Son, or the love of Christ in laying down His Life, would prove enough to kindle a flame, and they would begin to cry aloud for mercy forthwith. I have seen a whole school of more than a hundred children like this at the same time." Parson Haslam went occasionally to neighbouring parishes; preaching, for instance, to three thousand people on the common at Mount Hawke, where "several hundreds fell upon their knees simultaneously, and many began to cry aloud for mercy. The strange part was, that the power of the Lord appeared to pass diagonally through the crowd, so that there was a lane of people on their knees six or eight feet deep, banked up on either side by others standing. It extended from the left-hand corner near me, to the right-hand corner in the distance." This was the meeting which continued uninterrupted indoors for eight days. Haslam left on the first night, coming back "again and again to see how they were going on; *but the people were too absorbed to heed my presence*". The italics are mine.

Of the durable effects of these intensely emotional experiences it is impossible now to form a just estimate, but not long ago a Methodist minister who had "travelled" in Cornwall recalled, at a Croydon service which he was conducting on his ninetieth birthday, that he knew one Cornishman who had boasted of having been converted twenty-two times. The temporary effects of the revivals even upon weak and unstable minds were no doubt innocuous enough; but in one instance which has come to my notice they were disastrous. At the Cornwall Assize of 1824 a nineteen years old girl was indicted for the murder of her brother, aged under seven, by strangling him with a silk handkerchief. She had been attending revival services, and had been in the crowded chapel for over eight hours when, one night, her mother went to find her. In evidence the mother said that she got her daughter out of the meeting as soon as she could, "but she had lost her cloak, bonnet, handkerchief, and pattens, and was extremely disordered in her dress. My daughter's conduct, after attending the revival, was quite different to what it had usually been. Next night she came home from the meeting in a violent agitation, praying in a horrible manner for the conversion of her father and mother. Before the death of my son, I apprehended my daughter would do me some violence. On the preceding Monday she came home and sat by the fire in a melancholy way, and said, 'Mother, I am going out of my mind'. "

In his summing-up, Mr. Justice Burrough told the jury that the girl's delusion was such that "she first murdered her brother and then contemplated self-destruction, conceiving that by committing those high offences she should be securing a way to heaven". It appeared to his lordship that "this young female had been in the habit of attending religious meetings, as they were called, where the wildest and most extravagant excitements were used that could possibly operate on the minds of the weak and lead them from a just sense of the importance and duties of religion . . . He would therefore warn the pastors of those congregations against continuing those practices as being derogatory to true religion, and dangerous to the safety of the community." The girl, needless to say, was found not guilty, the jury believing her to have been insane when she strangled the little brother to whom she had been so devoted.

The year of this remarkable trial was the year also of the first appearance on the Bible Christian local preachers' plan of the name of William Bray, better known to his contemporaries and to Methodists today, as Billy Bray, the Twelveheads miner, of whom Charles Henderson once opined, that had he lived a dozen centuries earlier he would have been numbered among the Cornish saints. Billy Bray was by far the most individual and successful evangelist of his times—a dark little man, with searching eyes, sharp features, and, in repose, a strangely grim mouth. He was a Cornishman of the Cornish; though it was certainly not true of him, if it is of the rest of us, that he was fitful in his labours, given to unsparing spurts and then to periods of prolonged relaxation. Those who see us like that, argue that the Cornish climate is too soft to encourage steady, unremitting effort such as the people of the robust north and east regard as normal.

I do not commit myself to this theory; but if I were advancing it, I should strengthen my case by pointing out that there cannot be a regular rhythm in our traditional pursuits of mining, fishing, and farming. Pulse and limbs must respond with haste to the sudden discovery of the rich lode of mineral, the appearance of a vast shoal of pilchards or herrings in the bay, and the "catchy" weather on the land. And flesh and spirit, for the heavy exactions made upon them, in their turn demand compensation. Hence these alternations of furious activity and "takin' it aisy".

Billy Bray had a seemingly bottomless well of energy. He worked at the mine eight hours of the twenty-four; over long periods gave another eight to collecting and transporting material and building one or another of the three chapels for the erection of which he was largely responsible; and in the season four hours had to go to "tilling his piece" and other such jobs at home. On Sundays—when he refused to go to work—he had often a score of miles or more to walk over hilly country, and three meetings to address. Nor was his a sober tread. Cottagers outside their dwellings of cob and thatch, or moorstone and slate, fellow miners on their way to work, and farmers feeding their pigs and poultry, must often have seen the little man in his black Quaker coat, a trifle too large, and his white "praicher's" tie; dancing towards them —"catching up his heels", as he called it—along the lanes or over the tracks of the downs. Billy Bray covered few miles without dancing. Inevitably, there was the comparison with David, and he would exclaim, "Why shouldn't *I* dance so well as David? David, you say, was a king. Well, bless the Lord, I am a King's son." So he danced on his way in the candour of morning or the shadows of evening—and no daughter of Saul was there to look upon the dancing and despise him in her heart.

Sometimes, as I descend the steep hill below Baldhu Church, from Cross Lanes to Twelveheads, and pass the cattle-shed which was Billy Bray's cottage, I wonder how I should react if it were possible for the little evangelist to emerge and meet me in the way. There would, I fear, be moments of acute discomfort for me; and part of me, like an anemone in a pool among the rocks, would close up swiftly at the first probing question about my soul. If he carried me about in his arms as he did, in jubilation, the Baldhu parson on learning of his conversion, I should be full of embarrassment and resentment. The state of my liver would largely determine my response to the inevitable criticism of my pipe or cigarette. "I don't b'lieve our Father meant for men to smoke," Billy once declared. "If He did, He'd have put a hole in the top of their heads; for 'tisn't no heavenly architect that'd leave the smoke go out the front door!"

Something in me would respond instantly to the merriment in his eyes, to occasional flashes of wit, the broad flow of humour, the ready similes and metaphors, the obvious sincerity of purpose, and the simple faith which impelled him to such prodigious labours. ("The Lord put it into my head to build a Chapel . . . So my little son and me went to work and got some stone.") His fellow miners must have appreciated his metaphors; as when he told them he was "working for that powerful Company, the Father, the Son, and the Holy Ghost—and *that* Company will never fail". One can feel the sense of security and continuity this would give to men who, all too often, found themselves suddenly idle because the company employing them had "gone scat".

To have won for himself a place among the Cornish saints it would have been desirable, if not necessary, that Billy Bray should have performed a miracle or two. Perhaps he did. Many certainly accounted a miracle—the greatest, it was said, ever performed at Helston—his extraction, towards the cost of his Great Deliverance Chapel at Carharrack, now a cattle-shed, of a sum of two shillings and sixpence from a notorious miser. Billy Bray was born in 1794 at Twelveheads, and he died there in 1868. He is buried in Baldhu Churchyard, where the pines in a great wind echo the roar of the sea. In the years of his exuberant service most Cornish people were familiar with his name, and it is still a household word in parts of the county, as well as in places where Cornish people have settled beyond the sea.

In the November of 1823 when Billy Bray was converted, Robert Stephen Hawker, an undergraduate at Oxford and a month under twenty, was married to the forty-one years old Charlotte I'ans, and went honeymooning to "dark Tintagil by the Cornish sea". During the late spring of 1868 when Billy Bray died, Hawker was collecting his poems for the volume by which he is best remembered, the *Cornish Ballads*. The two men never met, may not even have known of each other's existence: the one a poor miner, with a tiny cottage in a deep and desolate mining valley in West Cornwall; the other the poet-vicar of Morwenstow, living in that vicarage the chimneys of which are models of church towers, among them Cornish towers in parishes where Hawker had previously lived, and over the front door of which is the tablet inscribed

> A House, a Glebe, a Pound a Day;
> A Pleasant Place to Watch and Pray.
> Be True to Church—Be kind to Poor,
> O Minister! for evermore.

No other two men of their times in Cornwall can have been more utterly unlike than the High Church medievalist parson of Morwenstow and the Bible Christian evangelist of Twelveheads, and for that very reason I wish that their mutual friend, Haslam, had contrived a meeting and kept a record of their conversation. In the mass, and in the abstract, Hawker detested Dissenters. "John Wesley", he once declared "years ago corrupted and degraded the Cornish character; found them wrestlers, caused them to change their sins, and called it conversion. With my last Breath I protest that the Man Wesley corrupted and depraved instead of improving the West of England, indeed all the Land. He found the Miners and Fisherman an upstanding, rollicking, courageous people. He left them a downlooking, lying, selfish-hearted throng." How can one help loving a Romantic of such verve? His parishioners, Dissenters and all, certainly loved him. It was a leading Wesleyan who came over with his newly purchased machine to cut the glebe hay, "although", Hawker commented, "I never spare heresy or schism ministerially".

And when, one August day, fire broke out at the vicarage, and Hawker fell into a faint on remembering how little water was available, Dissenting heretics rushed with the Church's faithful to their vicar's aid. "Anything more noble than the conduct of the people was never seen," wrote Hawker to a friend. "They risked life and limb, and the Dissenters were conspicuous among them all for vigour and zeal." Nor were these the only qualities they shared with the Churchfolk. When it was all over, the fire subdued and the furniture and other things saved, Hawker's flock, to a man, exhibited a quality which, while not peculiar to the Cornish, is in them most marked. "The delicacy, too, with which, when the fire was stopped, they went away, as if not to intrude even for praise, was very striking."

Church and Chapel—in no other county can the people have been, until recent years, more sharply divided in this way than the Cornish. The division extended into the more remote as well as into the primary social and economic relationships. Much depended, at one time, upon the answer to the questions, "Be y' Church or Chapel?" Even at Padstow, with its long tradition of good fellowship as a community, one was constantly, in boyhood and for some years afterwards, becoming aware of that division; but with us it was never so sharp and disconcerting as in many another place. Our little town did not reflect Bishop Phillpotts's picture of a Cornwall in which "Wesleyanism is the established religion". But the picture in general was faithful enough, and the Churchpeople were often a minority; in consequence, presenting to the world a more militant aspect than if they had been a complacent majority. There is a story I have heard or read about the vicar of such a parish who was waited upon by a small deputation of Nonconformists, one of whose leading men had died. So spontaneous was the vicar's consent to read the burial service at the forthcoming big funeral that one of the deputation expressed gratified surprise that he had not flatly declined to bury a Chapel man. "My dear fellow," the vicar answered promptly and with vigour, "I could have no greater pleasure, believe me, than to bury the whole lot of you!"

The Cornish are great ones for funerals, and possibly I should share this characteristic had it not been for a thing that happened to me when I was a small boy. A little girl playmate had died, and I was a bearer at the funeral. There was four of us boys, one at each end of two short poles from which the little white coffin was suspended. I was the smallest and most nervous of the bearers, and we had carried the coffin a long way. As we were passing through the south porch of the church the pole slipped from my grasp. Though nimble-witted enough to regain my hold quickly, I was horrified and humiliated by the incident; and even now funerals are associated in my mind with those black, tearful moments. I attend as rarely as I can—which is not at all Cornish. Quite recently I heard of a Cornishman who accounted as featureless that Sunday afternoon when there was not a funeral in the district to attend. An obituary notice in *The West Briton* of February 21st, 1843, ran: "At Bodmin, on Friday last, Mrs. Peggy Arthny, aged 78 years.

Cornish cottage at Zelah, near Truro

This old woman was especially fond of *grave doings*, having been an attendant for a number of years of every funeral in the town."

A very impressive funeral was that of Lord De Dunstanville, best-known of the Bassets of Tehidy, near Camborne, whose barony was of Pitt's creation, sixteen years after Basset had entered Parliament as his father's successor in representing Penryn. His baronetcy was the reward nineteen years earlier for his initiative and zeal in marching to Plymouth, when it was threatened by a combined French and Spanish fleet, a big contingent of the Miners' Militia, who contributed notably to the defences. (Cornish miners had a proud record in this form of service, and also in tunnelling, and so on, to facilitate the capture of besieged fortresses.) Nobody now reads De Dunstanville's treatises on politics and agriculture; and in Cornwall he is chiefly remembered because of his solicitude for the miners' welfare. The obelisk on Carn Brea is the county memorial to him. It was erected in 1836, the year after his death in London, whence his body was brought, at a walking pace, by road to Cornwall, with plumes and pennons, outriders and ten pages on horseback, and a procession which took twelve days to reach Tehidy. At Launceston, Bodmin and Truro, the coffin was placed for the night in a hotel, and the townsfolk were allowed to file round it. There were twenty thousand people present at the funeral at Tehidy.

Eleven years later there died at Pengreep, in the mining parish of Gwennap, a successful merchant, Mr. Collan Harvey, aged 76 years, whose "integrity in all his business transactions had kept pace with the rapidly accumulating wealth". Fifty carriages bore the wealthier people in the funeral procession, "while not fewer than ten thousand of the labouring poor paid the last tribute of respect to their kind friend and benefactor". It must not be supposed that the Cornish, in attending funerals in such great numbers, are only demonstrating gratitude to prosperous benefactors. The year before this big funeral at Gwennap there had been one almost as largely attended at Sithney, several miles to the south-west. A ship, in which was the captain, his wife, and a crew of five, had been driven ashore at Porthleven, and only one member of the crew had been saved. The bodies of the other six, all "foreigners", were taken about three miles inland to Sithney Church-yard for interment, "and the melancholy procession was attended by at least eight thousand persons".

Reserved, I think, for the funerals of celebrated old local preachers were the big processions headed by a long double row of singers, who led in slow time and a minor key such hymns as the one that began:

12

*Cornish Wrestling: the fateful moment
before a fall*

> Ah, lovely appearance of death!
> What sight upon earth is so fair?
> Not all the gay pagans that breathe
> Can with a dead body compare!

Since the Cornish set such great store by funerals, it is distressing to recall that two Cornishmen of genius and humble birth went to nameless graves unattended save by the handful of workmen who bore their coffins. One, Richard Trevithick, inventor of the high-pressure steam engine, with a score of other great advances in engineering, died penniless at Dartford, where he seems to have been working on the marine engine which rendered practicable under steam the first crossing of the Atlantic. On that April day in 1833 half-a-dozen mechanics from the factory at Dartford were the sole mourners of the vivacious, lovable, blue-eyed giant—a formidable wrestler in his younger days—whose restless genius drove him ever ahead of the invention upon which he was at the moment engaged, and whose name stands in the first half-dozen engineers of the world.

There is a statue of him outside the Free Library at Camborne, not far from the cottage in which he lived and which is in the care of the Cornish Engines Preservation Society. In swallow-tailed coat and breeches, and holding in one hand a model of his locomotive, he looks up Beacon Hill to the top of which at Christmas, 1801, his "puffing devil" carried, at more than a walking pace, its ten or dozen passengers. One remembers the prelude to that great achievement, in Trevithick's little home, where the model locomotive had as stoker Davies Gilbert, faithful friend and adviser and afterwards President of the Royal Society, and as engine-man Lady De Dunstanville of Tehidy. And one thinks of Trevithick returning from those eleven adventurous years in South America, his passage money home having been paid by a friend, and his sole possessions the clothes he wore, a gold watch, a pair of dividers, a magnetic needle, and a pair of spurs.

Camborne Church bells pealed out a welcome, and the homes of the great ones of Cornwall were open to receive him, after he had rested awhile with the wife and family of six whom he had left, with characteristic impetuosity and improvidence, quite unprovided for while he earned the ten thousand a year which, he supposed, would be his abroad. But money never lured him anywhere; it was his genius that drove him. Of all the Cornish giants of the past, real and legendary, Trevithick is the one I should like most to have known.

In the year of that funeral at Dartford there came to Place House,

Fowey, the home of the Treffrys, a fair-haired, round-faced, power-fully-built boy of fifteen, bringing with him a chisel and a tender bud of genius. This was Nevill Northey Burnard, a stonemason's son, from the upland parish of Alternun, with its "Cathedral of the Moor". He had come to do some of the fine work in stone and plaster in the restoration and enlargements upon which Squire Treffry had embarked. Already, while a mortar boy for his father, Burnard, with nails finely ground, had carved in slate a head of Homer which is now in the library of the Royal Cornwall Polytechnic Society at Falmouth. The boy remained at Fowey for two years, busy with his chisel and his drawings and the books in the library of Place. A year after his depar-ture he sent to the Polytechnic Society's annual exhibition a bas-relief in slate of the "Laocoön", which he had copied from a woodcut. With the silver medal of the Society, it won for him also the warm interest of Sir Charles Lemon, M.P., of Carclew, who enabled him to realize his ambition of seeking fame in London.

Sir Charles took him to Chantrey, in whose studio he worked until he could confidently leave the master for a studio of his own. Com-missions began to flow, then to pour in, and for thirty years this "powerful, pugilistic-looking fellow", as Caroline Fox described him when he was twenty-nine, with "mouth open and all sorts of simplicities flowing out of it", was among the first two or three sculptors in the land. There was a place for his work in the Royal Academy, but he loved to exhibit also in his native county, to which he was constantly returning. Some of that work is among our treasures now: for example, the statue of Richard Lander, the Truro explorer, which, in granite, looks from its tall Doric column down the gracious Lemon Street. There is also his superb bust in marble of Richard Trevithick in the County Museum and Art Gallery at Truro, which has a collection of the great inventor's letters to Davies Gilbert. And at Truro, too, in the chapel of *Lis Escop*, formerly the Bishop's Palace and now Truro Cathedral School, set among the pleasant greenery of Kenwyn on the northern outskirts of the city, is a copy of the bust of John Wesley which, at eighteen, Burnard had carved for the meeting-house of his moorland home.

In middle life it became all to clear that the witty, tousle-headed, loquacious Cornish giant—to sit to whom had been at one time in London almost as fashionable as, many years before, to the painter, John Opie, "the Cornish Wonder"—was becoming hopelessly addicted to drink. There came separation from his wife, the loss of friends, the telling diminution of commissions, and at last utter failure.

When Burnard turned westwards from London for the last time, it was as a tramp. One winter night in 1875, unkempt and weather-beaten, he knocked at the door of the Crow's Nest, a house at St. Cleer, about ten miles from his birthplace on the northern edge of the Bodmin Moor. Kindly people took him into their family circle, and there he stayed for a few months; drawing, and writing witty verse, and talking, talking—and remembering the child Lottie, in whom death had taken from him his treasure.

Nothing could stay his waywardness, and from the affection and solicitude of St. Cleer he took to the road again, becoming one of the little band of dissolute outcasts who frequented mumpers' inns and shuffled at last into the workhouses. It was in the workhouse at Redruth, on a November day in 1878, that Burnard died. They were at that time carrying out some small restorations of Camborne Parish Church, and the stonemasons were busy there when a pauper funeral arrived at the gate. The coffin on the parish hearse was met by the curate, who turned back to the churchyard and called the workmen together. They remembered, did they not, he asked, the stone medallion over there with the finely wrought head of a former vicar? They remembered. Well, that had been the work of Nevill Northey Burnard, a great master of their craft, and a fellow Cornishman withal, whose body lay now at the gate awaiting burial. Would they not like, as their last tribute to him, to carry him to the grave? Reverently they performed the task.

It is all too unlikely, but I hope that kindly curate lived to become a bishop, and that handful of workers master stonemasons, greatly prospering; and I wish there had been at Camborne then a rectangle of slate, going begging, and a stonemason's boy with impelling talent, a chisel, and a nail or two finely ground, with which to inscribe upon the stone a few simple memorial words, and to fashion at each corner cherubs and seraphs, in the carving of which that other Cornish boy of the distant moorlands had once found the delight of the true artist.

How different had been the last years and end of "Jan" Opie: those busy, happy years in the studio or at the writing-table at No. 8 Berners Street; and, not long before his death, the delivery before the Royal Academy, as its professor in painting, of his "Discourses on Painting". Then the illness, with the six physicians in attendance, and, when their efforts were of no more avail, the burial by the side of Barry and his fellow Westcountryman, Reynolds, in the crypt of St. Paul's. There seems never to have been any waywardness in Opie, and the worst fault people found in him was the forthrightness which, even from the most delicately minded and evasive of the Cornish, issues on occasions with the force of an unpolished pebble from a sling, and which in Opie was habitual. With him, though, the pebble had sometimes been polished in the brooks of Babylon. One day he was passing the Church of St. Martin-in-the-Fields, where he had married his first wife, Mary Bunn, who had later run off with another man. Said Godwin, the unbeliever, as they went by: "Ah! in that church I was christened." "And I was married in it," said Opie grimly. "They made unsure work there, for it holds neither in wedlock nor in baptism."

"Unsure work"—there spoke Jan Opie, the 'prentice boy to his father, a skilful and thorough carpenter and builder, down home-along in St. Agnes Parish, at Harmony Cot, that "sequestered cottage, white-washed and thatched", looking one way to the slow rising Beacon and the other to where now on the high ground are the austere church of Mithian and the solemn pines. Jan Opie must often have been warned against doing unsure work in wood by that prosaic and puritanical father, who was constantly being astonished and antagonized by his son's love of art. "That boy will come to hanging," he exclaimed when Jan, who had sold one of his paintings for five shillings, came rushing home, shouting, "I'm set up for life! I'm set up for life!" Later, the 'prentice boy went over to Place at Padstow to paint some portraits there, including one of the Prideaux dogs. Returning home in a costly new coat, lace ruffles, and silk stockings, he scooped a score or more of guineas out of his pockets on to the floor, crying "See! I'm wallowin' in gold!" He was much elated by success, but as easily depressed by doubts and set-backs.

It is all so Cornish that; and with our mercurial temperament went also in John Opie the shrewdness of the Cornish, expressed by him in one of his early letters to his mother from the far city: "To be known, is the great thing in London." And on that score he had no reason to complain. On the contrary, within a few months of his arrival with Wolcot ("Peter Pindar"), who had befriended him in Cornwall, Opie was "known and talked of by everybody". As his father had predicted, he came to hanging; but in the Royal Academy and not in Bodmin Gaol. The great and the good flocked to have their portraits painted by "the Cornish Wonder". Over five hundred of his paintings have been catalogued. (How many had Thackeray in mind when he wrote contemptuously in his *Four Georges:* "Far better for our eyes to contemplate whitewash . . . than to look at Opie's pitchy canvases"?) There are, I believe, about two dozen in Cornish houses, and the County Museum and Art Gallery at Truro has seven, one a portrait of the artist. As a boy, and using a good old Cornish phrase, Opie had declared, "I love painting better than bread and meat." In delirium on his death bed he was painting still, and repeating (as though to forestall Thackeray): "It wants more colour in the background."

The Cornish, especially the women, "do dearly love a bit o' colour"; but precious little of it Jan Opie can have seen in his youth in St. Agnes Parish, then grim and scarred with mining. No wonder he should have insisted so much in his *Discourses* upon colouring as "the sunshine of art"; and no wonder, reared as he was among those mine-heaps and so near to the northern cliffs with their wild grandeur, that the delicate touch and charm he so much admired in the work of others should so often have eluded him. Suppose John Keats had been born and reared in those wild and desolate surroundings . . . he might well have been. His father's home is said to have been there; but the young ostler was evidently pushful, and to better himself went off to London. By the time of the premature death of the owner of the "Swan and Hoop" stables in Finsbury, Keats—I think the name had been Keat in his St. Agnes days—was right-hand man. He married the widow, "a lively woman, passionately fond of amusement". He himself was cast in another mould, "a man of remarkably fine common-sense and native respectability"; but the two seem to have got along well together and John was the fifth of their children.

If Opie lived for painting, John Keats lived with even greater intensity for poetry, and in him there was the magic, the delicacy, which his Celtic origin might also have assured to Opie. It has often been remarked that the Cornish, a people in whom there are many poetic qualities and who have been cradled in a land of legend and romance, have been curiously deficient in poets of distinction. We can, at least, claim a half-share in Keats and in Matthew Arnold also. And who shall say to what degree their mother's Cornish temperament and ancestry enriched the work of the Brontës? But directly, till within living memory, Cornwall's contribution to English letters was small, as it was to English music—for after the delicate and charming pieces of Giles Farnaby, of Probus, which so much delighted Queen Elizabeth, no mean judge, there is silence, though William Beale, of Landrake, born 1784, wrote some charming madrigals in the early nineteenth century. To English seamanship, on the other hand, Cornwall has contributed directly and with distinction through Grenville and Hawk, old "Dreadnought" Boscawen and Exmouth, and—one must add—the bullying Bligh of the *Bounty*; besides scores of less known figures, the captains and mates, some of them among the first to sail round the world, in the days when our supremacy at sea was being established.

If the names of these admirals are not unfamiliar to students of English history, neither, one may suppose, are those of Sir John Eliot and Sidney, Earl of Godolphin; while for the name of John Couch Adams, of Laneast, the moorland parish adjoining that in which Burnard was born, there will always be a place, as discoverer of the planet Neptune, in the story of the heavens. No less secure among the illustrious in science is Humphry Davy, son of the wood-carver in the little village of Ludgvan, overlooking Mount's Bay and the slow-curving coast to The Lizard.

It is pleasant for us in this remote peninsula sometimes to think of these distinguished men as they were when their powers were at the zenith and their fame was established: Godolphin in conference with Marlborough or having an audience of the Queen; despatching Boyle, the Chancellor, to persuade Addison in his garret to write a poem celebrating the triumph of Blenheim; or slipping away happily to Newmarket, or to hazard a few guineas at the cock-fighting. And one thinks of Humphry Davy, far less a man of the world than Godolphin, but more handsome and vivacious, being fêted by the savants of Paris; receiving a rich service of plate from coal-owners and miners as a token of gratitude for his safety lamp; or delivering, in full court dress, the seven annual addresses as President of the Royal Society, among whose Fellows so many Cornishmen have been numbered.

But I like to think, too, of Godolphin in his Cornish home, with its terraces under the hill and its colonnade of granite—Lord High Treasurer of England, but a good neighbour in that south-west corner of the Duchy. There were then no regular conveyances west of Exeter, where letters and packets were allowed to accumulate for some time before the post brought them into Cornwall—a Cornish innkeeper's son, Ralph Allen, friend of Pope and Fielding's "Squire Allworthy", had yet, to his own and the nation's great profit, to revolutionize the English postal system. Godolphin hired a weekly messenger to bring from Exeter his dispatches, letters, and a newspaper, "and on the fixed day of their arrival, all the gentlemen assembled at Godolphin House from many miles round, to hear the newspaper read in the Great Hall".

I like to think of Davy as the bright-eyed boy with the wavy brown hair, holding forth—in a voice which was then not at all pleasing—to a crowd of his schoolmates marshalled in front of the Star Inn at

Penzance; or, when he could muster no such audience, wandering along the shores of Mount's Bay, declaiming and gesticulating to the unresponsive waves and sky.

Six years before Davy's birth, Ludgvan Parish had lost by death its rector of the previous fifty-two years, Dr. William Borlase, first of Cornish antiquaries, and a parson who, even at the worst period of Churchmanship, was able to draw to his church at St. Just (of which parish he was vicar for forty years) a Sunday morning congregation of a thousand. Much fun has been poked at the old Doctor because of his obsession with the Druids, but the importance of his *Cornish Antiquities* and his *Natural History of Cornwall* is not under-estimated. His account of the Scilly Isles Dr. Johnson described as "one of the most pleasing and elegant pieces of local inquiry that our country has produced". In my mind Dr. Borlase is linked with a Cornishman of a later generation, and I should guess, of less unbending nature: Dr. Jonathan Couch, of Polperro, "Q's" grandfather, who also made valuable contributions to natural history, in particular as an ichthyologist.

Neither Borlase nor Couch, though their gifts might have taken them far, was much away from Cornwall. The county has been fortunate, indeed, in having had many sons of diverse gifts who have been satisfied to cultivate and employ them this side of the Tamar rather than in the busier world of men. Gifted sons of the future, though they may love Cornwall no less, will look naturally to the larger world for the exercise and rewards of their talents; but we may yet hope to breed a few who will be content to remain, as Pope once wrote of Borlase, "In the shade, but shining".

INDEX